Summer Of The Dragon

Don Goodman

Cover Photo by John Moran.
www.JohnMoranPhoto.com

Design & Typography by
Nina Sutherland Photography & Graphics
www.ninasutherland.com
(404) 840-4283

Production and Publishing by
Gainesville Association for the Creative Arts
P.O. Box 12246. Gainesville, FL 32604
(352) 378-9166

To my daughters, Alexis and Summer,
who have blessed my life beyond measure.

Acknowledgements:

The manuscript of *Summer of the Dragon* was entrusted to only a few individuals, and I am indebted to them for criticisms that improved the final draft. Chief among these is my wife Jordan, who was a participant in/accomplice to many of the events and whose better memory rendered them more accurate, if occasionally less fantastic. Her counsel and encouragement were invaluable and her generosity in sharing her recipe for lima beans with devil's dung could incite a culinary revolution or, at the very least, her exclusion from polite society. Norman Jensen also provided valuable comment and welcome encouragement. I am especially grateful to Gabe Duclos for providing an account of the execution of my crocodilian assailant while I was occupied with surgery and morphine induced fantasy.

I am deeply indebted to Florida's de facto photographer laureate John Moran, for allowing me to grace the cover of this book with his remarkable image of dragons at Alachua Sink, the visual equivalent of William Bartram's eloquent depiction of the same more than two centuries ago. An image of the most notorious dragon described in these pages was captured on canvas by Sean Sexton and in photographic copy by Dr. Jim Castner, both of whom kindly assented to the reproduction of their work. My late friend Gary Branam is given posthumous thanks for his wonderful photograph of Grundoon and for many happy memories. Two other photos are reproduced with the permission of The Gainesville Sun.

I also wish to extend special thanks to Dr. William Eyerly, Executive Director of the Gainesville Association of the Creative Arts, and to Nina Sutherland, for orchestrating the multifaceted process of bringing this book into print.

Finally, I am grateful my daughter Alexis for providing the inspiration for putting pen to paper in the first place. One lesson of life's carousel is that neither we nor our children can ever know the other's full journey. The many cycles we share begin long after we first embarked on our journey and—barring some tragedy—end long before they complete theirs. It is for this reason that we write biographies, memoirs and family histories—to acquaint our children with the people we were before their appearance transformed us into parents. Certainly, this is what inspired me, and why I thank Alexis, without whom, these words would be left unwritten and unread and the carousel we share much less fun.

Preface

One of my earliest recollections—possibly the earliest —was turning over a soggy board to discover two salamanders curled beneath. I was no more than three years old, but still have a vivid recollection of the incident. My innate response was one of great excitement; I picked up the moist creatures and ran to show them to my mother who, as always thereafter, was willing to indulge—even encourage—my fascination with wild creatures in general and reptiles and amphibians in particular, a fascination that made the moment preeminent in a lifetime of memories.

It is tempting to assume that my reaction was the typical and perhaps universal response of an innocent and inquisitive young mind unsullied by the prejudices against many lower vertebrates that are so senselessly harbored by so many adults. Certainly, young minds are more likely than those of adults to see such creatures as they are, and not as we have learned them to be, often in error. But, in fact, I now recognize that my level of fascination with these new animals was well above the norm. Of three siblings, only my sister, two years my junior, seemed inherently hard wired to respond to such surprise encounters with anything more zealous than a sideways glance or casual comment before returning to affairs of greater import. To me, there simply were no affairs of greater interest than chance encounters with—and later purposeful searches for—salamanders, frogs, lizards, turtles and especially snakes!

In my youth, I encountered few people who were truly thrilled by such things, certainly not sufficiently so to scour Kennett, Missouri's modest public library for any reference to snakes and frogs and such. In fact, I became locally notorious as a snake collector, at least to the degree that folks thereabout knew to call me when there was a snake to be captured or, more commonly, posthumously identified. On several occasions, townsfolk captured reptiles for the express purpose of delivering them to me, including a disheveled lizard that had been apprehended by vacuum cleaner. At that point in my life, I was unaware that other youths in other towns were cultivating the same fascination-bordering-on-obsession that had seized me that day I first laid eyes on those two squatty bubble - eyed salamanders. Although their experiences differed in details, they likewise sparked an innate and unquenchable thirst for more.

At the same time and a world away, Jill Jordan, twenty one days my junior, was a little girl struggling with a less tolerant parental attitude that held little affection for reptiles in general and an unyielding opposition to having them around the house. Not that the environs of Niagara Falls, New York harbored an extensive herpetofauna. Still, it was doubly difficult for her to discern any scrap of encouragement for her interest in scaly creatures because the prevailing opinion in this and most American households was that nothing good could come of it, especially for a girl. Both of her sisters were content to play with stuffed toys, but Jill liked turtles and lizards as well; and the sight of a snake would leave her trembling with excitement. In our photographic archives is an otherwise warm and cheerful Jordan family portrait that was sabotaged by a skinny and sour little waif who refused to smile because, while her sisters were allowed to pose with their stuffed animals, Jill was forbidden to hold her rubber lizard.

This was the same rubber lizard she requested at bedside to cheer her through a difficult recovery from a tonsillectomy. She would have preferred to possess a living lizard, or better yet, a snake, but that was well beyond the realm of possibility. And on one occasion, the allure of things that creep and crawl excited in her a passion that not only blurred the boundaries of propriety, but incited actual criminal behavior. She was only six years old on that summer day when she beheld a creature so wondrous that she was seized by the irrepressible yearning to have it for her own. It was a toad; a huge, wise, squat, warty toad. Sadly, it was in the hands of a pudgy and clearly undeserving boy who had just caught it near the edge of a small pond that she happened to be bicycling past. Summoning all of the tact and persuasiveness a six year old could muster, Jill tried to wheedle it out of his clutches but without success. At this point, desire and frustration conspired to put her actions beyond her control; this was not a Barbie doll, but a toad!

Abruptly, she snatched the coveted amphibian, leapt onto her bike and pedaled away from her startled victim as fast as her legs would carry her. The image of this brazen toad thief was irrevocably seared onto the soul of that incredulous boy as he stared, mouth agape, at the receding spectacle. Otherwise, that might have been the sole episode of the incredible purloined toad caper. But, in fact, the paths of the toad catcher and the toad thief crossed again and it happened, of all places, in a church. When her family moved to a new house on McKoon Avenue, Jill found herself face to face with her victim as she was being introduced by the Sunday School superintendent to her new church's classmates.

Any prospect of redemption she might have harbored was abandoned the moment she watched an expression of astonishment spread across his face as his eyes grew into saucers.

"That's her!" he sputtered, pointing a quivering finger at her like a pistol. "She's the one who stole my toad!"

Despite repeated demonstrations of this passion throughout her childhood, it was not until she was enrolled in graduate school, where she was studying fish, that her parents finally accepted the fact that their daughter was an incorrigible naturalist. In the face of constant exposure to attitudes and subtle pressures intended to extinguish that spark, Jill knew with an inborn certainty that her happiness was somehow bound to an exploration of the natural world.

Why are some people so enthralled by snakes and toads from the time of their earliest recollections while others are disinterested or even terrified? Education and exposure may promote a tolerance for or even fascination with such creatures, but they fan a virtual flame in the hearts of people like Jill and me. Others leave the womb hard wired with the same obsession for other disciplines like art, music or physics. Why it should be so would likely remain a mystery even if the brain could be disassembled neuron by neuron, but it certainly makes the world a more interesting place and guarantees a continued quest for knowledge that, day by day, is providing a better understanding of our place in a very grand scheme.

In the decades that followed, Jill (who later adopted "Jordan" as her given name) and I pursued paths in our study of nature that drew us ever farther south and finally converged in Gainesville, Florida in 1967. The allure of the natural world that neither of us could resist is what ultimately drew us together and has so immeasurably enriched our lives. It seems altogether fitting that the first to sample our wedding cake was a little night monkey who had just mastered the operation of the bedroom door knob. And along the way, that path has conferred other experiences so wonderfully bizarre that they cannot be left untold. This is the chronicle of those special times.

Contents

1

The Unnatural Side of Naturalists

Jack Russell Terriers do not suffer in silence! Their DNA is so tightly wound that they respond to every slight—real or perceived—with yowls sorrowful enough to curdle milk. Living with Katie, our Jack Russell Terrier, has taught me that frenetic bouts of yips, barks and howls may be nothing more than a response to a bird flitting in the underbrush or even a leaf falling. Still, on this day, I was able to discern from the pitch and delivery of her wails that Katie's anguish was of physical, and not psycho-pathologic, origin as she leapt frantically about in a tangle of catbrier and shrubby undergrowth. Over the past 25 years, we have lost two other small dogs to rattlesnake bites and this was paramount in my thoughts as I dropped my garden trowel and sped to her rescue.

Soon enough, I learned the secret of her misery as I too stepped into the yellow jacket nest whose infuriated residents clung to the two of us wherever opportunity allowed and unleashed a measure of torment that obviously represents millennia of evolutionary refinement, though I contemplated that well after the encounter. The combination of legion numbers, barbed stingers, painful toxins, and sheer relentlessness routed us completely, our only ambition being deliverance from our shared agony as we tore through the catbriers away from the furious yellow maelstrom. I broke a swift stride only to slap or flick away individual tormentors whose stings were intense enough to be perceived individually through a sea of pain.

Jordan, who was working nearby in the garden, came running when she heard the commotion. The sight of the two of us leaping about like crazed banshees to Katie's now nearly stratospheric howls of sheer misery brought to her lips the barest suggestion of a smile, which she wisely suppressed, as she rushed in to help us annihilate the last few kamikaze warriors. I counted thirteen stings and Katie required generous measures of sympathy and comfort for several hours. Even into the evening, recollection of the dreadful trauma overwhelmed her, as she lapsed into bouts of whimpering, often escalating into mournful wails and other bids for sympathy and solace.

Later, as I related the episode to Dan, a young friend, I shared my plans for dealing with the nest of insects whose admirably coordinated assault had reduced two higher vertebrates to whimpering ninnies. Tomorrow evening, after the wasps retired for the night, I would don a headlight, sneak out to their nest and plop around it an open ended cylinder of chicken wire fencing three feet high. Around the upper rim of the fencing, I would have woven a strip of bright orange plastic flagging to make it conspicuous to anyone not legally blind. My goal was to leave the yellow jacket colony intact while sparing all other sentient life forms the prospect of suffering the regrettable fate that befell Katie and me.

It was obvious, from his puzzled countenance, that Dan did not find in my strategy the vicarious closure he sought since there was nothing that exacted retribution from the offending colony. The yellow menace was still unhumbled and intact, save the loss of a few compatriots to our chaotic flailing, despite the vast array of chemical and incendiary munitions at my disposal.

Nonetheless, I was content to leave vengeance to the gods. In fact, I felt no animosity toward my erstwhile attackers; they were, after all, simply defending their colony from a much larger home wrecker. And self defense is both laudable and defensible in any court of law or arena of objective public opinion. My principal intent was to recruit this horde of warriors for my battle with the caterpillars that can otherwise reduce a garden to mush. The fact is, yellow jackets are excellent agents of caterpillar control, and having an army of alert, airborne death dealing warriors patrolling my garden in search of the leaf shredding gluttons is more than compensatory for the temporary—if intense—pain accrued in discovering their domicile. They will execute their quest for food—including caterpillars—with the same focused intensity they expend in repelling intruders like Katie and me. Regrettably, their tenure in service to my garden will last only a year or two before they pull up stakes and move to greener pastures.

Dan's concern—more accurately, suppressed frustration disguised as concern—is that having yellow jackets for neighbors will inevitably result in additional painful mishaps, a circumstance that could be averted by a preemptive strike. But, in fact, yellow jackets are not the least bit aggressive away from their hive. One can stand quietly a few feet away from the portal to their subterranean nest and watch their comings and goings with complete impunity, and the chicken wire barricade insured this measure of separation.

It is this sort of dispassionate scheming that sets naturalists apart from humanity's mainstream, whose inclination would be to blast the bejeezus out of those yellow bastards. Naturalists' view of the natural world is frequently flavored by a familiarity with living beings and their interactions to such a degree that, for all practical purposes, they dwell on a different planet. And this necessarily results in responses to specific incidents—protecting rather than eradicating a nest of yellow jackets for instance—that are so greatly at variance with the norm that they are beheld by society at large as truly peculiar, if not bizarre. The truth is that naturalists' perception of a particular circumstance is often accurate and rational, but in most instances, this will put them at odds with prevailing attitudes that tend to be anything but objective. They will thoroughly enjoy a trek through a north Florida hammock that is home to many wildlife forms—including rattlesnakes, stinging insects, poison ivy, banana spiders and such—precisely because they are familiar with the true nature of these life forms and can place their relevance into a proper and non-threatening perspective.

Nonetheless, it is a perspective that can result in experiences that are almost inconceivable to normal folks who subscribe to society's prevailing biases against snakes, spiders and the like. An incident that lays bare this disparity of tolerance occurred several years ago at Kanapaha Botanical Gardens, where I am the director. Before the construction of a new visitors center, our base of operations was a small wooden building that housed an entrance counter, gift shop, two restrooms and a room that served as both an office and for tool storage. Even then, we accommodated outdoor weddings but obviously lacked the sort of dressing chamber many brides consider indispensable.

On this day, a resourceful bride had elected to utilize our small ladies' restroom for just such a function, an exercise complicated by a gown nearly equal in volume to that of the small room. Suddenly a blood curdling scream filled the adjacent hallway into which she promptly tumbled with limbs flailing and layers of satin billowing. We knew instantly that she had caught sight of Whiskers, the room's resident wolf spider. Whiskers is generally retiring and discreet, spending daylight hours behind either the mirror or the space separating the door jamb from the wall. But when night falls, she is transformed into the alert and nimble predator that we count on to patrol the corridor of our little building in quest of roaches and other unwelcome arthropods.

Our bride, it seems, did not share the fondness we held for our spry and hairy warrior. She had grasped the mirror frame to straighten it a bit and the disturbance caused Whiskers to bolt from her sanctuary and scurry across the wall. Eda, our ever resourceful volunteer admissions attendant immediately set about salvaging a potential public relations nightmare by acquainting the trembling young lady with Latvian tradition which holds that encountering a spider on your wedding day should be counted a blessing. Even so, however, the bride-to-be seemed willing to forego such encounters at the expense of any good fortune that might accrue.

For sheer terror, this episode pales in comparison to an incident—related to me by a herpetological colleague, Duke Campbell—that befell an elderly woman whose misfortune derived from her apartment's proximity to that of one of Duke's fellow UCLA graduate students who kept a number of snakes. More precisely, it derived from their apartments' shared plumbing. One of his pets, a six foot anaconda, was experiencing difficulty shedding its skin, a common problem for captive snakes. The accepted treatment for this condition is to allow the snake to soak in a container of water to soften and loosen the skin and thereby facilitate shedding. So he half filled his bath tub with lukewarm water and released the snake into it. Wild anacondas spend much of their time in the rivers and sloughs of the American tropics and this individual readily submerged and lay coiled on the bottom as his keeper departed, taking care to close the bathroom door behind him as he headed to the sofa for a nap.

An hour or so later, he was awakened by shrill screams emanating from the apartment one wall away, the one whose bathroom backed up against his own. Speculating, from past experiences, that one of his snakes was likely a party to the disturbance, he raced to the bathroom, threw open the door and spied the aft portion of his anaconda sticking out of the toilet. His snake, it seems, had departed the tub to investigate yet another repository of water and had gotten more than half its body down the toilet before becoming stuck. The good news—for the snake, not the neighbor—was that it was able to break the surface of a new found pool of water beyond the tight and imprisoning tunnel where it could catch a breath of air. Initially, the little pond was in darkness, but light suddenly flooded in as an overlying cover was flipped up to reveal the startled face of a little old lady. The huge snake head opened its mouth menacingly, and that's when she screamed, her initial concern with using the facility now irrelevant.

Regrettably, the snake was truly stuck, seemingly incapable of moving forward or back. Ultimately, its release was secured by a plumber who pounded a hole in the wall and, with a ball peen hammer, disassembled the network of pipes that held it captive, before presenting a substantial bill for services to the anaconda's owner. It's hard to imagine how the lady ever found the strength of character to use a toilet seat again since any attack would come from the rear undetected. Eve at least got an apple.

When I was a boy, I collected reptiles—lizards and turtles, but snakes in particular. And one of the lessons known to all who engage in snake husbandry is that the teeth of serpents are slender, sharp and recurved—the better to hold their prey—but delicate and easily ripped out by something that pulls away sharply from an unsuccessful strike. And the resulting wound is prone to a bacterial infection that can quickly spread and even result in the reptile's death unless aggressively treated. While I endeavored not to be bitten by my snakes, it happened sometimes and, in order not to indirectly inflict injury to the snake, I always held my hand motionless while enduring the bite rather than yanking back, an action that carried the likelihood of pulling out some needle teeth as well as ripping my skin. This non-reaction to snake bite never ceased to astound most observers, despite the fact that it was clearly the most prudent thing to do. Getting bitten by a snake after all, is an experience I always compare to scratching my skin on the loose edge of a piece of screen wire, nothing more.

My restraint, though, is truly conservative relative to what passes for normal behavior among hard core herpetologists. In the annals of legendary snake fanciers, there is an extraordinary but authentic tale of one true believer who carried a concern for his pets' dental hygiene to a much greater extreme. Several years ago, police were summoned to a Cincinnati apartment by a man who had calmly requested their assistance in disengaging from a python that was attempting to swallow him. Upon their arrival, officers found a middle aged man who was unexceptional but for being entangled in the coils of a 16 foot Burmese python that had attached its mouth to the top of his head and was attempting to swallow him whole. It had reached his eyebrows and appeared incapable of proceeding further, but also refused to release its grasp.

In a matter of fact tone, the man explained to the officers that they were witnessing a simple case of mistaken identity in that he had been handling a rabbit that was the snake's intended meal and had inadvertently acquired rabbit scent on his body. The snake smelled rabbit, struck and was now attempting to ingest its prey as it had so often before. It doubtless sounds preposterous, from the human perspective, that a 200 pound, clothed and largely hairless man could be mistaken for a 3 pound fuzzy bunny, but snakes are not overly thoughtful creatures; they are slaves to instinct. After all, what besides a rabbit would smell like a rabbit?

The potential ingestee explained to police the potential for a bacterial infection if the uncoupling was not performed properly and that his call for assistance was to achieve this end with the least possible trauma to the snake. Whenever officers tried to pry the snake's mouth free, they were admonished for unnecessarily brutality by the man it was swallowing. Finally, the python apparently tired of the impasse and voluntarily surrendered its grip. Except for a great many puncture wounds on his scalp, the rabbit scented man was unharmed.

The foregoing is not, for humanity as a whole, a plausible scenario. Most people would likely die from shock upon encountering—much less being bitten by—a Burmese python. And if they possessed the strength of will to remain conscious, their sympathies would clearly not be with the snake. To a naturalist, however, the snake man's concerns were perfectly understandable and his actions appropriate, even commendable. I once had two water snakes, one attached to each hand, attempting to swallow the frogs I had been handling and now smelled like. So I understood his concern and felt his pain.

Part of being a naturalist necessarily entails getting bitten now and then. Whenever we probe too deeply into the affairs of other creatures, there always exists the possibility—or likelihood—that they will register their displeasure with tooth or nail. Where naturalists congregate, in fact, conversations regularly touch on the latest calamities to befall one or more of their ranks who crossed the line of interspecific sensibilities and got nailed by a wood rat or stabbed by a heron. In some cases, it is fairly easy to predict a bit of bloodletting as, for instance, when a physiological ecologist tries to determine the rectal temperature of a wolverine. Sometimes, though, there's just no reckoning when an episode of routine field work will serve up a laceration or two.

My initiation into the ranks of the bioperforated came at the age of four when I opened a kitchen cabinet to see a mouse scurry behind a large metal pot. I immediately coveted this tiny furry creature for a shoe box pet and focused every fiber of my being on apprehending it. I considered my prospects to be promising because it did not run out the other side, meaning it was hiding behind the vessel immediately before me. I had only to encircle it with my arms; it would inevitably end up in one hand or the other. Poor dumb creature! The reasoning behind my capture strategy was half right. Very briefly, the fingers of my right hand clutched the little rodent before it exercised the universal right of self defense and bit the hell out of me. This was the first of a substantial and varied assemblage of creatures that would exact a mouthful of me in the years to come.

Usually, these episodes of bloodletting were the consequence of minor indiscretions or interspecific misunderstandings; like picking up a baby blue jay that had fallen from its nest only to become the target of savage aerial bombardment executed by an admirably protective mother, also a childhood memory. Perhaps the most notable bite I sustained in my childhood, though, occurred when I was about 15 years old. My mother had finally acquiesced to my unrelenting badgering for permission to buy a boa constrictor from a snake dealer in Florida. In retrospect, I can see that the only alternatives left to her were strangling me in my sleep or selling me to gypsies, because I was truly insufferable. Thus did I acquire a magnificent specimen about eight feet long and the circumference of a fire hose. Boas are notoriously gentle snakes and mine was no exception, at least until the day I inadvertently crossed the line.

I kept my boa in a renovated walk-in closet outfitted with a large limb where he lay coiled and presumably content most of the time. Most snakes don't move about very much except in quest of food or a tryst and this was certainly true for my boa. Still, I sometimes took him outside to crawl around and get a bit of exercise. On this fateful day, I had an hour to kill before my paper route and fell asleep on the front porch in a rocking chair while my prize serpent crawled slowly and with obvious deliberation across our front lawn. Shortly, I awakened to the sight of a boaless lawn and set about in a panicked state to find and recover him. When I finally thought to look up, I spied him right away about 10 or twelve feet above the ground on the branch of an elm.

I nimbly leapt to grasp a lower branch with both arms and pulled myself up across it, then astraddle it, and on up to the next limb. One of my boyhood strengths was tree climbing and I whiled away many pleasant hours in the canopy of my favorite elm, among others, with my shoes parked at the base. I was a veritable monkey once I had bark underfoot, the scourge of nestlings everywhere, and I was confident of easily retrieving my snake. I soon learned, however, that disengaging a muscular eight foot reptile from a tree is not as simple as plucking an apple. I had only one hand available for the effort since I had to use the other to cling to the tree. Whenever I had uncoupled a foot or two of its cylindrical trunk from the limb, it clung ever more tightly with the rest. And when I abandoned that newly freed section to deal with the rest, it would reattach to deny me any net gain. With the reach of one hand, I simply couldn't be in enough places simultaneously to dislodge a husky eight foot strip of pure muscle intent on maintaining its grip.

Determined to prevail and with judgment clouded by frustration, I stood erect on the limb below the boa and gave a strong yank with both hands spread as far apart as possible. I felt his grip loosen and pulled forcefully once more. This time I pulled the snake free of its perch; but before I had time to relish my victory, became aware that I was falling backward with no free hand to grab a branch and abort my fall. I had somehow forgotten that our battle was being waged in a tree 10 feet or so above the ground. That realization dawned painfully as I crashed through a barrage of green boughs and fissured branches and was stopped abruptly by a collision with terra firma that left me gasping for breath.

Because I landed on my back, I had a commanding view of misfortune yet to come, for it came from above. My bruised body was positioned to break the fall of eight feet of twisting, thrashing, contorted and now angry boa that was plummeting directly toward me. When I felt the bulk of his body strike my chest, I groaned and lifted my head in time to see him coil minimally, open his mouth and hurl a loop directly at me. I had time only to press my chin into my chest so that his teeth stabbed the top of my head—not my face—each of the three times he struck. Clearly, I had it coming. Thereafter, his docile demeanor returned and he never attempted to bite me again. If only we humans could learn so well to let bygones be bygones.

Fortunately for naturalists, their frequently unconventional behavior is generally indulged by the larger society that has come to accept these types of eccentricities as harmless aberrations of a noble quest for knowledge. This has been brought about, for the most part I believe, by exposure to television nature documentaries that depict such undertakings as acquiring a full set of dental impressions from a large crocodile under primitive field conditions as altogether normal and necessary to our understanding of the world, if not the very survival of humanity. I can recall an instance in my own past where this charitable indulgence served to my advantage and possibly spared me bodily harm. Jordan and I—zoology graduate students both—decided to abandon our colleagues to collect some Mediterranean geckos on campus. I can't remember exactly why we undertook this particular mission, but the prospect seemed altogether normal to our compatriots in building "I" as we grabbed our flashlights and a cloth "snake sack" and exited, announcing our intention to collect a few geckos, much as mathematics students might run out for doughnuts.

Mediterranean geckos are not native to Florida or even the New World. Like a large number of exotic species that now call Florida home, they escaped from—or were released by—someone long forgotten, and found the region to their liking. The original animals not only survived but reproduced and, over time, colonized much of the University of Florida campus, especially the older buildings near the center of campus. They were most commonly seen, in fact, on the walls of The Hub, a low long building that, at that time, housed both a bookstore and the campus bank. Far from the rocky Mediterranean cliffs that are their ancestral home, the rubbery little lizards seemed content, running up and down the building's rough brick walls in quest of small moths and other nocturnal insects.

The front of the building faced a road and sidewalk that were well lighted, not a circumstance conducive to the activities of a nocturnal creature that preferred dim and quiet conditions. So we ambled to the back of the building where the prevailing light came from interior security lighting left on here and there coming through the windows. It was a balmy evening, the sort of situation that would bring out geckos. The geckos were mostly situated near the windows where they could capture insects attracted by the light. We donned our headlights, leaving both hands free, and set about grabbing lizards.

We had collected three or four animals when I spotted one that was larger than any we had seen and, needless to say, I had to have it. It was high, near the roof eaves, and out of reach, so I pulled myself up onto a window sill and was attempting to balance myself on this narrow ledge when I heard a loud male voice bellow from somewhere near but unseen in the darkness, "Freeze!" It was not until that moment that I realized that my conduct might be subject to misinterpretation, perhaps even arouse suspicion in someone not inclined to skulk about in the shadows collecting nocturnal lizards, in this specific circumstance a campus cop with his gun drawn.

I was, after all, silhouetted crouched on the sill of a bank window holding a cloth sack and wearing a headlight. In retrospect, I considered it remarkable not to have been shot on sight, a clearly justifiable reaction, given the circumstances. Instead, the officer listened patiently and politely as we offered an alternative explanation to what seemed an open and shut case of attempted breaking and entering and showed him our bag of geckos as corroborative evidence. Because his beat was a college campus where such improbable shenanigans were not uncommon, he accepted our story without reservation, admonished us for what he suspected to be trespass and allowed us to continue on our way.

Naturalists' penchant for collecting is at the heart of many a memorable tale. One of the professors on my doctoral committee, Dr. Pierce Brodkorb, was an internationally renowned avian paleontologist, which is to say his research entailed the collection of bird skeletons. There's more to it than that, of course, but many professional biologists are avid collectors. Instead of collecting baseball cards or coins, however, they tend to specialize in a group of animals or plants and assemble as large a collection as possible. In Dr. Brodkorb's case, the collection's repository was a foul smelling office-laboratory on the second floor of Flint Hall that housed an enormous collection of bird remains—mostly bones—packed away in boxes and tightly closed jars of macerating bird carcasses. Maceration involves soaking the carcass of an animal in a container of water until the flesh falls away from the bones. Then, Dr. Brodkorb would lock his office door, open all of his windows and pour off everything pourable and retain the bones, which were then set aside to dry and minimally deodorize before being cataloged and filed away with his other treasures.

The occasions on which these "pour offs" were allowed—basically in the evenings and on weekends—was a matter of department policy. This schedule, established after long and difficult negotiations, reflected the best compromise between Dr. Brodkorb's admirable, if odoriferous, pursuit of knowledge and the threats of the building's custodial staff and others to either resign or murder the old man and macerate his corpse.

To Pierce Brodkorb, happiness was a dead bird. And never was this judgment better confirmed than by the events of one simmering summer day when I and a number of other grad students took the day off to float the Ichetucknee River. En route, just outside Fort White, I spied something checkered black and white beside the road that had to be either a dead loon or a kaffiyeh blown from the head of a Palestinian motorcyclist. I had never seen a real loon, but knew them from photographs and nature documentaries as denizens of northern rivers and lakes, capable of unleashing shrill and blood curdling screams that terrify the uninitiated.

We drove back for a closer look and determined that it was, in fact, a dead loon. As I subsequently learned, these birds regularly mistake moonlit highways for rivers during their nocturnal flights and seldom survive attempts to alight on the surface of nonexistent water or the traffic thereafter. They are superb swimmers but, apparently, not especially clever. However one happened to end up here on the shoulder of Florida Highway 27 is anybody's guess, but a cursory olfactorial investigation suggested that the demise had occurred several days earlier.

Here again is an incident that clearly separates naturalists from the general ranks of humanity. Members of the latter would never have noticed the loon, never have stopped and driven back to check, and certainly would not have considered collecting it as a gift to Dr. Brodkorb. We did all of those things. Among the four of us, it was not too difficult to come up with a cloth snake sack large enough to accommodate the dead bird. We then closed the trunk on the neck of the sack and drove on with our cargo suspended from the rear of the car, confident that no one would purloin our fetid prize while we frolicked in the Ichetucknee River. The whole affair took less than 10 minutes.

By the time we arrived back at Flint Hall, it was almost dark. Apparently, it was not a "pour off" night and Dr. Brodkorb was nowhere to be found. So I tied the drawstrings of the loon bearing sack to a low branch of a pine tree just outside the main entrance to Flint Hall and departed. By the time I arrived for classes the following morning, the bag had disappeared. Dr. Brodkorb had spied it upon his arrival and knew from the putrid bouquet that it was intended for him; it was already macerating away and Dr. Brodkorb was grinning from ear to ear at his good fortune. Imagine! A dead loon!

Another of the University's gifted eccentrics is Carter Gilbert, a man with an encyclopedic mind and near total recall of baseball statistics and fish taxonomy. His ability to engage effortlessly in discussions of sports doubtless disguises the "Mr. Hyde" component of his nature; his penchant for collecting, classifying and preserving—not eating—fish by the thousands. His reputation as a man obsessed was assured by his innate response to an accident that occurred on a seining trip with colleagues from another institution. As they transported their large glass specimen jars up the slippery rock slope to their vehicle, one member of the party slipped and fell. Upon hearing the unmistakable sound of a glass shattering and the thud of an interrupted stride followed by a groan, Gilbert gave voice to his manifest concern, "Whose jar was that?"

But perhaps the greatest collector of all was Tulane University's Dr. Royal D. Sutkus. His passion for collecting and preserving virtually any life form within reach was so obsessive that it made Dr. Brodkorb macerating dead birds seem like Norman Rockwell material. I had heard of Sutkus' legendary zeal for collecting and preserving critters—mostly fish, but much besides—but had never been collecting with him. Jordan, however, took a field biology course with Dr. Sutkus during the summer of 1967, during which they traveled across the South, virtually annihilating populations of fish by seining and also grabbing any reptiles, amphibians, mammals and birds that crossed their path, all in the name of science. The swath of destruction they cut through the South that summer made Sherman's march seem like a Cub Scout hike.

The justification for murdering and preserving so many animals was that Tulane's zoological collections needed a broader sampling of specimens for study of their geographic range, anatomical variability and so on. It was often unclear how the collection of hundreds and hundreds of individuals of the same species of fish from the same site would advance science more substantially than a more modest sample, but it was not the place of lowly graduate students to question the actions of a legendary terminator like Sutkus.

His exploits in quest of specimens were often genuinely remarkable. When more substantial munitions were unavailable, Sutkus once beaned a groundhog with a rock. He had a particular fondness for squirrels and once leapt from a still moving vehicle he was driving—yelling as he departed for his startled passenger to grab the steering wheel and assume control of the vehicle—to disappear into the forest in quest of a squirrel he had spotted. Once he had skinned and prepared squirrels for his enormous collection, he would spend hours brushing their coats of fur with a toothbrush, quite possibly his own, so that not a hair was out of place.

These tales and others just as remarkable were related by colleagues at a celebration of Sutkus's 80th birthday. Many former graduate students, including Jordan, were invited to the affair and I tagged along since, after all, it was in New Orleans. It seemed that gars were among Sutkus's favorite fish species and an enormous and expertly carved smoked specimen was the centerpiece of an elegant hors d'oeuvres table. Speaker after speaker regaled the assemblage with astounding stories of Sutkus's often remarkable exploits in quest of specimens. Trespass was frequently involved and he was apparently cited for illegal discharge of a firearm while shooting at bats. But the evening's highlight was a colleague's scholarly presentation comparing the bulk of Sutkus's cache of fish specimens with those of other renowned collectors. He employed graphs, charts and statistical analysis to demonstrate definitively that Dr. Sutkus had killed more vertebrates—mostly fish—than anyone else in recorded history. Hitler in hip waders.

Of course, it could be convincingly argued that many field taxonomists are really hoarders rather than naturalists. They just happen to collect animals instead of stamps or campaign buttons. But, in order to keep and display their specimens, they are compelled to preserve them. Theirs is a special joy derived from a satisfaction of seeing row upon row, shelf after shelf, of jars—ideally, uniform in style and size—filled to the brim with preserved fish. Or lizards. Or snakes. Or drawers of stuffed mammal or bird "skins." These things afford bio-collectors with the same sense of satisfaction that a gardener might derive from the sight of a shelf full of jars bearing newly prepared blackberry preserves.

In the vast majority of cases, naturalists outgrow the regrettable obsession to possess the animals they fancy, finding fulfillment instead in simply observing them in the wild. Sometimes, in fact, satisfaction can arise from more indirect evidence of their presence; their songs, calls and cries; their footprints, etc. An acquaintance has so refined a sense of appreciation for such things that he gets teary eyed recounting the time he wiped from the soles of his shoes fresh evidence of one of Florida's few black bears. The beauty of some things simply transcends the grasp of the unsmitten.

It is not surprising that so much of humanity's mainstream is puzzled by the proclivities of people who catch geckos or seine fish or defend the welfare of snakes that are trying to shallow them. It is unfortunate, though, that so many are so estranged from the natural world that they are incapable of experiencing the sense of awe and wonder that lovers of nature take from the sight of a snake or the call of a barking tree frog. Unlike sports or literature or art or music, the natural world comprises a reality that is independent of human enterprise and would persist if we vanished tomorrow. We share our lives and our planet with them; they are our neighbors. And like all neighbors, they should at least enjoy our respect.

2

Grundoon and Friends

Jordan found little Grundoon in an outdoor market in Panama in the summer of 1968. She was attending a summer field course in tropical marine ecology, one of several courses offered through the Organization for Tropical Studies. This program is operated by a consortium of universities that included the University of Florida and its purpose is to teach Gringos about tropical ecosystems. I was attending a different OTS course next door in Costa Rica.

Grundoon was a coati mundi, a tropical American member of the raccoon family, not that this relationship is readily discernible except, perhaps, by her faintly banded tail. But the tail isn't bushy and soft; it is short haired, skinny and usually held ramrod stiff, often straight up. In this way, their tails serve as flags, visual signals to help keep the members of their group together in their jungle home. Coatis, at least the females, are social animals, moving about in "troops," as mammalogists say. This is why they make, for a non-domesticated species, such good pets; they enjoy company. In the wild, of course, this would be the company of other coatis, but when the young are separated from their own and sold at market, they quickly bond to people as well.

We were already somewhat familiar with coati ecology and behavior because one of our colleagues at UF, Dr. Jack Kauffman, had studied them extensively in Panama, had followed them around in the jungle, often clad essentially in shorts and canvas shoes, and had published his work in an extensive species monograph. The only reason his work is not as widely celebrated as that of Jane Goodall is that coatis don't use tools. Yet. If they or their raccoon cousins ever evolve opposable thumbs and abandon their richly anarchistic nature to engage in cooperative ventures, they'll become the dominant life form in a matter of weeks and we'll all be working for them. Nonetheless, even without these enhancements, they're curious and intelligent little scamps; you can see it in their eyes. Jack had kept one for a pet and would become bright and animated whenever he had the opportunity to talk about her. With little prodding, he would whip out of his wallet a picture of his beloved pet sitting impatiently atop the clothes drier, chattering in mildly distressed tones so Jack said, awaiting the return of the security blanket she kept with her at all times it wasn't part of the wash cycle.

We don't know how Grundoon came to be separated from her mother, but it would not likely have been a heartwarming tale. In much of Latin America, there exists a wide tolerance for practices Gringos tend to codify as animal cruelty (not that we don't also turn a blind eye where commercial gain is involved), and it is undoubtedly a good thing that she joined our household for the sum of $25. Grundoon was a tiny thing. Coatis tend to be thin and wiry anyway, not soft and cuddly like their raccoon cousins, and she was just a wisp of one. But she was completely tame, and Jordan found the coarse rope tied around her tiny neck was completely unnecessary. She would sleep with Jordan and follow her everywhere as befits a smart and social mammal.

And Grundoon was smart. She was also very bonded to Jordan and didn't like my intrusion onto the scene when I visited Jordan in Panama later that summer after my field course ended. In fact, we had to confine her to the bathroom to have a little non-threesome time and even then endure her squeaks of protest. Otherwise, she would use her long snout to wedge herself between us doling out tiny nips and squeals of outrage whenever we tried to modify the arrangement.

When we returned to the University of Florida late that summer, we moved into a wonderful old wood frame house south of town right on the edge of Paynes Prairie. It was one of three structures just off US 441 on a parcel owned by a relentlessly Baptist couple. Behind our house, beyond a fence, was a large pasture that they also owned and beyond that stretched Paynes Prairie. At that time, Paynes Prairie was a commercial cattle ranch, but within a decade, it would be purchased by the state as a nature preserve with limited public access and managed with the goal being restoration to its original state. Or, at least, the condition described by naturalist William Bartram when he visited "the great Alachua Savannah" just prior to the American Revolution. Anyway, it seemed then, and still does, an amazingly enlightened and commendable goal, especially in a state like Florida where everything is up for sale.

Restoration efforts went so far as to include the reintroduction of bison which, unfortunately, hasn't worked out as well as hoped. The parent stock from the western plains, the only stock left, was not the same as the eastern woods bison which was never abundant and, as so often seems the case, had been eliminated altogether by early European explorers and was gone by the time of Bartram's visit. In particular, they didn't possess a resistance to bruscillosis, a respiratory illness that afflicted a number of the reintroduced animals. Today, only a tiny herd of bison remains but the prairie teems with alligators, deer, snakes, sandhill cranes and much more. It is one of America's natural treasures and we lived right next to it.

As it turned out, Jordan and I really liked procyonids, members of the raccoon family procyonidae. I returned from Costa Rica with a kinkajou, a somewhat monkey like procyonid, and we shortly acquired a baby raccoon. We turned our back porch into a rumpus room for our pets and built a large walk-in outdoor cage as well. Kinkajous are arboreal and strongly nocturnal, meaning they prefer to climb and leap about, often dangling from their prehensile tails, especially at night. And so we ultimately gave him up to a more promising situation, but not before he bit a fellow graduate student—for no good reason as nearly as we could tell—and left a slow healing wound that bought him a deferment from the draft at the height of the Vietnam war, an estate envied by many colleagues living under the cloud of conscription.

Grundoon and Pooh, our raccoon, accompanied us for long walks on the prairie. As she ambled along with us, Grundoon proudly held her tail aloft and often ran ahead a bit or made brief diversions to investigate objects of interest. She also used the opportunity to locate and devour delectable tidbits, especially insects. Her particular relish was reserved for large crunchy beetles which she would munch and chew with lips smacking and eyelids half shut in sheer ecstasy. She quickly learned that there was a ready source of these treats, and various other grubs as well, under the dried cow pies that littered the pasture between our house and the prairie. Thus, we traversed the pasture at a more leisurely pace than was our inclination rather than endure Grundoon's chittering of bitter complaint that would invariably punctuate a hurried passage through such a potential cache of culinary treasures.

She became very proficient at processing cow pies and was a marvel to watch. Coatis have long noses that terminate in what appears to be a massive black rubber stopper. As they snuffle along the ground, they move the black stopper to and fro, up and down. When this animated snout detects a crunchy beetle or other delectable morsel, the long curved nails of their forepaws begin to dig furiously. However, if the item of interest lies beneath a fibrous cow pie, Grundoon would flip the pie with one paw, as proficiently as a short order cook flips a pancake, grab the coveted arthropod in her teeth and eyelids at half mast—begin smacking and crunching away with a delight that left us envious. Jordan and I always enjoyed our jaunts immensely, but we always suspected that our enjoyment was eclipsed by Grundoon's.

Author with Grundoon circa 1973
Photo by Gary Branum.

Some insects employ noxious odors to repulse the attentions of potential predators, but this never deterred Grundoon. She regularly encountered our massive, inept and flightless woodland roaches, called palmetto bugs, and learned early on that they discharge a pungent, vaguely almond scented spray that makes them even more disgusting. Grundoon would hold a palmetto bug under her front paws, rolling it toward her while slowly moving backwards, like someone rolling a small barrel toward herself. Eventually, after the spray had been fully discharged into the coating of dust and the dust rolled away, she would devour them with the same enthusiasm we might reserve for a chocolate eclair.

Ultimately, we learned what everybody who keeps wildlife pets eventually learns: In the long run, they don't usually work out. The delightful spirited nature that attracts us to them includes elements that are too often incompatible with the order and predictability we try to bring to our lives. Coatis, for instance, don't like the sound of certain specific noises, jangling keys in particular, and learning about these eccentricities can be a painful experience. She also had the always entertaining, but frequently painful, habit of treating us as "security trees" to be quickly scaled to the shoulders when she was startled. That, at least, is better than being a "pissin' tree," a fate that befell a fellow graduate student who turned out to be the preferred urination site for our pet flying squirrel, Schultz. Upon awakening from a nap in my shirt pocket, he would glide silently to Tom's pants leg, urinate, and be gone before Tom could bellow, "keep that animal away from me!" Wildlife pets wreck things, bite people and create disorder generally. Most endings are not the ones we hope for. At best, we usually end up hoping they've been reintroduced into the wild incrementally enough as to wean them away from dependence, that they picked up the skills they will need to survive without us.

In the case of Grundoon, she got miffed and ran away from home. We'd had her for perhaps 6 or 7 years, had moved to Puerto Rico and back, and were renting a house from another of Gainesville's innumerable slumlords several miles west of Gainesville. Grundoon had her own tree house in a large red mulberry tree that stood beside our house; later, in fact, we discovered that the house was leaning against the tree and that was likely what kept it standing. The arrangement gave her freedom and kept her dry and comfortable when we weren't around and, of course, she also had the run of our house when we were.

Then, I went away to the Galapagos Islands for a couple of weeks. Jordan was to pick me up upon my return to Miami where we had decided to spend a couple of days in nearby Lighthouse Point with her grandparents. So, before leaving, I transformed an unused carport into a giant walk-in cage with slide-in trays at the bottom where a neighbor would leave food and water. Grundoon did not like the arrangement. When we returned to throw open the door and fuss over her, she loped off with no expression of excitement, chirping a squeak of profound indignation, ascended the mulberry tree and retreated into her tree house. She refused our subsequent attempts to make amends and invitations to join us in the house, and condescended only to reach down from the roof to accept a banana, one of her favorite foods, squeaked again and was gone. For good.

For the next two weeks, we searched and called, advertised and set catch 'em alive traps baited with her favorite foods and the perfumes she loved to rub into her tail. We received reports of sightings for months but were never able to locate her. Finally the sightings stopped, though not until she had made it through the winter on her own. We missed her sorely and had a hard time accepting the fact that she was truly gone from our lives. Because coatis are intelligent and resourceful and because north Florida is covered with a promising mix of woodlands and cow pie infested pastures, we hope she lived out a full life and eventually got over a grudge only a procyonid could hold so uncompromisingly.

Regardless of the ultimate outcome of a particular wildlife pet experience, those who succumb to the temptation to bring the critters into the family always have wonderful stories to tell. Our own include the time Jordan and I returned to our prairie side home late one night to find no trace of lights, a situation that did not improve even when we entered and flipped the light switch. We did, however, hear water running as well as frantic scurrying and general pandemonium. There was no doubt what had happened; our merry band of procyonids had somehow opened the door to the back porch and were enjoying an unsupervised romp.

Quickly, we shut the front door behind us to prevent their egress to share their frolic with our long suffering neighbors, Ransford and Carola, who had borne the brunt of their past excesses. We could tell that the electricity was not totally out, but took little comfort since the tip off was the faint sound of some sort of distressed appliance emanating from the vicinity of our bathroom. I splashed about in the thin film of water that covered the living room floor bumping objects that shouldn't have been there until I found another wall switch and—risking deliverance by electrocution —flipped it.

We gasped as one! The water was not a pool, but a stream, and its source was our bathroom sink; for the first time, I was thankful we had only a single bathroom. The anguished appliance was my electric razor, switched on and gurgling angrily on the surface of an overflowing sink clogged by every item from the medicine cabinet above that had not been knocked to the floor. The lamp that should have lighted our way when I first flipped a switch was but one of many furnishings overturned and broken. All accessible foods had been opened and sampled at the least and often smeared about just for the hell of it. Everything, not just the floor, was wet because the kinkajou, raccoon and coati were leaping about on everything in a superexcited state, likely the high point of their lives.

The mystery surrounding their unauthorized entry into the house was solved some days later when we witnessed the kinkajou wrapping its prehensile tail around a door knob and executing a body roll to effect its rotation. That was when we realized that a more secure mode of door closure was needed and built a large walk-in enclosure for them under an imposing live oak in our side yard.

Of the many and varied comments elicited by an introduction to our extended family, one is memorable. One of the three little houses was rented to Mike, a medical student who had a penchant for experimenting with drugs and, it subsequently turned out, for inadvertently burning down his rental units, possibly related enterprises. A favorite pastime was taking long walks onto the prairie and engaging in long reflections on the plants and animals he encountered there. The prairie is a wonderfully fruitful place for such an undertaking; it is brimming with wildlife of all sorts, carnivorous plants, luxuriant lotuses, and, above it all, the sonorous trumpeting of sandhill cranes in the sky.

One day, as Jordan and I were embarking on a stroll, we spied two figures out on the prairie walking our way. One we could identify as our neighbor, but we did not recognize his companion. We worked our way through the pasture as briskly as Grundoon would allow without excessive protest but were still among the cow pies when our two parties converged. Mike introduced his friend and began describing in excited tones the glorious purple thistles blooming on the prairie rim. His account was so animated that there was little doubt his perception had been psychotropically enhanced. Meanwhile, his friend's mouth hung open; his wide eyes were riveted to Grundoon, a bizarre apparition snuffling around with a long, black rubber stopper nose, banded tail held stiffly up and flipping dried cow pies. Finally, in a barely audible tone, he said aloud to himself, "Man, that sure is a funny lookin' dog!"

We have kept many other creatures as well and most come with such tales. The first to sample our wedding cake was a little owl monkey, but it was unauthorized and, after the frosting was rearranged a bit, nobody knew better. And there was the crow—a wonderful, mischievous, neighborhood terrorizing crow—whose penchant for stealing shiny objects regularly complicated the lives of all who knew him. As when he found and absconded with the house key we'd left for a neighbor so she might gain entry to our house to feed the fish and parrot while we were away; ah well, a brick worked just as well. Or the time I returned to my lawnmower repair project from a lemonade break to find all four absolutely critically essential bolts had vanished; I returned in time to watch helplessly as he indifferently released the last one from his perch 80 feet up in a sweet gum tree and intently watched it plummet into the thick layer of leaf litter below, before flapping away in search of new amusement.

Catherine Hayes, a neighbor, once recounted her harrowing encounter with our sinister bird. She was carrying two bags of groceries, one in each arm, when the bird appeared from nowhere, alighted on her shoulder and proceeded to furiously tear away the end of a cellophane bag that protruded from her groceries and gobble down as much bread as possible while, with both hands occupied, she hurried to her door shrieking at him and trying to shake him loose the entire time. He flew away only when she reached the door and set the bags on the stoop.

We were witness to another interaction between the villainous crow and our victimized neighbor. Mrs. Hayes stopped by our greenhouse one day to buy a plant for another neighbor whose brother had just died after a long illness. She had a cake offering on the front seat of her car, but felt a need to bring something living as a token of sympathy and support. We spoke about matters of life and death, how death often comes unannounced and can be such a surprise, even when one's health is failing, and, of course, the finality of it all. After selecting a nice

Chinese evergreen, she opened the front door on the passenger side of her car and set it on the floorboard. She then closed that door and returned to the driver's seat, put her car in reverse and glanced into her rear view mirror. And screamed. Then she leapt white faced out of her car. She had found herself face to face with the crow hunkered down on the seat back glowering at her as only a crow can hunker and glower. After all that talk of death, Mrs. Hayes was not prepared for this apparition of death incarnate. When she regained her capacity for coherent thought, she discovered that the wax paper covering her cake bore numerous puncture holes through which the bird had devoured generous chunks. Fortunately, a few swirls in the icing with her index finger disguised the depredations of our black trickster.

It is unfortunate that not everyone is amused by such clever and mischievous antics since crows share their playful roguery with everyone, taking no account of age, gender, race or even degree of armament. And thus it was that our amusing black clown disappeared on the first day of the fall hunting season.

We also had a wonderful, though generally misanthropic, yellow head Amazon parrot, a wedding gift, who would sing her heart out (and we have the tape recording to prove it) whenever she heard Barbara Streisand perform and who yelled, "I'll get it!" whenever the phone rang. I also credit our parrot with inciting the highest peak of alertness I have ever observed in a vertebrate in a situation not involving electric shock. As a young bird in Costa Rica, Lorita had been pinioned, ie. endured a process whereby certain wing muscles were severed to render her incapable of flight. This also rendered her incapable of settling a score with our black cat, Beans, who endlessly taunted her from atop an aquarium hood by flicking his tail in her face across an unbridgeable chasm just beyond the reach of her massive beak. Nonetheless, her perseverance and resolve were both commendable and inexhaustible. She would climb out her cage's open door, clench her claws into its iron lattice and extend her body horizontally with neck outstretched and nut crunching jaws agape. But with every fiber of her being focused on delivering a bone crunching chomp, she still fell tantalizingly short.

Until one day. The established scenario was unfolding predictably, with Beans' tail slicing lithely through the air a micrometer from the tip of Lorita's slashing hooked beak. And then the great cosmic crap shoot delivered the grand convergence Lorita had hungered for so fervently and so long. The white tip of Beans' black tail snapped whiplike into a cubic inch of empty space a microsecond before Lorita's crushing gape slammed shut across it. For a long second, Beans looked as though his tail had been plugged into an electric socket. There was a gravity defying moment when his entire body stood rigidly in space, unsupported, with his head and legs extended straight out from his bristly torso like the discharge from an exploding black cigar held tightly in Lorita's beak. For the remainder of a loud and talkative day, her parrotspeak talked of nothing else as she savored her triumph. From that day forward, Beans and his crimped tail gave her very wide berth.

These days, we are content to enjoy our two dogs and three cats. Their behavior is less enthralling and far more predictable but undeniably less life-complicating. We genuinely miss that special spark that domestication extinguishes, but the predictability it brings to the mix is more than compensatory. If there is good news in the realm of wildlife pet keeping, it is that most animals are being captive—reared these days rather than being removed from the wild which was the norm only a few years ago. Perhaps commercial selection will one day produce a coati mundi that is not so easily offended, perhaps as forgiving as a golden retriever. If so, I'd like to have my name at the top of the waiting list; I'm ready to try again!

3

Dillers, Salamanders and Toads by the Gallon

Until the age of 22, I was a Missouri boy. Then commenced my love affair with Florida. It was in the summer of 1966 that I drove down to Gainesville in my first car, a 1962 Chevy Biscayne, a fine vehicle—until I got my hands on it—that served me throughout my graduate career. To a lifelong Missourian, Florida offered the prospect of a second childhood; or at least the opportunity to experience for the first time many strange and wonderful animals and plants. For a time, the world was new again.

Some elements of the fauna and flora were Missouriesque, but more were altogether new to me. Shortly after arriving, I encountered my first armadillo. It was unmistakable, with armor plating on all dorsal surfaces, including a triangular plate that stretched from one membranous ear to the other and narrowed down to the tip of its long and pointed nose. Like much of the local population, this armadillo was dead, having expired some hours earlier in a manner altogether orthodox for its kind—it placed second in a clash with tire tread.

Armadillo corpses are a common sight on Florida's road shoulders, especially following evenings when showers have softened the topsoil in which they love to snuffle about in quest of earthworms and other invertebrates. A popular prank for a time was to place beside their carcasses, conventionally belly up, feet extended ramrod straight and long slender tongue hanging from a slightly agape mouth, a beer bottle to suggest a demise attributable to inebriation, a gag their youthful perpetrators found endlessly hilarious.

But this lifeless creature was a new sight for me, having known armadillos only as prepared "skins" in the drawers of the University of Missouri's mammal range. While it was a marvel to behold, this armadillo pancake was the first of a great succession of the armored mammals that would cross my path in the coming decades, most often serving posthumously and randomly as speed bumps or adorning road shoulders until being spirited away piecemeal by throngs of appreciative vultures. But mostly, I remember them as enemy combatants in many conflicts where my garden was the field of combat.

Unlike many other animal species in which individuals are distinguishable by variation in size, coloration, body proportions or such, adult armadillos seem to be manufactured like cookie cutter copies, except that the armored tails of some have been abbreviated by dogs able to reach far enough into their burrows to worry away the aft portion of an otherwise gracefully attenuated extremity. In fact, stub tail armadillos are fairly common because the species' only defense against predators is a swift retreat into their burrows where they hunker head first against the tunnel's terminal wall huffing and grunting loudly, but making no attempt to fight their pursuer even as they are being nipped and gnawed. In the recesses of their earthen sanctuaries, nothing worse is likely to happen, given their full body armor and massive claws that keep them tightly embedded and resistant to extraction.

Armadillos are not possessed of great cunning, a frailty that is reflected in a countenance that seems to be limited to two expressions. When plowing the topsoil with their long snouts, they are oblivious to goings on around them and not easily distracted; at these times their demeanor is one of intense focus as their tiny black eyes sparkle in anticipation of an earthworm or other delectable morsel. When affairs of the larger world intrude upon their limited consciousness, however, they wear a startled expression that could only be accentuated by a cartoon bubble above their heads bearing the word "huh?" If they sense that danger is at hand, arnadillos execute their singular defensive maneuver—running like hell, bouncing without injury off anything standing in a straight path between them and their burrow; a bowling ball with a tail.

Being devoid of fur and poor thermoregulators, armadillos don't emerge during cold weather, but huddle in their burrows, doubtless dreaming of earthworms or, perhaps, simply lost in thought. But during Florida's abundant warm balmy evenings, earlier if they've discerned that rain has fallen, they lumber from their lairs and begin another night of dismantling the earth's crust in quest of insects, worms and other culinary delights. This is where they run afoul of the considerable tolerance borne by most gardeners for our wild friends. They lack the sensitivity to skirt our flower beds and vegetable gardens as they snuffle about and can destroy a sizeable planting in the course of an evening's rambling. Though they usually den alone, it is not uncommon to see a number of armadillos working in close proximity. This is especially—and depressingly—true during Florida's frequent droughts since they often converge on the only moist ground available, our gardens and lawns, ripping up considerable expanses with their massive claws whenever they sniff out a promising tidbit.

Several years ago, I faced down an imposing armadillo horde that was waging an assault on Kanapaha Botanical Gardens. Nightly, they were ravaging several plantings, particularly the sedum ground cover in our rock garden. I suspected that there might be a burrow or two in our large thicket of a native Florida yucca called Spanish bayonet, an impenetrable—to people, not armadillos— green wall by virtue of the long and sturdy spines borne on the tips of its sword like leaves. At the suggestion of a fellow armadillo battler, I purchased a catch—'em—alive trap called the armadillo special. Its design was basic—a central floor plate that tripped a wire causing the doors to slam shut—but was longer, long enough to allow the full body, tail and all, into the wire tunnel before its doors closed. The mesh was of a heavy enough gauge to withstand the considerable force an armadillo could bring to bear on it with its powerful claws.

I set the trap on a well worn trail bearing an armadillo's trademark "tail drag" impression etched along its length between the Spanish bayonet wall and the adjacent lawn. There was no need to bait the trap, even if I could figure some way to affix bugs and earthworms to the trip plate, because armadillos are creatures of habit and will use the same trail day after day even if a hardware cloth tunnel suddenly appears on a section of its length. The next morning, I found my trap closed shut with an armadillo inside. I removed the 'diller and reset the trap on an adjacent runway in case there might be another. On the second morning, I had a second armadillo. And on the third. And fourth! In eleven days, I caught nine armadillos, the entire hole-in-the-wall gang of sedum despoilers. I then moved on to other areas where they had visited less severe damage and reset my trap. In the course of that summer, I trapped more than 40 and removed them from Kanapaha.

The only real talent involved in trapping armadillos is determining where to place the trap. If an activity trail is evident, and they are unmistakable, especially given the clearly discernable "tail drag" impression on bare soil portions of the trail, the trap needs only to be placed in the center of it. Otherwise, it is best to locate the burrow, which is not as difficult as it might seem, and set it there. Armadillos' sole defense comes from their inaccessibility in the recesses of their earthen burrows, and they maximize this advantage by siting its entrance against a tree trunk, fallen log, boulder, building or other object that complicates excavation by a pursuer. Searching out such sites within a few hundred feet of 'diller damage, an astute trapper will usually find the offender's den without difficulty.

If there is more than one path radiating from the tunnel's entrance, it is a simple matter to narrow the animal's options by using sections of wire garden edging as a guide fence to the trap entrance, thereby sparing the miniscule brained creature the burden of indecision. A raccoon would never fall for such trickery, but then they are brilliant by comparison. When no den is evident, it is possible to erect wire edging drift fences that radiate from both ends of the trap into areas being visited by armadillos, but it may take several nights before their evening jaunts bring them to one of the fence guides and thence into the trap.

Jordan related the story of a fellow graduate student at Tulane University, Johnny Pagels, who was conducting research on armadillos. To recognize his study animals individually, day or night, he painted numbers on both sides of their carapaces with brilliant luminescent pink paint. In the course of his field research, Johnny parked his car in the Louisiana sun one sweltering day and returned hour later to find the vehicle's interior dazzling pink. After scraping a bit of paint from the windshield, he drove it to a body shop to get an estimate of the cost of restoring the interior. After examining the vehicle, the shop's body painter, barely suppressing a grin, quipped, "Well, at least it was a nice color."

One of the most amazing things about armadillos, other than the incredibly long time it takes for the bony carcass of a dead one to be fully incorporated into a sandy road, is that females bear litters of identical quadruplets. This is because their offspring are derived from a single fertilized egg that cleaves and separates twice. And young armadillos look like miniatures of the adults, not like the juveniles of most mammals that are readily distinguishable by their relatively large eyes, endearing countenance and different body proportions. They don't engage in play or show evidence of affection to human surrogate parents or to each other; they seem reptilian in both appearance and sociability.

Florida hosts another armored creature that lives in burrows of its own excavation, and it really is a reptile. I first learned about the gopher tortoise from a landlady who kindly tutored me as yet another in a long succession of student tenants on Florida's many natural glories. Although she disliked Spanish moss, because it reminded her of "old gray beards," she nonetheless seemed to take a balanced view of the natural world and was surprisingly knowledgeable about many aspects of the state's natural history. Thus, I became increasingly bewildered as she told me of a type of "gopher" that was common on most of Florida's sandy peninsula. We Missourians are regrettably well acquainted with burrowing rodents called pocket gophers because they cause significant damage to vegetable gardens and landscapes alike. But they don't bear the hard protective "shells" that Mrs. Bates assured me encased their Florida relations. When I fished for some clarification, she readily admitted that these armored burrowers differed greatly from northern gophers. In fact, she acknowledged, "Northern gophers look more like our salamanders."

Now, I was completely perplexed and momentarily assumed my landlady was demented. Salamanders are lizard-like amphibians; admittedly, some are burrowers but they are amphibians nonetheless. Still, my every attempt to resolve the enigma generated only additional descriptive characterizations that made my brain ache and left me with the impression I was trapped in a conversation that was the zoological equivalent of "Who's on first?" Only weeks later did I learn that some locals refer to Florida's native gophers as "sandymounders," because of their propensity for pushing surplus soil up and out of their sandy tunnels to create conical mounds at the surface. And over time, "sandymounders" has been corrupted by many into "salamanders." Indeed, northern gophers and Florida's sandymounders are alike. And to Mrs. Bates, a gopher is the abbreviated term for a gopher tortoise.

When the strictly vegetarian gopher tortoise lumbers from its dark burrow into the brilliant Florida sunlight in quest of food, its cold blood is warmed and it becomes quite animated. If disturbed, it races like an armadillo directly toward its burrow. Unlike the "diller", though, it can withdraw into its portable fortress when the need arises. It is unfortunate that neither of these evolutionarily refined responses is equal to the two forces that have reduced its populations so dramatically that it is now considered a threatened species. And both forces are aspects of human activities.

The first, incredible as it seems, is the slaughter of these slow and gentle creatures for food. I suppose it should not be surprising that a society that farms ostriches for meat would also have among its ranks folks who consider the small quantity of meat to be gleaned from the considerable effort required to dismantle a gopher tortoise worth the effort. But, in fact, these lumbering reptiles have long been counted as a delicacy in corners of the rural South that are visited by poverty as evidenced by the regular employment of homemade tools concocted solely for extracting tortoises from their burrows without a resort to excavation.

The second, and principal, cause of their population decline is the ever present and ever menacing habitat destruction that attends the ever present and ever menacing spread of human populations. Whether for more orange groves, cattle ranches, roads, residential developments or whatever, the sandy well drained habitats preferred by these ancient reptiles are being destroyed; and with it go the creatures that call it home, including the tortoises themselves and the myriad other creatures that find refuge in their burrows. It is perhaps the harshest indictment of official Florida's capitulation to forces plundering the state's natural treasures that its official regulatory guidelines actually have language defining the circumstances under which living gopher tortoises, perhaps decades older than people operating the machinery, can be entombed—there to suffer the torment of slow suffocation—if their presence complicates development and construction. Even crimes against nature can secure the legitimacy of official sanction in a state whose very soul is up for sale.

Not just gopher tortoises are lost when their burrows disappear because these tunnels are home to many other life forms. These include animals as diminutive as crickets and gopher frogs and as majestic as two of our continent's most colossal snakes. The massive indigo snake is North America's largest serpent, sometimes attaining a length exceeding eight feet. It is also one of the nation's most strikingly beautiful reptiles, encased in an armor of large prismatic blue-black scales. And, regrettably, it is also one of the rarest due to the same habitat destruction that plagues gopher tortoise populations and also to a gentle nature that makes it especially desirable as a pet.

Another regular lodger in the gopher tortoise's bustling lair is the eastern diamondback rattlesnake. This huge reptile is undeniably the world's largest rattlesnake; specimens longer than eight feet have been recorded and their heavyset bodies, beautifully patterned with vivid diamonds, make them seem even larger. They are often excitable when disturbed, throwing their massive trunk into coils that writhe protectively around a huge head, with eyes alert, tongue aflicker and a pillar of rattles held high and buzzing with passion that would shame a cicada. It is unquestionably one of the planet's most magnificent life forms and an encounter with a large one in the wild will leave any naturalist breathless and exhilarated. Civilians, on the other hand, tend to treat such chance encounters as horrifying life threatening ordeals.

Several years ago, while liberating some coontie plants destined to shortly be sacrificed at the altar of coastal Florida's relentless condominiumization, I encountered the freshly shed skin of a diamondback rattlesnake about four feet long. When I picked it up, I found it to be still damp with the aqueous lubricant that shedding snakes secrete between their two skins to facilitate separation. I knew, therefore, that it was very recently shed, since the waxing sun would certainly dry it to parchment within 30 minutes. Still, it was another five minutes and two excavated coonties later before I spied the snake, lying alert but motionless less than ten feet from the skin and the site of my activities.

I am regularly astonished at how a brilliantly marked animal, whether rattlesnake or tiger, can blend so well with its surroundings as to become virtually invisible. Here again, a stunningly bold reticulate pattern of black diamonds set in brilliant contrast to a backdrop of lighter colors, yellow in some specimens, nonetheless utterly vanishes into a mosaic of leaf litter, twigs, palmetto fronds and a miscellany of other earth tones. The snake remained motionless until I nudged it with the handle of my shovel in an attempt to persuade it to crawl elsewhere since it was in close proximity to a coontie I coveted. It slowly relaxed its coils and disappeared into the brush with a calm demeanor, never once becoming agitated or lifting its rattles to sound an alarm—a perfect gentleman.

Not all of Florida's sometimes subterranean fauna resorts to the considerable bother of excavating a burrow at all. The spadefoot toad is seldom seen above ground except following the heavy rains that bring it to the soil surface to breed in the short lived temporary pools left behind. A light shower, or even a steady rain does not provide a stimulus that is adequate to trigger the breeding fervor that results from a torrential downpour. On the evenings that follow such a deluge, the strange choruses of male "storm frogs," as they are called, fill the night air with an otherworldly din that conjecture might deem the warbled groans of distressed trolls. Despite the unsavory characterization however, this clamor wafts through the night air to alight as seductive whispers on the ears of female toads who rush headlong into a wet and amorous rendezvous. And that results in the deposition of long gelatinous strands of fertilized eggs, and presumably no hangover.

This procreative blitz is essential in environments where pools and puddles last only a few weeks. In fact, the metamorphosis from egg to tadpole to froglet may be completed in as little as 15 days and only a thunderous downpour, not merely a spirited shower, will produce a sufficient body of free water that will persist for such an interval in the sandy soils that are home to these reclusive creatures. It is true, of course, that they could work their magic in permanent water bodies like more conventional amphibian stock, but then these environments also harbor all sorts of predators and parasites as well as competitors.

On the heel of each hind leg, the spadefoot toad possesses its species' trademark, a raised black crescent that it wields like a spade to shovel dirt aside as it corkscrews itself into the moist soil to begin a life underground. In sheer numbers, an emergence of spadefoot toads can sometimes assume the magnitude of a plague that would overwhelm a pharaoh. Unquestionably, the most vertebrates of any kind that I have ever observed firsthand were spadefoot toadlets that materialized two weeks after Hurricane Frances sideswiped north Florida in September of 2004. Upon returning from an overnight visit to south Florida, I spied a dark mass of raisin sized objects swirling at the surface of our pool. The leaf skimmer basket, it seems, was already filled to the brim with the mass, innumerable spadefoot babies, leaving the balance to be swirled about. After emptying the basket's quart of toads into a bucket, I replaced it to screen out more while accelerating the process using a deep bodied blue net normally employed to scoop up leaves that had fallen into the pool.

By the time I had filled my net, the skimmer had collected another quart of raisin toadlets so I added the contents of both receptacles to the ghastly heap of corpses that filled the bottom inch or so of my white five gallon plastic bucket and went back to work. As I netted these mostly dead and bloated bodies from the water surface, a multitude of recruits emerged from pool side vegetation and plunged into the water like so many suicidal lemmings.

I began to push my net across the pool's bottom collecting the countless waterlogged toads that comprised a second layer of victims. When I finally emptied my net into the bucket for the last time, it was filled more than halfway with the tiny creatures. I estimated the aggregate to be three gallons or more, the only time I have ever employed volume as a unit of measure for any animal species. And the sad truth is that an imminent death in one guise or another awaited the vast majority of the participants in this great migration to nowhere. This is the supreme Malthusian truth that attends all such reproductive excesses. But while it represents a personal tragedy to many a toad, it is, in a demographic sense, simply the result of a genetically ingrained response proportionate to an extreme meteorological stimulus.

I briefly entertained the notion of preserving these three gallons of toadflesh and contributing them to the Florida Museum of Natural History's herpetology range. This would substantially eclipse the collection's celebrated series of 478 mud snakes, mostly juveniles, collected one rainy night in 1956 on Paynes Prairie following a hurricane, an affair that gave rise to the local oft repeated (in herpetological circles) maxim, "on a rainy night, you can slam on your brakes on Paynes Prairie and slide all the way into Micanopy on dead mud snakes." But I had more pressing concerns than locating a suitable receptacle and a drum of formaldehyde. After all, we had just recovered electrical power and water following two back-to-back hurricanes and had much order to restore. Unless we installed a generator before the next loss of power, we would face the prospect of rinsing off after the abbreviated lathering that passed for bathing in such circumstances, not with clean pool water, but with frog broth. And there was the nagging doubt that neither the lot of mankind nor the store of scientific knowledge generally would be substantially advanced by three gallons of toad preserves on a museum shelf.

Even so, I eventually surrendered to a growing curiosity about how many individual toads were in that estimated three gallons I removed from our pool. So I purchased a box of raisins and counted the number required to fill a level cup—780. Employing this as a representative measure and disregarding compaction, which would yield an even larger figure, I determined that there were approximately 12,480 animals per gallon or 37,440 altogether in my three gallon bonanza.

Within a matter of days, the plague abated as toadlings everywhere were compelled by their nature to corkscrew themselves into the earth, there to feast and grow and mature and await a drenching heaven sent summons to emerge. In the months ahead, my daily rescue mission afforded me a privileged view of the intense winnowing process that brings such a population back into balance with the resources that sustain it. Following rains, I invariably found immature spadefoot toads paddling about and grappling to ascend our pool's sheer concrete face, but progressively fewer in number and larger in average size, no longer raisin frogs, but prune frogs, then plum frogs. What fates had befallen their more numerous and less fortunate contemporaries it is not possible to discern. But clearly, their individual misfortunes served to improve the prospects of their surviving compatriots and their species.

In the 40 years I have called Florida home, the state has undergone many changes, virtually all attended by negative consequences for its ever diminishing natural areas. Lifeless armadillos still line the roadways, particularly in rural areas while truly desirable species like gopher tortoises have become rare or, like the indigo snake, extremely rare. Regulatory protections doubtless serve to decelerate these population declines but, in the absence of a change in humanity's basic values, they are little more than a holding action. The relentless loss of habitat necessary to the survival of these creatures insures a future when their populations are limited to a few tracts of land that are mostly publicly owned but mostly inaccessible to the public.

It is a truly peculiar network of neural synapses that enables humanity at large to profess unlimited and selfless love for its children and grandchildren while continuing to selfishly squander the world's limited resources in the same manner as its parents and grandparents. Perhaps these two incompatible value systems reside on neural networks that are separated by that deep cleft in the center of the human brain. Though neural anatomy repudiates such a straightforward physical basis for the dissociation, it seems to me a fitting metaphor since, for a species that reasons, the chasm is unaccountably deep.

It is regrettable that natural selection acts to improve the prospects of individuals, not species, and, even then, their immediate prospects only. Evolution has not equipped us to concern ourselves with long term prospects for survival, not even the foresight to discern the ongoing collapse of our ecological support systems all around us. How else could you explain our willingness to breathe polluted air and drink impure water or, incredibly, buy bottled water? To wage war to keep oil gushing rather than adopting energy efficient automobiles and lifestyles, until it's all gone, all the while pretending it somehow won't happen? To even consider colluding in the extinction of half the planet's life forms, when we fought like hell only a few years ago to save the bald eagle and the timber wolf, all because we won't voluntarily limit human population growth? Clearly, as a whole, and whatever we may say, we don't love our children enough to accept the painful consequences of putting our house in order now so they don't inherit a planet in ruins.

All of these fellow creatures—armadillos, gophers, diamond-back rattlesnakes, spadefoot toads—are products of unique evolutionary pathways, each with unique adversities and pitfalls, bottlenecks and compromises, triumphs and limitations. At a time when largely unchecked human population growth pushes one species after another into the abyss at an ever increasing rate, we are finally beginning to ask whether this loss really matters. The unspoken assumption, of course, is that we're asking whether it matters *to us*. Doubtless, it would matter profoundly to the individuals facing annihilation and represent an insult to any underlying creative intelligence. But these are entities whose concerns we tend either to ignore or rationalize into irrelevance. Does their loss really matter *to us*?

While some life forms, like watermelons and poodles, significantly impact the quality of human life directly, most species do not. We have limped along fairly well without the dodo and the demise of the dusky seaside sparrow did little more than moisten the eyes of ardent bird watchers. Collectively, we clearly value our comfort and security above the continued existence of any species that might limit our access to crude oil, even to squander chasing leaves around our driveways with a leaf blower when a leaf rake would suffice. And we know from experience that the web of life is not woven so tightly that the loss of one thread—or a thousand—will necessarily create an irreparable tear or result in ecosystem collapse.

But their loss *should* matter. Beyond our selfish concerns of utility, all species are manifestations of unique genetic blueprints derived from unique evolutionary pathways. Their paths diverged from our own long ago, in most cases long long ago, but they are linked nonetheless. It is this uniqueness that gives every species an innate value that is equal to our own. We may ponder whether human life has value and meaning; but mosquitoes don't! Every time they sense a puff of our carbon dioxide wafting by, they give chase precisely because they know our lives have value. To them. By only one uniquely human quality do we invest ourselves with the authority to judge their worth to be subordinate to our own; but arrogance is not a virtue.

4

Snake Stories

While all of the earth's creatures may enjoy the favor of God, few enjoy the sanction of humanity. The reasons for our uncharitable nature are as numerous and varied as the groups of organisms that offend us and betray a level of intolerance that is unbefitting a species that celebrates its capacity for reason. Even many who grow misty eyed at the plight of whales and sea turtles would not refrain from stomping the earth's last cockroach. Efforts to explain this prejudicial nature invariably fail when it is deemed to somehow be an expression of logical judgment because, in fact, logic is not involved. Prejudice does not result from ruminations of a rational mind, but rather as an expression of our darkest fears colored by an ignorance of the natural world. We loathe what we loathe without giving it much thought one way or the other.

As a class, birds have fared well. We hold them in such high esteem that we enact legislation to protect them, build structures to house them, market foodstuffs to supplement their natural diet and put their likenesses on our stamps, coins, and paper currency. Butterflies, too, are generally exalted and there is a temptation to attribute these affections to a respect borne by earthbound mortals for those possessed of a capacity for flight. But then there are bats—filthy, rabid, mangy, hair entangling bats. Even though they are kindred mammals, bats fail to enjoy the respect accorded our feathered friends. Because they flap about at night, perhaps? Then what of owls, also nocturnal fliers, who enjoy universal veneration as noble and virtuous creatures? No, it simply isn't worth pondering; there is no uniformly applicable standard to explain the disparities we know as bias. We like owls because they're birds and butterflies because they're butterflies and hate bats because they're bats. We don't like bats more when we learn that many species eat mosquitoes, but, thus informed, realize we'd like them even less if they didn't.

Still, we offer vindications for our prejudices, even though they tend to be rationalizations and not truly logical judgments. Sadly, we seem willing to cling to any justification that ennobles our prejudices, even those devoid of a factual basis. For instance, hunters regularly give voice to the claim that, without their benevolent intervention, deer herds would swell insufferably and overpopulate their environment And while this is doubtless true, it overlooks the fact that natural predators would perform this function had their populations not been decimated by hunters. Population control, man's stewardship of the natural world, provides exoneration, not inspiration; hunting down animals and blowing their brains out is the motivating factor.

In the realm of those creatures that have fallen altogether from our graces, none are more reviled than snakes, with spiders the likely contenders for a distant second place. There is no logical explanation for this attitude as their endeavors work largely to human advantage, as do those of spiders. It is our collective assessment that they simply lack virtue. Clearly, it is unreasonable to expect logic to play a substantial role in the judgment of countrymen who embrace a scavenger for their national bird.

It is not generally reasonable to think badly of snakes, but we usually stoop to the occasion, even if reason need be abandoned. Virtually any serpent encountered in the vicinity of water is routinely branded a water moccasin, the nominal justification for its annihilation by any means necessary. Many snakes that avoid damp areas fare no better; they are deemed to be copperheads—even where they don't occur—also grounds for death by thrashing. Those who subscribe to these conventions generally refuse to abandon their misinformation when challenged by those who know better, as evidenced by an account related by a snake hunting companion of my youth.

Dolph came upon a scene of carnage that is duplicated daily wherever fishermen gather to fish and swap lies. A benign banded water snake had just been pummeled to a nearly unrecognizable heap of blood, scale and sinew by two locals who mistook involuntary writhing for defiance and heaved yet more stones on the dead reptile. Too late to intercede on the serpent's behalf, Dolph resolved to at least cast some light to dispel this mental darkness and perhaps spare other water snakes this regrettable fate. He explained to the baffled pair that the reviled creature was not a water moccasin but an innocuous water snake, likely their ally by virtue of its consumption of shad and other "trash fish." As evidence, he picked from the mangled mass a head whose dangling eyeballs bore clearly recognizable, if bloodshot, round pupils; those of water moccasins, he explained, were elliptical.

He opened its mouth to confirm the absence of fangs that even the witless know water moccasins possess. As a final proof of his identification, he apprised the men of a distinguishing anatomical feature; below the anal plate of a water moccasin's belly, the scales are whole and undivided, whereas the remains of this poor snake exhibited the clearly exonerating divided scales of a harmless water snake.*

Dolph abandoned the field of slaughter content in the hope that his intervention might deliver other snakes from a similar fate. He was not long able to entertain this lofty self delusion, however for, as he strode away, he heard one of the men exclaim to his comrade, "He don't know a damn thing about snakes! I know a water moccasin when I see one!"

And so they do, at least in their hearts for these are affairs of the heart, not the head. Given the passions involved, it is not surprising that the realm of bio-folklore abounds with strange and fanciful tales that bear witness more to the fertility of the human imagination than to the nature of snakes. Herpetologists might deem life inordinately richer if half these lies were true.

Many of these colorful tales are generic, as I learned in my boyhood travels in quest of snakes. Even where "milk snakes", a colorful species of king snake, don't occur, folks are familiar with their regular recourse to entering barns to suck milk from cows. And well beyond the range of mud snakes, the much maligned scapegoat of the ensuing myth, hoop snakes are said to take tail in mouth and roll down hills in pursuit of prey or flight from danger. A regular embellishment of this tale puts in the path of the cartwheeling serpent a tree that sheds its leaves and withers when stabbed by the "stinger" these snakes are alleged to bear at the end of their tails. The facts that snakes don't have stingers, can't milk cows and aren't possessed of the skeletal integrity to survive a hoop roll are no more relevant than the negligible probability of finding a bat tangled in your hair. This is not biology, but a glimpse of the fears that dwell in the shadowy recesses of the human psyche.

* While these diagnostic features are useful for postmortem assessments, they are of limited value in the field where the human predisposition is to thrash first and ask questions later. Moreover, counseling that water moccasins have heart shaped heads does a disservice to harmless water snakes, whose defense posture involves flattening both head and body to appear larger and more formidable. Probably the most useful distinguishing field characteristic is the prominence of the serpent's eyes when the head is viewed from above. In harmless water snakes, the eyes protrude outward and upward in the manner of frogs. In water moccasins, however, the eyes are not visible from above, as they are overlain by the superocular scales; they appear to be embedded in the side of the head, not on top. If opportunity permits, potential snake pummelers should be further advised that moccasins are rarely seen abroad during daylight hours because, as their eyes' elliptical pupils attest, they are nocturnal creatures. Finally, they will profit from heeding the universally ignored but nonetheless universally meritorious counsel that inaction is preferable to snake—flogging because it precludes the prospect of snakebite if things go awry.

The human faculty for exaggeration is inordinately challenged when reckoning the length of snakes. It is my observation that the scale of the misrepresentation is generally a function of venue—whether the individual describing an encounter with the serpent en exaggerato relates the account indoors or out. Outdoors, the snake seems almost invariably to have been crossing a road when encountered and almost as invariably spanned the road's width entirely, often with a coil or two to spare on the shoulder. This means its length is a function of the width of the road. For indoor accounts, the critical determinant of length is the distance separating the narrator from some structure, particularly a wall. Chronicles of these tall tales are richer because they are most often related at social functions, where the likelihood of tongue-loosening inebriation as well as varying proximity to several walls increase the likelihood that the reptile was enormous. "It was...It was...Why, it was from here to the wall!" they stammer, spattering beer in a sweeping gesture toward a wall ten feet or more distant. These claims might be deemed more credible if those peddling them at least took a thoughtful step in any direction before bellowing their delusions.

And what soldier has abandoned the jungles of Asia without hearing accounts of the deadly "five step snake," also known as the "five second snake" to those who measure post bite longevity in time rather than space. Both refer to the limited time or tread that remains for the unfortunate mortal bitten by this serpent, whose poison is apparently more potent than any known to science. Another tale that bears testament to the toxicity of snake poison involves a cowboy who dies after being bitten on the ankle by a rattlesnake whose fangs penetrate his right boot. Years later, his son puts on the boots and, after complaining of a stinging sensation on his right ankle, collapses and dies. It is subsequently discovered, of course, that the son's death is attributable to a prick by one of the fangs that had felled his father and still remained lodged in the boot. There is even an infrequently recounted sequel wherein this curse strikes yet a third generation of a family that seems to economize on expenditures for footwear, but this seems to speak more to congenital stupidity than venom potency.

And then there was the motorist who ventured upon a rattlesnake, a large one, stretched completely across a country road. Before he could flatten the reptile with rubber tread, it struck the car's right front tire. Instantly, a torrent of pressurized air rushed through the snake's hollow fangs, inflating its whole body, resulting in its explosion and, apparently, vaporization, as not a trace of its existence remained. The fact that poison ducts are not connected to the body cavity is an inconsequential trifle to those who defend the veracity of the account. After all, the tire was flat and the absence of a carcass a logical consequence of the blast. How much proof do you need, anyway?

When snake maligners recount truly fantastic tales, they are usually careful to distance themselves from personal experiential knowledge of the encounters they report, generally, those of casual friends or second cousins. This affords exoneration in the event the story is debunked by the occasional listener who is familiar with the natural history of reptiles or who simply recognizes baloney, however thinly sliced. Consequently the infrequent account of an individual who assumes direct responsibility for its accuracy is all the more memorable.

Perhaps the most remarkable such narrative in my experience was related by the father of a boyhood friend. In his youth, he told me, he was being pursued across the lawn by an older brother with whom he was engaged in a game of tag. His escape strategy entailed diving into a dog "wallow" that breached the base of an otherwise impenetrable multiflora rose hedge, executing a wriggling belly slide and emerging on the opposite side to taunt and further elude his pursuer. He was hurling headlong in mid air when, to his horror, he beheld a snake coiled in the depression that was his target. Out of sheer terror, he resolved not to touch the reptile, or even the ground, and sailed through the breach to land running on the other side. Confronted with my objection that this was clearly impossible as it violated immutable physical laws, he fixed me with a riveting glare and said simply, "I did it!" That's a level of snake avoidance that's even more astounding than my high school buddy Ronald Abmeyer's crossing 25 foot wide Cane Creek to escape a water snake and only getting one foot wet.

Believe it or not, snakes are more than just legless lizards and there are many species of true lizards—with moveable eyelids, external ear openings and other features lacking in snakes—that have lost their limbs over evolutionary time. And when the inventory of slanderable snakes is exhausted and beer remains, some will slander them too. "Glass snakes" or "joint snakes," so the story goes, are so named because of their sinister ability to break into segments when threatened and scatter in all directions to elude capture. One portion of the tale is not without foundation, because some legless lizards, like many other lizards, when threatened, are capable of separating their bodies from their inordinately long tails to produce the appearance of a snake breaking in half. Unencumbered by cephalic guidance, the hindquarters thrash about and further fragment with a genetically preordained fervor that distracts the adversary while the more prudent forequarters retreat with little fanfare to fight another day, or at least grow a replacement tail.

Snake vilifiers, though, insist that the tale is only half told. For it is the "snake's" dastardly intent to reunite its fragmented being after the storm has been weathered, an ambition conventionally foiled by the incarceration of any segment of the disjointed reptile, preferably in a glass container. The remaining pieces inevitably reassemble into two sections only to suffer the anguish of an inability to incorporate the one remaining and painfully visible fragment needed to unite them and make the body whole once more. Such is the futility of resisting a species of such superior intelligence.

Will humanity's fear and suspicion of snakes ever diminish? That seems unlikely, given the innumerable wrongs these reptiles have committed against us, a species possessed of inherent intellect and virtue. After all, nothing positive could come from fraternizing with a life form that hangs out under flat rocks and leaves a trail of slime as its trademark. Truly, there is little prospect of a reconciliation between the blameless ranks of humanity and the unholy agents of Satan.

At least that's how many in the mainstream apparently see it. And regrettably, this is a fair characterization of the estrangement that has passed for a relationship with snakes since the time we first descended from the trees and began to survey the world around us. Such biases are established early and not easily changed. So it is usually futile to argue with advocates of these beliefs and often dangerous as well, so strong do emotions run where snakes are concerned. Though it may be unrealistic to expect our race to afford snakes the loving embrace conferred by its subset of herpetologists, it should nonetheless be possible to summon the discipline to spare them the unwarranted curses and injury that have so long been their lot.

Educational programs that reach into our classrooms seem to be the best approach to fostering a reassessment of prejudices that would otherwise become the birthright of unborn generations of potential snake thrashers. Even an uneasy peace is far preferable to a perpetuation of the groundless suspicions that pervade our relations with snakes and estrange us from them. Otherwise, I doubt that we, as a whole, will ever see beyond the scales and limblessness the singular splendor of which serpents are possessed.

Within my lifetime, I hope to witness the issue of a postage stamp bearing the likeness of a banded water snake, an act that would symbolize a long overdue tribute to the splendid and long suffering creature that has so long been persecuted for being the water moccasin it is not. But even more, I await a like tribute to the species whose inglorious notoriety has made it symbolic of our unfounded intolerance, the water moccasin. For this would herald a welcome ennobling of the human heart, the dawn of a new day of coexistence with snakes—and spiders and bats—whose presence has gone uncelebrated for so long.

5

Gardening in Purgatory

To gardeners in northern Florida, it seems psychohistorically significant that the concept of purgatory had its origin in a church whose spiritual center, Rome, is located in a similar climatic realm. For zone 9, the U.S. Department of Agriculture's meteorological euphemism for purgatory, is peopled with those who know the endless toil and seasonal calamities that attend gardening on Florida's, northern peninsula. Despite seasonal variations in soil and rainfall, zone 9, where, by definition, winter lows normally bottom out at 20 degrees F., may be considered generically purgatorial because its winters, however glorious, are either too cold or too hot to satisfy so many of America's most beloved 'mainstream' landscape plants, especially those dear to the Yankee malcontents that constitute a major, and vocal, demographic component.

In zone 8 just to our north, many harbingers of spring find a home in the wooded hills of Georgia. Jack-in-the-pulpit tubers stir in their earthen womb to send aloft yawning inflorescences as they awaken from their cold slumber. And patches of spring beauty arise from nowhere to spread their pink lace on the leaf strewn forest floor. In short order, they are joined by bloodroot and trilliums, and then columbine, whose dangling flowers are a welcome sight to nectar seeking hummingbirds en route from their winter home on the Yucatan Peninsula to northern climes. Gardeners set about tending radiant beds of tulips, jonquils, lily-of-the-valley, hyacinths and myriad other glorious species that grow from bulbs or rhizomes whose dormancy needs cannot be satisfied by the on-again off-again dalliances with cold that pass for winter here.

To the south, in zone 10, the marvelous tropical ornamental plants and fruits that would be killed by our occasional dip into the low 20s add to the landscape a splendor that is beyond the reach of zone

9 gardeners. So we forsake tulips altogether, or indulge the sacrilege of growing them as annuals, and drag in the dracena with every freeze warning—purgatory by any gardener's reckoning. When one adds to these woes the local tragedies of soil, mostly ancient sand dunes, and the predictable late summer drought, it often seems that hell, and not purgatory, is a better characterization of our climatological predicament.

At certain times, though, this wretched state of affairs is not immediately obvious. In an early spring that is not hijacked by one of the region's notorious late freezes, a ground hugging multicolored cloud bank materializes beneath oak canopies everywhere as azaleas burst into bloom! For a few precious weeks, these Asian beauties flower so profusely that their foliage is overwhelmed by a soft floral shroud of white, red, lavender, yellow, or variations thereof. At such times, a drive through some older neighborhoods can be a transcendent experience that leaves retinas raw from overstimulation. Shortly thereafter, meadows and roadsides begin to blush with the glow of phlox, an exquisite wildflower whose color spans the transition to summer. These blushes deepen into carpets of pink, purple and white that are doubtless the most striking offered by any wildflower in homage to spring in north Florida. In midsummer, great masses of flowers weigh down the boughs of crape myrtles to brighten our streets and yards for another six weeks.

But that's it! For the remaining weeks and months, not much of horticultural consequence goes on in the region as a whole. Right in the middle of this horticultural morass is Gainesville, known as Hog Town until 1853 and affectionately called Hogtown by many even today. Gainesville has its share of gardening gurus, collectors and specialists, some of whose landscapes are nothing short of spectacular. But, for the most part, homes large and small have traditionally been encircled by "McLandscapes," assemblages comprised of a relatively few species known to thrive in purgatorial situations—liriope, crinum, pittosporum, African iris, sago palm and the like. These veritably indestructible selections are also favored for cemeteries, parking lots and other situations here where commitment to maintenance may be lacking, or at least questionable. This tends to confer a visual monotony that is testament to the exercise of caution, rather than daring, that pervades the practice of the horticultural arts in zone 9.

Given this bleak picture, it is reasonable to ask why any rational person might consider undertaking the development of a substantial personal garden, let alone a public botanical garden in this climatic realm. And yet that is exactly the mission Jordan and I undertook back in the summer of 1977. Certainly, it would have been easier to do our sowing and reaping a few hours drive either north or south. This presupposes, though, that climatological considerations weighed heavily into our decision to live and garden in this part of the world. In fact, the decisions and judgments that define our lives seem always to be infinitely more complicated affairs, and in our case, suitability for gardening was not a major consideration. For we were here not as horticultural pioneers, but as malingering students, survivors of Hogtown's academic mill, the University of Florida, spewed out, diplomas in hand, at a time when job prospects were grim.

Still, we were not altogether without prospects and I made the plunge first. Upon graduation with a doctorate in zoology, I had job offers from Arlington College, in Arlington, Ohio, and InterAmerican University in Hato Rey, Puerto Rico. Figuring, incorrectly it turned out, that any university would be more exalted than a mere college, I fled to the tropics where I taught for one year at Inter American before being unceremoniously discharged for rabble rousing. Specifically, I attempted to help organize a badly needed teacher's union at an institution reputed to have a 50% faculty turnover annually. That year I learned much about the world in general and academics in particular.

And so I returned to sunny Gainesville to lick my wounds and get back on course. My alma mater offered me an interim appointment to give me a year to get back on my feet, to toe the straight and narrow, while Jordan finished her dissertation. If their goal was to financially underwrite my rededication to the glories of academic endeavor, however, they squandered their investment as we grew ever fonder of the oasis that is Gainesville and decided not to seek jobs in other locales we considered unlivable—much of the deep South and Midwest, the far North and, of course, Texas. At year's end, we didn't land a position at either of the two schools to which we applied and elected instead to settle in, at least for the time being, in the one place we both loved.

But how to make a living? If knowledge of biology was a marketable commodity, we wouldn't have been in this predicament and that was all we really knew and loved. Almost. It seems everywhere we went, we always dragged along a host of critters and plants. The animals, mostly captive raised, included a coati mundi, ferrets, a kinkajou, parrot, various snakes and miscellaneous vermin. Their various antics and endeavors always seemed to eclipse our efforts to control them with the effect of keeping us perpetually in hot water with neighbors, employers, and others capable of influencing our credibility and fortunes. The plants, however, invariably thrived under our care and were much admired by all. And thus we decided to grow and sell plants—house plants—to all who had ever admired our own, to our friends, and to their friends' friends. If we wouldn't be rich, we could at least make ends meet.

And it worked. We built a small greenhouse and propagated everything that was readily available at the time—peperomias, pileas, begonias, airplane plants, succulents, cissus. We sold plants only in clay pots, as we hated plastic, and even made macrame hangers to support some of our hanging baskets, going so far as to select specific twines and colors to match or complement the foliage or flowers. In those days, before the central Florida horticulture giants caught up with demand, it was a seller's market and we could peddle virtually everything we could grow right from our greenhouse once a month to a public that began lining up early to have first crack at whatever new items we were offering. It was the first golden age of gardening and we were on the ground floor. It seemed we had only to capitalize on our collective green thumb for sustenance and watch the Nixon administration flail and sink into the abyss for entertainment. All was well in the respective realms of horticulture and politics.

In retrospect, it seems obvious that if we had understood anything about economics or had been even modestly ambitious, we could have grown into a horticultural giant ourselves, as some of our contemporaries did. After all, the reason our customers flocked to our doorstep was that we served up two commodities in short supply—sumptuous plants, always with something new, and credible advice on growing them. But we were always dabblers who enjoyed the gabfest with our customers more than managing and growing a business. And this is what finally steered us away from commerce and nurtured an interest in growing plants for educational display.

The sad truth is that not everyone has a green thumb; many, in fact, possess the touch of death. As a consequence, we became accomplices to the mercenary practice of phytocide, regularly taking a few pieces of silver to look the other way while our customers returned monthly to purchase replacements for plants they had managed to annihilate in the same period we had spent grooming to life's prime their now doomed successors. Month after month, they appeared at our doorstep cash in hand, smiles on their faces, with gripping tales of woe and misfortune, often involving pets or children, that had reduced their latest crop of houseplants to fleeting memories. Blame was seldom acknowledged since buyers tended to see themselves as victims of some grand cosmic crap shoot rather than causal agents; but most accounts were laced with an innocent optimism that this time would be different; that, whatever else happened, the new peperomia would not end up in the blender.

Certainly, their accounts filled the entertainment vacuum created by Nixon's resignation and variations and twists in their telling seemed endless and frequently imaginative. Still, they were insufficient recompense for the haunting image of green tangles of foliage crushed at mid stem and dangling from the back door of a station wagon lumbering out of our driveway as its beaming driver waved, "see you next month!" And there was no doubt we would.

So, in addition to selling plants, we began to teach a community education course through Santa Fe Community College to provide instruction on the basics of plant care. The course was quite popular; so popular, in fact, that additional sections were scheduled to meet a burgeoning demand. People everywhere seemed intent on growing plants in their gardens, homes and work places. We taught the basics of soil preparation, watering, fertilization, light, pots and potting, propagation and much more. Generally, we brought flats of plants to these sessions for 'show and tell,' and ended with a question and answer segment in which we mostly addressed the causes of whatever disasters had befallen their plants in the week since we last assembled.

Shortly the Alachua County Older Americans Council asked me to bring our dog and pony show to their clients and I gratefully accepted the invitation. My most memorable recollection from that era was one that deepened my understanding of how terribly estranged we are from so many other creatures with whom we share the earth. As was usually the case, I transported a varied assemblage of plants to acquaint the class with the vast array of species that can be pressed into service to make our lives more pleasant, or to demonstrate principles of propagation or whatever. On this fateful day, a little anole, a native lizard, had come along as a stowaway in the masses of stems, flowers and leaves that filled my tray of demonstration plants. We all were unaware of its presence until it was startled by my movements, leapt to the floor and darted away from me and toward the audience of oldsters. I smiled, pointed to the little hitchhiker and prepared to remark on our indebtedness to these creatures for their role in insect control. Then a lady in the front row matter of factly bellowed, "I'll get it!" as a sturdy black shoe came down on it with an obliterative force sufficient to crack a coconut, leaving no doubt of the lizard's fate, except to which surface the liquefied remains now stuck.

And so, one evening over dinner, Jordan and I took stock of our vocation. On the one hand we liked growing plants and were good at it. On the other, our operation had become an assembly line affair whose green harvest provided a fleeting ambience to our customers' homes, way stations on the road to compost. Often, our prized specimens ended up under the benches, playing second fiddle to mundane plants that needed the bench space and access to light it afforded to become marketable and thereby support our habit. If only we could find a way to employ our talent for growing plants and our love of learning and teaching about them to create a job that celebrates the green kingdom without exploiting it. The obvious solution was to work at a botanical garden, just as an animal lover might find fulfilling employment at a zoological park. Though obvious, this insight came with a problem of its own: There existed no such facility hereabouts and we were quite committed to a life in north Florida's Eden. And thus did our stock-taking lead Jordan to suggest the obvious solution to a vocational dilemma—maybe we could start a botanical garden here in Hogtown! After all, every botanical garden in the world exists as the manifestation of somebody's enterprise. Why not ours?

And thus it was, in the summer of 1977, that we set out in our vintage (i.e. un-air conditioned) Datsun, baby Summer in arms, to visit kindred institutions, and there to hopefully gain an understanding of the promise and pitfalls of the path ahead. In the course of a sweltering extended weekend, we met with the directors and/or other administrators of Marie Selby Botanical Gardens in Sarasota and Fairchild Tropical Garden in Miami to lay out our vision and solicit their counsel. We were pleasantly surprised to learn that we enjoyed their support all around and were encouraged to proceed. Their common concern was whether a city with Gainesville's demographic profile possessed the resources to underwrite such a venture, but left that ours to discern.

That fall, Jordan and I conscripted my old major professor and mentor, Dr. Archie Carr, and two others who had a serious interest in horticulture and the five of us incorporated to become the North Florida Botanical Society. Dennis Comfort, a local attorney contributed his services to draft the Articles of Incorporation and, on September 15, I drove to Tallahassee to file them with the Secretary of State. Our schedule was too tight to entrust the document to the Post Office because it was essential that we be incorporated by September 16, the deadline for submission of a CETA grant proposal. CETA, the Comprehensive Employment Training Act, was a public works program that provided federal funding to cities and counties and to non profit organizations, like the North Florida Botanical Society, to provide temporary employment and job training skills to unemployed youths. That was back when Jimmie Carter was president and such public works programs were fashionable, before the nation became mired in compassionate conservatism and disadvantaged youths were set adrift.

In short order, we were able to identify a piece of property that seemed to be the perfect site for our undertaking. Some years earlier, local government acquired 250 acre Lake Kanapaha and substantial chunks of the surrounding uplands, the holdings of a single family, by exercising the power of eminent domain. Thus did they avert the bother and tiresome litigation that would ensue from dealing with numerous small land owners to acquire the property to site a second wastewater treatment facility, the better to accommodate the county's explosive growth. The City of Gainesville constructed the Kanapaha Wastewater Treatment Plant on property just west of Lake Kanapaha, while the lake itself, as well as substantial upland portions, became the property of Alachua County. In the construction process, workers unearthed a wealth of artifacts from an aboriginal encampment and a report of the subsequent archaeological excavation was recorded in The Florida Archives.

It was a parcel of county land on the southern flank of the lake that we had in our sights. In addition to a commanding view of the historic lake, the land offered a mix of rolling pasture land interlocking with beautiful hardwood forest and several sinkholes—as much variety as one might hope for in this corner of the world. And an ideal setting for a botanical garden.

From the beginning, we named our undertaking Kanapaha Botanical Gardens. The site is located on the southern edge of Lake Kanapaha and it seemed appropriate to employ a title that held some geographic significance. And historic significance as well; two Timucua Indian words, meaning "palm leaf" and "house" are spliced together into "Kanapaha," which, therefore, loosely translates as "palm thatched house," a reference to the style of habitation utilized by the region's earliest human residents. Because there was a Timucua village on its western shore, the lake was called Lake Kanapaha; the lake with Indian houses. As members of the race whose forebears had eradicated the Timucuas and stolen their land, we felt an obligation to keep at least a vestige of their language alive. A few years later, Alachua County designated a nearby parcel of land Kanapaha Park despite our objection that having two parks bearing the name "Kanapaha" would result in confusion, an obvious prophecy that has subsequently been fulfilled.

Kanapaha Botanical Gardens could not have developed at all without the CETA program, as it allowed for the employment of a work force to transform a parcel of county owned land into the Eden it has become. In fact, a substantial amount of juggling was involved in bringing together all of the elements necessary to the project and, at one point early on, all balls were in the air at the same time. The CETA grant proposal was an application for money that would pay the salaries of youths who would polish this county owned diamond in the rough. However, it wasn't until two weeks after the grant submission deadline that the Alachua County Commission acted on the request for a lease that would make the site available, and early the next year before the lease was signed. Still, the CETA grant was approved and the County did lease the land so all ended well.

Or should I say all began well? Affixing the appropriate signatures to these documents authorized the commencement of work, but the work was yet to be done. The CETA grant provided minimum wage employment for three workers and a barely more ample stipend for their crew leader—me. Although we originally had almost no tools or supplies, we set about our task with great enthusiasm. And the first thing we did was to transplant several types of bamboos into our bamboo garden-to-be. On March 8, 1978, one day after starting work, the four of us were in Savannah, Georgia, in a borrowed truck, digging bamboos to plant at Kanapaha.

The U.S. Government maintains agricultural research stations in various locations for the purpose of conducting research into ventures that are of potential economic significance to the nation's agribusiness industries. The Coastal Research Station in Savannah, widely known as the "Bamboo Station," was charged with the mission of researching the economic potential of cultivating bamboos, particularly for pulpwood production. Consequently, the station had under cultivation what, at that time certainly, was the nation's largest collection of "running bamboos," the type that spread everywhere in blazes via underground rhizomes, or "runners." Everyone has heard horror stories about the consequences of unfettered bamboo growth; of unstoppable shoots that crack sidewalks, fracture foundations, impale children and pets, destroy lives and so on. The truth is, these tales are frightfully exaggerated and it is possible to limit their spread with the use of subterranean barriers; and anyway, bamboos produce shoots only for a period of approximately two months each year.

These bamboos were grown in stands that were kept square and, presumably, separate by occasional disking between them. This turned out to be a recipe for tax subsidized disaster, and by the year of our arrival, several stands had been invaded, if not overrun, by their neighbors and had become hopelessly intermixed. Our intention was to relocate a specimen or two of everything of ornamental value for public display at Kanapaha Botanical Gardens.

That was the theory. But it soon became obvious that we hadn't come prepared for the task at hand. We learned soon enough that shovels, the only tools we brought along, are of value only in the final phase of the effort, prying clumps from the ground after their rhizomes have been severed from a tangled subterranean network. The net effect of prying prior to this is breaking the handles, rendering them useless for anything more practical than banging against your head in frustration, a surprisingly cathartic exercise. It seems that severing these tough and woody rhizomes, often a foot or more underground, required chopping or sawing, not digging. And so, before destroying our last intact shovel, we elected to drive into Savannah to buy two axes. After that, we were able to extricate a number of specimens—white bamboo, giant timber bamboo, sweetshoot bamboo and some of the incomparably beautiful black bamboo, so called because its mature canes are shiny jet black.

We trimmed the plants, muscled them into the back of our truck, swaddled them in a shocking orange army surplus parachute we'd brought along and set out in high spirits with our booty. When we sailed past Florida's agricultural inspection station at the border, an agri-enforcer gave chase on a broccoli green motorcycle and pulled us over. We explained our mission and implored him not to unwrap our plants because it had taken considerable time and bother to find a way to enclose them without exposing a loose edge of the parachute that could be pried open ever wider by the probing wind on the long drive home. We rifled the glove compartment and managed to locate a sheet of our new Kanapaha letterhead, legitimizing our claim that nothing less than a noble pursuit of knowledge inspired our journey, even if we did look and smell like a band of grave robbers. Besides, what could possibly account for the long, straight contour of the bright orange shroud but bamboo canes except, perhaps, a giraffe beset by rigor mortis? Ultimately, the official was content to settle for a tactile examination through the nylon veil and agreed with our contention that only bamboo could be possessed of stems so relentlessly cylindrical and regularly segmented—a commendably insightful judgment. He then allowed us to continue our journey with a promise to visit Kanapaha one day when his travels brought him our way.

The bamboos were planted in the area designated for our bamboo garden, but had to be watered from five gallon buckets, since we had no irrigation system in place. We were also aware that the clock was ticking; within a year or less, we had to surround each type with subterranean barriers to prevent their invasive spread and intermingling. But, for now, we were content. Three days after the commencement of our efforts, development of Kanapaha's gardens was underway!

Sustaining ourselves during the early years of Kanapaha's development required a fair measure of juggling and flexibility. In the best of times, my work as supervisor of YCC or YACC work crews provided a salary barely above the minimum wage salaries paid to those enrolled, making it necessary to seek a supplemental income. So both Jordan and I signed on as part time biology instructors as Alachua County's 'other' college, Santa Fe Community College. Santa Fe has always relied heavily upon non faculty instructors to teach a large portion of its classes because they are not paid benefits; not even those who are hired "full time part time," a new entry in my extensive lexicon of academic oxymorons. While this was abusive to most of those involved and could only be sustained in a community with a large pool of qualified but unemployed instructors, UF faculty spouses, it saved SFCC a bundle each year. In some cases, individuals remained part time pawns in this game for years before realizing the system was premeditated with very little chance of leading to a full time position. For us, however, the system fit like a glove since the relatively high hourly rate of pay enabled us to earn the supplemental wages we needed in relatively few hours each week, leaving time for Kanapaha labors. For several years, we handed off little Summer between us like a football as we met our respective classes and were able to keep her with us most of the time.

For the next two years, we focused our efforts on improving the site and developing the infrastructure that would be necessary for such an undertaking. The meadows were beset by bull nettles, prickly pear cacti and sandspurs, plants that often made traversing them a painful experience. Often the flattened pads of cacti laid low and were not easily seen amidst the grasses and forbs, but controlled burns blew their cover, making them conspicuous in a sea of blackened ash and stubble. They were then dug out and discarded by the truckload.

The bull nettles were too numerous to dig out so we resorted to the use of a systemic herbicide dyed with red food coloring to turn their white flowers pink so we could identify individuals we had already treated and didn't inadvertently spray the same plant twice. Sandspur eradication entailed hand to hand combat for the most part. Some spraying was done in the early years, but eventually we abandoned this method as altogether too indiscriminate a killer and "scalped" them from the ground with carpet knives. Still, it wasn't until 2001 that sandspurs were finally eliminated and we had attained our goal of making the entire site safe for barefoot strolls.

We planned to develop an herb garden, a hummingbird garden, a rock garden, palm hammock, water lily pond, vinery and, in the largest of our several sinkholes, a sunken garden. But before we could indulge the pleasures of gardening, we had to build sidewalks, erect fences on our boundaries and, beneath it all, install an irrigation system. And so, while doing battle with noxious weeds, we began the construction of a loop of sidewalk to connect these gardens-to-be. Fortunately, we were able to expand our work force through another public works program, the Youth Conservation Corps. For a matter of several years, public works programs allowed us to keep as many as twelve people on site, always at least eight, and this enabled us to make steady progress.

What our workers lacked in experience and skills, which was considerable, they made up for with a generous measure of youthful enthusiasm and inventiveness. When one young firebrand used his own initiative and our wood router to engrave "welcom" on the thick plank that comprised the top step of the stairs to our trailer-office, I declined to comment on its potential as an ankle turning health hazard and simply observed that it was regrettable he had run out of space before completing his thoughtful greeting. His puzzled countenance was my first clue that he was unaware that "welcome" ended in a silent "e." I learned that day that "free labor" can be a mixed blessing; sometimes you get what you pay for.

After a bit of research, we decided to stretch our dollars by constructing sidewalks from soil cement, a mixture of nine parts soil free of organic matter to two parts cement mixed to uniformity with a masonry hoe in a mortar box. A local cement provider sold us cement at cost and the Alachua County Public Works Department hauled in truckloads of soil. Sometimes we had to screen the soil through a galvanized grate to remove stones and organic matter, but for the most part this was unnecessary. The dry mix was then wetted to the consistency of soft molding clay, dumped into preconstructed frames, tamped, leveled and broom finished. When everybody was feeling well, we might get twenty feet done in a day; but the days when everyone simultaneously felt well were few and far between. On most days, we did well to complete twelve.

Those days were the most repetitively boring of any experienced in the development process. Many a long day of soil cement construction yielded to slumber that was consumed by dreams of soil cement construction, only to end with my awakening to yet another day of soil cement construction. This drudgery was quite a lot to expect of new recruits working for minimum wage and I'm still surprised I didn't mysteriously disappear to re-emerge later when the soil cement was eventually smashed apart for removal or repair. I wondered if Jimmy Hoffa ever managed a soil cement crew.

As the sidewalk increased in length, the day's work site grew ever more distant from the mixing station so that we found it necessary to roll the heavy and tipsy wheelbarrows up a ramp into the bed of our pickup truck for transport, two per trip, to the pour site. When our route took us uncomfortably close to the base of a tree, we left a gap to be completed with a wooden segment whose frame could be modified through time to conform to the tree's root growth, thereby damaging neither sidewalk nor tree. Over time, we experienced more cracking and pitting than would be expected of commercially poured concrete, but then again, we couldn't afford commercially poured concrete. And we did, after all, have hard surface, and not just wood chip, trails, a distinction of great importance to those with physical handicaps.

As word of our venture began to spread, a local builder, Phil Emmer, contributed the chain link fencing materials we needed to secure our vulnerable western border and, later, a construction trailer that we renovated for service as an office and storage space. And then Newberry based Carlon Company contributed the PVC pipe we needed to get an irrigation system underway. It was a triumph to see water surging from the spout of an impulse sprinkler in the new bamboo garden fully 1000 feet from our well as we inaugurated the new system. Antique bricks for the herb garden and bamboo garden walkways were mined from hills of rubble that represented the remains of deconstructed brick buildings and cobblestone streets stockpiled by the City of Gainesville on a site near the town's airport. They had to be excavated, stockpiled, cleaned and transported, but at least their cost could be paid in sweat, our most abundant commodity. Little by little, we were able to obtain the materials we needed to keep our work force busy and continue the development of our green dream.

One of the biggest challenges turned out to be one of our greatest triumphs, especially for the early years. We aspired to provide boardwalk access to a lakeside cove and into the depths of our sunken garden-to-be, but lacked the expertise to design the structures or the materials to build them. And it was a remarkable collaborative effort that gave substance to that dream. Orjan Wetterqvist, a UF landscape architect, contributed a substantial amount of time and creative energy to draft the necessary construction documents and a materials list. Owens-Illinois, the county's largest land owner, agreed to donate and deliver to Griffis Lumber Company, a local saw mill, the necessary logs and the mill processed them as a contributed service. Koppers, a local industry that sold telephone poles and other pressure treated lumber agreed to provide pressure treatment for whatever wood we delivered to them. The transport of these materials was provided by another local lumber company and the Alachua County Public Works Department. Thus did the generosity of a varied coalition provide us with 34,000 board feet of pressure treated lumber, enough for boardwalks in our sunken garden and water lily pond and a facade for the construction trailer that served as our office in the early years.

And so it went. The trailer office was succeeded by a wooden building that was contributed, relocated as a contributed service and renovated for service as our entrance building with a $10,000 grant from The Stanley Smith Horticultural Trust. The old trailer stood in place as a storage structure and reminder of old times until it had to be removed in 1994 to make way for the construction of a paved entrance road, a vast improvement on the old historic "Stagecoach Road," a limerock washboard (known affectionately at Kanapaha as Tobacco Road) that provided access to our facility for many years and destroyed the suspension of many vehicles.

In 1983 we asked the Alachua County Commission to add a contiguous 29 acre parcel to our original 33 acre lease so we would have enough space to develop an arboretum. By that time it was obvious that this intact parcel, located in fast growing western Alachua County, would otherwise end up as soccer fields and such. The County Commission approved the addition.

Creative juggling was the template for the evolution of Kanapaha Botanical Gardens. We were not blessed with a wealthy benefactor or endowment, as is the norm, and there were difficulties to be sure, but the outcome was never in doubt, at least not in my mind. On October 19, 1986, after nine years of development, Kanapaha Botanical Gardens was officially opened to the public in a dedication ceremony attended by a thousand people.

Somehow, we had managed to accomplish most of what we set out to do that evening when we sat down to plot a course that would allow us to rescue our beloved specimen plants and put them back on our benches in places of sunny prominence and still have a career in horticulture. Some of the difficulties we encountered attest to the youthful optimism and naivete that gave birth to a quest so impractical and quixotic that one of more mature discernment might have dismissed it as altogether delusional. Thank heaven for youthful optimism and naivete! The difference between success and failure of this improbable scheme had less to do with merit than with persistence since it required sweat and inspiration in approximately the same proportions as Edisonian genius, although without the genius. The key, it seems, was pounding our heads against the same wall long enough to reduce it to rubble. In the end, with the support of many and a fair measure of luck, Kanapaha joined the ranks of Florida's botanical gardens, in the process providing us the vocational venue we sought in the Eden we love and call home, another jewel in its exalted crown. The phytocide we have left to Wal-Mart.

6

Student Days in Hogtown

Over the past several decades, generic Floridazation has corrupted so much of the state that many of its cities and towns have become virtually indistinguishable. While Gainesville has not yet been completely transformed, it is daily divesting itself of the unique qualities that endeared it to generations of students and civilians alike. Some of the most egregious defilement occurred half a century ago when aesthetic judgments critical to the town's character were being made by people who considered vinyl upholstery to be chic. It was then that the majestic live oaks lining University Avenue, Gainesville's principal east-west thoroughfare, were sacrificed to a street widening project. The splendid red brick courthouse hub that anchored its modest downtown was razed and replaced by a drab, characterless box that blights the town square to this day. Only decades later was tribute paid to the late grand edifice with the construction of a red brick clock tower across the street bearing the original timepiece that once chimed the hour from its towering summit. And the stately Thomas Hotel was rescued from the wrecking ball in an eleventh hour bid by the City of Gainesville to salvage at least a vestige of its former grandeur. In fact, the academic tenure of returning alumni can always be sorted chronologically by their accounts of which Gainesville they remember.

Still, it must be acknowledged that Gainesville has held the line better than most Florida cities in controlling growth and preserving historic buildings and natural areas. But a veritable flood of new residents has proven to be irrepressible and governments have continuously modified their growth management plans to accommodate new growth well beyond the capacity of the supporting infrastructure. Tampa long ago grew too large to meet the water needs of its citizens without importing from surrounding counties and regularly advances the notion of constructing a pipeline to divert water from the historic (Way down upon the) Suwannee River 100 miles to the north! It is only because ever vigilant environmentalists continually beat back these attempted piracies that the grand river still flows uninterrupted to the Gulf, where it nourishes invaluable nurseries of shellfish and other marine life.

The principal reason Gainesville has fared better than most in controlling growth is that the community is a hotbed of environmental activism, not sufficient to bring growth to a halt, regrettably, but at least to bring large natural tracts of land into public ownership, preserve historic structures and afford some protection to large trees. But well before these environmental protections were codified, there were individual acts of civil disobedience hereabouts that had the same effect, if on a limited scale. For instance, I once rented a little house west of Gainesville on Southwest Eighth Avenue, then an unpaved road, that was flanked on its south side by a row of power poles. I noted that the row of poles crossed over to the north side at one point for perhaps 600 feet before crossing back to continue its otherwise unbroken southern flank. I learned sometime later that the individual responsible for this strange anomaly was our neighbor and victim-to-be of several crow perpetrated indignities, a spirited lady named Catherine Hayes.

Years earlier, when the power line was being installed, she vowed to save a venerable live oak in her front yard that was slated for removal. So every day during the process, she ascended a ladder into the oak and spent the day in her daughter's tree house. Not only that, but she took her infant son with her along with provisions for the day. When the chain saws arrived at Mrs. Hayes' doorstep, workers recognized they could not cut down a tree bearing anybody, let alone a mother and infant. Workmen, their foreman and assorted higher-ups regularly appeared at the base of the tree to try to persuade her to abandon the vigil. When this failed, they threatened her with legal action, but were savvy enough to recognize a public relations nightmare when they saw it, a circumstance understood by Mrs. Hayes from the outset.

Entreaties to her husband got them nowhere as he characterized the action as solely her own and that, as they could likely discern, he was powerless to affect her conduct anyway. Finally, the electric cooperative relented and amended their installation project to cross over the road, bypass Mrs. Hayes' tree and then recross the road and continue on land lining the road's south side. Well before environmentalism became a cause, Catherine Hayes knew in her heart something apparently unknown to officialdom, that cutting down a majestic live oak tree to install a power line was not progress but a crime against nature.

One of the community's changes that is most apparent to former UF students who did their time in the sixties is the preponderance of apartment complexes and especially condominiums. In days past, there were a few apartment buildings but no condominiums; the notion that students were solvent enough to actually purchase housing was incomprehensible. Most of us rented rooms or buildings to call home as we whiled away our youth matriculating and partying. And this necessarily entailed weathering the eccentricities and vicarious parenting of landlords and/or landladies as part of the bargain.

It is true that the accommodations were not always stellar, but then the rents weren't either. While house hunting, I once inspected a 'rustic' rental unit whose bathtub appeared to be made entirely from iron oxide. And, for some time, we paid $40 monthly to rent a commodious old cracker house, one of three minimally renovated army barracks units that had been relocated to a site south of Gainesville. The front of the house was lamentably close to U.S. 441 but the back was a naturalist's dream as it abutted Eden—Paynes Prairie State Preserve— known to early settlers and eighteenth century English naturalist William Bartram's The Great Alachua Savannah. All three structures were sheltered by huge live oaks. There were a few mice in residence, but their tenure was very brief since Grundoon stopped at nothing, not even sofa upholstery, to seek them out and devour them with lip smacking relish, all before the sofa's stuffing had fully settled onto the floor.

Our landlord was friendly enough, as long as the conversation didn't veer too closely to matters of household improvements, always a taboo topic of conversation with the landlords I knew during my student days. But, we were free to remodel and were quite proud of the flourish with which we redecorated the dining room—Chinese red walls, paper lanterns, and a central door-turned-tabletop painted black and resting on cinder blocks with seating cushions strewn liberally around it.

The building lacked air conditioning but had an attic fan that blew warm air out with the effect of pulling fresh air in through the windows below. This feature, along with high ceilings, enabled generations of families to survive the otherwise inhospitable Florida summers prior to the advent of air conditioning.

It was not until we decided to grow a garden that we first found ourselves substantially at odds with our landlord. Although he lived and worked in Gainesville, he still fancied himself as somewhat of a weekend farmer and had a few chickens running about on the property we were renting. When he first spied us planting tomatoes, he laughed, "Them chickens'll eat them tomatoes. Wait 'n see!"

Regrettably, he knew what he was talking about. When the fruits first appeared and were still small, hard and green, showing no blush whatever, the birds began to peck them to death. Our landlord's only response was to chuckle anew and remind us this was the outcome he had predicted. And thus it was that Jordan and I decided to exact some vigilante justice; if we couldn't harvest tomatoes, we'd harvest chickens instead.

Our chicken trapping device was the essence of simplicity, relying on technology likely known to Neanderthals and perhaps even their Australopithicine ancestors. Corn kernels were liberally sprinkled inside a wire cage whose hinged door was opened wide. One end of a string was attached to the open side of the door and I was comfortably seated on our front porch about 20 yards away with the other end in my hands. A quick yank on the string would jerk the door shut trapping any of the birds that had been seduced by the prospect of an easy meal.

Raccoons or even squirrels would fall for such a ruse no more than once before they and their compatriots either gave the trap wide berth or devised a plan to snatch the corn without being captured. Not so chickens, whose legendary dim-wittedness was readily and repeatedly confirmed. There were five or six of the brainless birds to be dealt with, but we could only process and eat one at a time. So we would dismantle the apparatus for a period of days during which we enjoyed meals built around chicken entrees. When we were steeled for another series of chicken based dishes, we would open the cage door, reapply a smattering of corn kernels and yank the string yet again to capture the first chicken to realize that the feed box was open for business once more.

Within six weeks or so, the chickens were no more, a circumstance noted with puzzlement by our would-be farmer landlord. It was our good fortune that he was only marginally more astute than his erstwhile poultry, for when he dropped by to share his concerns, the sprung trap was still in evidence and enough feathers scattered about to suggest that a chicken had exploded. The only thing lacking was a sign with an arrow pointing toward the cage door and reading "chickens enter here." We suggested that the mantle of guilt likely was borne by a large and menacing black dog that we had seen roaming the neighborhood during the past several weeks, an imagined terror that seemed to afford him some closure. Our world was now safe for tomatoes.

That might have been the end of the chicken tale, but for one thing. A couple of weeks later, our neighbors' parents were visiting and brought along their dog, a large black German Shepherd mix. Attracted by a commotion outside, they gazed out a window as their dog sped by with our landlord close behind loudly bellowing hurtful epithets and brandishing a large stick. The gist of his tirade was that this was the chicken eating canine he had been hankering to thrash. Our neighbor's father had only the comment, "Who is that lunatic?" Had it not been for the memory of our lost tomatoes, I might have felt remorse.

Sometime later, we rented a small house from yet another weekend farmer who taught Soils Science at the University. It was directly across the street from Mrs. Hayes, the power line diverting ecoterrorist who was subsequently terrorized by our relentlessly mischievous crow. The rental house was on nearly an acre of land separated by a fence from his small pasture and extensive woods. Along with his cows was a bull that regularly jumped over or crashed through the rickety fence with distressing regularity to ravage our garden and litter the lawn with bovine pies. We were aware that cattle are the intellectual equivalents of chickens and would clearly fall for a box trap baited with corn, if only I could find a box large enough. As this wasn't practical, I instead surrounded our garden with an electric fence and bided my time, awaiting the inevitable convergence of rawhide and raw electricity.

I didn't have to wait long. Two days after installing the fence, I watched through our kitchen window as the bull, seduced by the prospect of a meal of collard greens, muscled his way through the fence. As he approached our garden, my heartbeat quickened at the prospect of sweet and impending revenge being visited upon our garden despoiler. This would be a lesson he would never forget. And thus did I gleefully summon Jordan to come witness our moment of triumph with that oft uttered and infamous prologue to disaster, "Watch this!"

Intently, we followed the movements of the unsuspecting bull as he grazed on our lawn, moving ever closer to the garden encircling fence. He kept his head down as he continued grazing and moving forward until it and a portion of his neck was thrust under the wire without making contact. Too late did I realize that my expectation of an uncomplicated, electrifying, lesson-teaching, revenge dispensing convergence was but one of several possibilities and, regrettably, not the one to be realized. He raised his head, now inside the perimeter of our garden, and made contact with 2000 searing volts of stark trauma. Instantly, his dull bovine countenance was transformed into an expression of intense mindfulness nuanced by panic and distress; he seemed more focused. With the first of several bucks, he managed to become entangled in the punishing strand and rushed headlong into our garden like a crazed bronco pummeling our produce into mush. I stood transfixed, frozen in horror for the few seconds it took him to complete the annihilation of our garden before recovering my wits and racing to throw the control switch. In a matter of seconds, my anticipated triumph, like our garden, was gone with the wind.

That little house stood silent witness to this sad episode as well as a lot of other memorable goings on; like the time I learned an important lesson about the use of heart pine, also called lighter wood or fatwood by the Crackers who clearly knew more about it than me. Like most vintage houses hereabouts, this little building was poorly insulated—actually not insulated at all—because winters are short and mild. The prevailing attitude embraced the practice of fighting cold with fire, and as long as the stoves and fireplaces were tended and judiciously poked, they generated enough heat to keep a house toasty with plenty left over to caulk the cracks.

Our little house was outfitted with a kerosene stove that was fueled via a copper pipe from a tank that rested on a metal stand out back.

The norm for the time, it was nonetheless unsightly and smelly, housing a stale flame that was devoid of cheer and vitality and barely visible through a scorched and opaque mica pane. With the great bounty of readily available firewood, it seemed wasteful and unnatural—an affront to our environmental consciousness—to entrust our comfort to the combustion of finite and soulless fossil fuels. If burning wood was good enough for early Cro Magnon man, it was good enough for us. It took a month or so, but while making the rounds of our regular Saturday morning garage saling, we came upon a sale item that seemed to fill the bill, a cast iron Cannon Army stove.

The disposition of this marvelous device represented the ultimate dilemma for the garage salesman, a recent UF graduate who was relocating to Alaska to work on the construction of the newly authorized pipeline that would carry oil from Alaska's North Slope. On the one hand, he was taking everything he owned in his VW van and doubted that it had the cargo space or the structural wherewithal to accommodate that much bulk and weight, or that his wallet was fat enough to get it there. But, on the other hand, having a reliable heat source was tantamount to survival in the icy north. In the end, his doubts about the stove's portability weighed ever more heavily and ultimately resulted in his reluctant decision to sell it to the first suckers to cough up $75; and that was us.

We jettisoned the kerosene heater and installed our weighty new acquisition. Though designed to burn coal, its basic function was to house a flame, however fueled, and to radiate a good portion of its heat into the surrounding space. So we cut our wood a bit shorter than conventional fireplace fodder, stacked it in the stove's belly, and applied a flame. In short order, we were basking in a toasty warmth that would have brought a smile to the face of Ben Franklin himself

We soon learned that, in truth, wood is not a free fuel. The cellulose itself was freely available all around us as a fruit of photosynthesis, but it had to be cut, split and dried, activities that involved the use of a chain saw and ax and countless calories of labor. All of this lent credence to the old adage, "If you chop your own fire wood, it will warm you twice." It is not surprising, therefore, that I frequently found myself down to my last few splinters of fuel and was compelled to scour the surrounding woods for dead and dry branches that could be easily deconstructed and pressed into service.

It was on a crisp December evening that I found myself trying to breathe life into a struggling flame that flickered weakly through a heap of hastily gathered tidbits. Just when the venture seemed destined to fail, I summoned the mental image of a substantial chunk of heart pine that I had bypassed many times on my forays into the woods. I'm not sure how it came to be where it was, but that concerned me little. I had lived in rural settings long enough to know that this special resin saturated pine wood was highly combustible; so much so that thinly sliced sticks of the stuff were bundled and sold, at flea markets especially, for use as kindling. And I was shortly to learn why I never saw it offered for sale in more substantial bulk.

I retrieved the resinous chunk from the woods, lugged it into our house, opened the door of the fire box and heaved it onto the anemic flicker, hoping the impact wouldn't undo the slight progress I had made thus far. It was small enough to fit through the opening, but just barely. As it turned out, my concerns about making things worse were well founded, but not for the reason I feared. For the first few seconds, nothing discernibly different transpired. Then the numerous thin trickles of flame coalesced into a bright yellow sheet that flowed upward around the pine heart, like an inverted waterfall. With frightening abruptness, the thin sheet became a brilliant molten torrent that gushed from the turban top into the stove pipe and was clearly visible through the numerous cracks and fissures that had previously escaped my notice. The gush was also audible, not yet a roar, but the forceful rush of a fire streaming from the volcano that was erupting just beyond the cast iron wall that suddenly seemed so thin.

For the first time since we gained possession of our prized stove, I began to frantically search for some way to reduce the intensity of the fire it housed; in vain it seemed, since every closeable portal for air intake was closed already. We were witnessing the uncontrollable emanations of an inferno housed in the little stove we had moved into our house amid so much naive gaiety. Now we were watching a Three Mile Island meltdown in our living room.

The room became sweltering within a very long minute or so

and, December or not, we threw open every window and door in the house. Fire shot out the top of the chimney and its every crack was backlit by fire. As a plastic light switch plate fully twenty inches from the stove began to trickle down the wall, we experienced a panic likely akin to that which must have consumed Mrs. O'Leary as she watched the Chicago skyline crumble. We applied wet towels to the face of the wall, lest it burst into flame, and steam hissed outward from the interface. Even our erstwhile neighbor Mike, an accomplished, if unwitting, serial arsonist, managed to be absent from the scene when his residences burned to ashes; we now stood at the crime scene, immobilized by fear with mouths agape and wide eyes fixed on the impending annihilation of our little house, actually, our landlord's house. How to explain all of this?

Then, as abruptly as it leapt to life, the inferno relapsed into a moderate blaze, then a pulsing flicker and was gone. Like a collapsing star, though with more flourish, it had burned itself out. We stood sweating before the near molten iron receptacle immensely relieved that serendipity had delivered us yet again from a foolhardiness that seems so often to pervade human enterprises, or at least ours.

But surviving landlords involved more than weathering meltdowns and matching wits with chickens and cows. Sometimes it involved matching wits with the landlord. Or, in one memorable case, the landlady. Mrs. Southerland seemed like a reasonably normal middle-aged divorcee out to make a few bucks by renting out the small garage apartment at the end of the driveway beside her home. Of course, at the outset of these relationships, people always seem to be reasonably normal, but then the same can customarily be said of ax murderers as well. Anyway, the rent was right and it was a short walk to classes at the University, just a few blocks from the University president's house, so I signed on the line.

It was not until several days after I moved in that I realized my immediate neighbor to the south, across my landlady's driveway, was a local celebrity of sorts, the Wicked Witch of the West. The Wicked Witch, Mrs. Southerland's sister it turned out, was not really wicked at all, but certainly looked the part of a witch as she patrolled West University Avenue between campus and her abode. She was invariably attired in dark—mostly brown—clothing consisting of a long straight dress, a tall hat, long brown coat, even during Gainesville's sweltering summers, and shoes substantial enough to be used to bludgeon a rhinoceros unconscious. Even so, she might not have been saddled with such an alias but for a face to match her attire, long and narrow with thin lips drawn tight beneath a long slender nose. She could be seen most any day either walking the sidewalks of University Avenue or standing on one of its corners conversing with a lamp post or staring at nothing, always with a bundle or two in hand.

Both Mrs. Southerland and The Witch seemed obsessed with my comings and goings so that traveling the length of the driveway between them was barely more relaxing than running a gauntlet. Whenever I pulled into the driveway, a crevice of light would appear in one window of each of the otherwise shuttered houses. It became immediately clear that I was the object of covert observation rather than someone about whose welfare they were concerned; for if I responded with a cheerful wave, the curtains would shut tightly, only to reopen at another window shortly thereafter. Once, in fact, I pulled my car into the driveway, surprising The Witch who was hosing away fallen leaves, apparently an obsessive behavior. As if under attack, she abruptly dropped the hose and, with a hurried shuffle, disappeared into the back door of her house. After I parked, Jordan and I went into my apartment and watched out a window as she reappeared and took up the hose and unconvincingly pretended to return to chasing leaves with water. Nonetheless in her distracted state, she riveted her eyes so intently on my apartment that she inadvertently blasted her face with the torrent of water. I took some comfort from the fact that she didn't melt.

I didn't really mind being obsessively scrutinized by two fruit loops and sometimes even reciprocated by directing the beam of my headlight into a face flattened against a window when I returned late from frog hunting, an action that always resulted in an abrupt retreat, akin to a vampire recoiling from a shaft of sunlight. I might even have lodged there longer if they had maintained the same degree of insufferableness. But, in a matter of a few months, I began to suspect that Mrs. Southerland was entering my apartment in my absence. Nothing was ever missing but I sometimes sensed a different style of disorder as though my clutter had been rearranged during my absence. I didn't have enough evidence to make an accusation so I set traps instead. In the first instance, I employed all of the resourceful ingenuity of a Three Stooges caper, placing a small plastic bucket of water above my front door balanced in such a way as to discharge its contents onto any unauthorized entrant. When I returned home later that day, the bucket lay on the floor with perhaps half its contents pooled on the floor. My assumption was that a wringing wet Mrs. Southerland quickly departed thinking that I would conclude that the trap went off on its own.

I further speculated that, next time, she would come in through the side door so I rigged it there instead. This time though, I upped the ante by arranging a shrewdly contrived apparatus that would reward the intruder with a can full of catsup. But the can was not set to tip over like the bucket of water, but instead delivered to the midriff—there to splatter upward—on a string that was activated when the door opened. Even if she stood behind the door frame to avoid a dousing, she would still get a face full of the red stuff.

It worked! This was clearly evidenced by a blotch of partially congealed catsup on the ceiling just inside the door. The edge of the red splotch facing the room's interior radiated outward but the edge closest to the door had a sharp border, as though something in the doorway had intercepted much of the thick red fluid as it spurted upward. We were at war!

All the while, we maintained the pretense of civility and our minimal interactions continued without any allusion to unlawful entry or catsup stains. That is until The Great Conflagration. In the days leading up to the main event, I returned from field work at the Archbold Biological Station farther down the peninsula near Lake Placid. With me, I brought twenty or so nearly ripe mangoes from trees that grew on the station grounds. Even though these were heirloom fruits not possessed of the genetic improvements of more recently developed varieties, they were, nonetheless, mangoes, the fruit of the gods. It is true that I would have preferred any of a number of newer varieties that were larger and whose flesh was uniformly soft and devoid of fibrous strands attached to their central pits and the turpentine undertaste that permeates the archetype. But even these small, turpentine suffused fruits bearing fibrous pits that necessitated a good post-consumptive flossing—even they were far superior in taste to lychees, pineapple, Concord grapes or to any of the other fruits that were tied for a distant second place in the assessment of my palate.

Fruit has always been my favorite category of food and mangoes are unquestionably far and away my favorite. My misgivings about eating them are twofold: (1) that I won't be able to stop, regardless of volume and (2) that the ecstasy they incite will cause my eyes to roll backward so far into my sockets that I may be unable to retrieve them and regain sight.

About half a dozen of these yellow gems remained on my counter top and I was already anticipating the gustatory orgasm that awaited me upon my return from classes. Their golden skins, already embellished by a rosy blush, were now beginning to flaunt the dark spots that herald the zenith of flavor. With quickened pace, I strode from car to apartment, threw open the front door and expectantly settled my gaze on the counter top where I beheld...nothing. Actually, there was something, but it was so much at variance with my expectation that I overlooked it at first glance: a note from Mrs. Southerland.

I was, of course, outraged by the obscene trespass; but my most immediate concern was the whereabouts of my coveted mangoes. I snatched the note from the counter and anxiously scanned it for information that might explain their disappearance and offer some hope of recovering them. The gist of the rambling missive was that my standards for cleanliness and organization in the maintenance of my rental unit (and moral character generally) were sadly inadequate, that she was assessing me a $25 fee for cleaning it and was holding my guitar hostage until I coughed it up. This was not the first, or last, time my standards of hygiene had been impugned although, in most of the other situation,s animals played a decisive role. In fact, I actually felt a tinge of vindication inasmuch as she would equate the value of a cheap guitar with the cost of bringing the state of my living quarters up to a socially acceptable level. I guess I wasn't such a bum after all.

But that wasn't the worst of it. Almost as an afterthought, she divulged her commission of unspeakable treachery: She had discarded the "rotting fruit" on my counter top. Savory mangoes with black spots, at the pinnacle of mellow flavorful glory....rotting fruit? Discarded? It was almost too much to bear. With the crumpled note in hand, I stood trembling with indignation at the scene of a crime against nature.

I strode the ten steps to her porch in five and pounded on the back door until she appeared and then denounced her conduct as loathsome and unspeakable, but it was clearly a waste of breath. She recited anew a slightly abbreviated, though still substantial and clearly rehearsed, inventory of my shortcomings in a tone suggestive of steam hissing from a volcanic fissure. In the clearly unenlightened state of one who had never allowed passion to infuse her relations with even as sensuous a fruit as mangoes, she had seen only decaying produce, not a portal to ecstasy. I then threatened to call the police unless she immediately returned my guitar, an ultimatum she dismissed as she retreated back into her kitchen with the screen door slamming behind her. As I stormed back to my little domicile, I became aware that The Witch was plastered to a window, relishing a ringside view of the gathering storm.

After reporting my grievance to the Gainesville Police Department, an effort that seemed to generate little sympathy but at least the promise of constabulary intervention, I placed a call to our good friends, Peter and Beth Westcott. Peter was a good natured fellow graduate student (and my best man to be) whose own unorthodox behaviors had placed him in many odd and often embarrassing predicaments, so I knew he would delight in an altercation involving police intervention, familiar turf for him. I was in good fighting form and confident I held the moral high ground, but I had often egged him on in situations where he might otherwise have capitulated and knew he would return the favor if I faltered. This was no time for moderation and two hotheads are better than one. He and Beth, accompanied, as always, by Rena, their witless German shepherd, arrived a very short time later. As they walked the gauntlet to my apartment, they felt the collective laser like gaze of two pairs of eyes burning into them.

Shortly thereafter, a patrol car arrived. With lights still flashing, it stopped on the road in front of Mrs. Southerland's house. I emerged and walked down the driveway to meet the officer who had responded to my call and enlist his assistance in retrieving my guitar. I was shocked to learn that this was not an officer from the Gainesville Police Department, but rather from the Alachua County Sheriffs Office responding to a call from Mrs. Southerland, not me. While I was still conversing with the officer, a second patrol car arrived, this time my officers from the Gainesville Police Department. The two officers suggested that I wait in my apartment while they sorted out matters of jurisdiction and the prevailing authority then spoke with Mrs. Southerland.

Apparently, our street was under the jurisdiction of the Gainesville Police Department as the Sheriff's patrol car departed and the GPD officer strode inside to meet with Mrs. Southerland. After 10 minutes or so, he emerged from the back door, guitar in hand, and was walking toward my door when The Witch threw open the window from which she had surveyed the goings on and shrieked to him, "Look out! They've got a dog! Get 'em with your guns!" Clearly, she knew that going in with guns blazing was the only way to deal with vermin like us.

I recovered my guitar and, as a matter of principle, maintained a residence there long enough to compensate for the value of a damage deposit that I knew wouldn't be returned, confident that it would take my banshee landlady at least a month or so to evict me even if she managed to establish cause. During the remainder of my tenure at Casa Southerland, my movements were monitored with a level of surveillance that would have shamed the FBI, but at least I lost no more mangoes to misguided judgment.

That was nearly forty years ago. Last year, I received a call from Mrs. Southerland. Clearly unaware that she was speaking with her erstwhile tenant, she offered to donate a palm to Kanapaha Botanical Gardens. I decided to drive by my old haunts to see the tree which, surprisingly, I could not recall. As I turned onto the old familiar street to have a look, I was suddenly transported by memory to an earlier time when I daily took that turn while returning from classes at the University. As I looked up the gauntlet driveway, I saw beyond it a cabbage palm standing beside the little garage apartment where the saga of the purloined mangoes had unfolded so many centuries ago. But the driveway was littered with a sprinkling of oak leaves, a sure sign that The Witch was no longer its neighbor since she would never allow such disorder where there was access to pressurized water. The little apartment seemed unchanged.

The little house that was the site of the great chicken massacre and the procyonids' night of frolic also stands unchanged, with U.S. Highway 441 out the front door and The Great Alachua Savannah out the back. The tiny brick gas station operated by our erstwhile landlord is still in downtown Gainesville, but has been moved a few blocks and now serves as a transit station for the city's buses.

Also unchanged is the little green house that was home to us when both Summer and the notion of starting a botanical garden were born. The road has been paved and the inevitable development that followed has left it one of few private residences on the road. One of the upscale residential communities that was developed on Catherine Hayes' former pasture land is named Hayes Glen. But the mulberry tree is still there—the one that held Grundoon's tree house and whose succulent fruit kept us red-handed each spring. It is comforting to know that, despite the state's breakneck pace of growth and development, there still remain some remnants of the old Hogtown we love. The road-crossing power line stands as tangible evidence that there have always been those who feel likewise.

7

Floating the Ichetucknee

Tony strained to intersect the last rays of the sinking sun as they streamed through the thick tangle of swamp vegetation that towered overhead denying him access to the warmth he so desperately sought. He spread apart his feet—toes clenched tightly into the inner tube's rubbery skin and pressed one hand into it as well to create a more stable tripod on the circular bladder that kept him a few precious inches above the frigid water that had already robbed his body of all residual heat. Just ahead was the slender sunbeam he ached to feel on his skin and he paddled vigorously with his free hand to claim it, if only for the brief moment of convergence the swift current would allow.

He paddled so furiously with his free right hand that the tube began to spin counterclockwise and he found himself staring at the left bank rather than downstream toward his goal. Pressing his right hand into tripod duty to free his left for paddling, he quickly compensated. His rapidly approaching target again came into view and seemed easily within reach; he had only to cease paddling and drift for a few seconds more to secure the divine warmth that would free him, momentarily, from the frigid circumstances that seemed to stretch out endlessly ahead. The rendezvous was a certainty. Then he saw it—a stocky brown snake draped on a gnarled branch a few feet above the water surface. He wouldn't even have seen it were it not for the coveted shaft of sunlight splashed against its rough scales, and now he was being carried by the swift waters right into it.

"No!" he shrieked in a tone of pure anguish. It was all he could utter before his desperate flailing to retriangulate on the tube and reverse course cost him his balance and sent him plunging into the cold waters of the Ichetucknee River.

Even in their shared misery, or perhaps because of it, the others in his party erupted into peals of laughter. "You jackass," howled Hope. "It's only a water snake."

Shivering, Tony struggled to climb back onto the tube. It was late afternoon, or maybe early evening—nobody had a watch—and he was freezing to death, too cold to fashion a response. This was the last of the increasingly desperate attempts to grab a smidgeon of sunlight that had consumed the last hour of their agony as they bobbed along into the cold, gathering gloom. Somewhere ahead was a bridge, and 100 yards from it, on a narrow dirt road, was their car. Or more accurately, one of their cars. In those days, it took two cars to float the Ichetucknee: one left at the Highway 27 bridge and the other to transport the whole party and a tube each to the spring "boil." Regrettably, these few particulars of logistics were the extent of their knowledge of tubing down the river. And so, with much gaiety, they had tossed their inner tubes into the cold headwaters of the great river and jumped in, squealing and shrieking, to reclaim them and begin the float. With the benefit of hindsight, they understood why, as they embarked on their float, one of the few malingering picnickers glanced at his watch and murmured something that elicited muffled laughter from his cohorts.

"It can't be much farther," said Hope unconvincingly. "It only took us 10 minutes or so to drive from the bridge to the spring and we've probably been in the water for three hours."

"Not that long," shivered Tony, adding the now obvious, "We should've started earlier."

Within 30 minutes, the long shadows had coalesced into a shroud of darkness. Towering hulks of cypress and gums lined the banks; behind them stretched the endless river swamp. The river was already swollen from recent rains and, as successive tributaries poured their contents into the main channel, the current slowed ever more. Even in the gathering darkness, they could sense that, wherever they were going, they weren't getting there fast.

After another 30 minutes or so, all light conversation had ceased and, between swats at mosquitoes, they spoke mostly to reassure themselves that deliverance was inevitable and imminent. How could it be otherwise? Around the next bend, or perhaps the one after, they would hear the reverberation of tires on the highway bridge and their plight would be at an end.

Hope was trying hard not to give voice to a terrifying thought that everyone now shared in silence: Could they have missed the bridge? Is it possible that, in the ubiquitous darkness, they had already passed under the Highway 27 bridge? After all, the narrow span principally carried traffic between barely existent Fort White and the even less substantial Suwannee Riverside town of Branford; it was conceivable that it might not convey a vehicle for ten or fifteen minutes at a time, during which they could have unknowingly passed beneath it en route to the vast Gulf of Mexico. The thought was terrifying but irrepressible, and they all listened intently for the slightest suggestion of vehicular traffic upstream as well as down. But for a long time, they heard only sounds that added to their collective sense of dread, shrieks of unknown origin emanating from a primeval swamp seething with alligators and snakes and the occasional splash of something or other into the water as they rafted past. They had become the Donner Party afloat!

Finally, they heard it, muted at first, then louder, then thunderous: the unmistakable sound of tire tread on pavement. Through joyous laughs and yelps, they paddled to the bank on the upstream side of the bridge where they could reclaim their car, each silently swearing a private oath never ever again to float the treacherous and terrifying Ichetucknee River. Ever!

So great was their misery and so solemn their oath that Hope responded with a spontaneous and nearly convulsive burst of laughter when I suggested one sweltering July day, that we escape the heat by floating the Ichetucknee. Never before had I known anyone to associate the Ichetucknee with anything other than exhilaration; jubilation; ecstasy; certainly not gloom and despair. But as she related her tale of that summer's misadventure, I came to appreciate her perspective. She had survived one trip through the valley of the shadow of death on an inner tube. And once was enough!

Today, the incomparable river is the centerpiece and namesake of a state park. It is no longer necessary to take two cars or even to take along your own tubes. Several mom and pop tube rental businesses line the highway through Fort White and their rentals include not only a diverse array of tubes but inflatable boats as well. At day's end, they pick up their wares, readily distinguished from those of competitors by colorful numbers and symbols spray painted on their sides, at the take-out point in Ichetucknee River State Park. Visitors have two options; they can park near the take-out point and ride a tram either to the spring boil or to one of two launch sites farther down the run. The former takes about 2 hours or more, depending on flow rate, and is wonderful and exhilarating; the latter are also wonderful and exhilarating, but more fleeting.

Ichetucknee Spring is a "first magnitude" spring, meaning more than 100 cubic feet of water per second gushes up from a great cavernous fissure that proves irresistibly alluring to cave divers from throughout the planet. In fact, the Ichetucknee is a first magnitude spring more than three times over; its average discharge is about 360 c.f.s. Many of Florida's springs, Juniper Springs and Alexander Springs, for instance, are dammed to transform a relatively modest discharge into a large impoundment for swimming before overflowing into their original diminutive channels, but no such chicanery is required to make the great Ichetucknee seem great.

While most springs empty into a relatively short run that connects straightaway with the dark waters of whatever river it feeds, the majestic Ichetucknee has excavated a three mile long channel that carries its crystalline waters through a lush and pristine river swamp en route to its rendezvous with the brown waters of the Santa Fe River just above its confluence with the Suwannee. As it transects this wild and enchanting swamp, the swift waters of the Ichetucknee increase in volume by accepting the discharge of lesser springs.

The trip is made effortless by the swift current that conveys anything buoyant with irresistible force. The water is crystal clear and surprisingly cold, a constant 70 - 72 degrees F year round. The center of the channel floor is mostly devoid of the lush vegetation that lines either side, scoured bare by raw aqueous force to expose native white sand, shattered shells, rocks, and even fossils, most famously mastodon and mammoth teeth and alligator coprolites (fossilized dung). Alligators occur here as they do in all substantial Florida waterways, although I've never seen one. Nonetheless the ubiquitous Florida Fish and Wildlife Conservation Commission warning signs are in evidence at various points advising tubers of the possibility of such an encounter and imploring everyone to avoid them and not to feed them.

Among the Ichetucknee's abundant wildlife are many fish species including some typically brackish water species like mullet and pipefish. Various turtles abound but the only ones most people see are loggerhead musk turtles clinging to underwater beds of filamentous algae or eelgrass. Despite the appearance, they are not grazing on the plants but rather hunting their principal fare, snails that do. Brown water snakes bask on branches along the channel, but most people never see them, because of their preoccupation with things below the surface and also because the reptiles' color and pattern make them virtually indistinguishable from the tangle of shoreline vegetation.

In the old days, before it became a state park, the river was uncrowded, though its bed was littered with discarded cans, bottles and other litter that appeared even larger when magnified by the crystalline torrent. At that time, it was possible to float the whole way without seeing or hearing another tuber, though this was often accomplished only by taking account of other parties' launches to guarantee adequate spacing. Those days are long gone. On one recent float, we had to endure a succession of religious hymns belted out at high volume by a church group bobbing along just ahead of us. I was hesitant to use a tranquilizer dart for fear of damaging one of their tubes, and had neglected to bring along a cyanide pill, so we found relief only by holding onto shoreline branches that held us stationary in the river's torrential flow until the raucous din receded downstream.

State stewardship is doubtless the best thing that could have befallen the lovely Ichetucknee since it has resulted in a clean up and enforcement of rules that prohibit tubers from taking potential litter with them as they float the river; refreshments can be purchased at a concession stand located at the take out point. The other positive impact of state stewardship is crowd control; the number of launches from the spring boil is limited to a thousand daily. Incredibly, visitation reaches that level on some sweltering summer weekends.

This prompted a friend who owns property near the river to plot a bit of ecoterrorism that was intended to reduce visifloatation on the grand river. His plan capitalized on the well known tendency of bull sharks, like pipefish and mullet, to swim upstream into freshwater rivers like the St. Johns and the Suwannee. His intent was to buy a large bull shark from fishermen in the Gulf town of Cedar Key and transport it by boat up the Ichetucknee in the dead of night. The subsequent discovery of a bull shark, even a dead one in the Ichetucknee's headwaters, would be well publicized and represent adequate cause for the cancellation of many planned float trips down the River. Apparently, the elements of his plan never coalesced or I would have read about it in the Gainesville Sun.

Through it all, the Ichetucknee River, has just kept on rolling along, clear, wondrous and cold; serving up shivers and youthful squeals of joy in the Florida heat. It retains all of the magic of those long gone sultry summer days when University freshmen with patch-strewn inner tubes strapped to their jalopies stopped to ask locals for directions to the great spring as a rite of passage.

8

The Catmobile

In the summer of 1966, following my senior year at the University of Missouri, I worked for the Missouri Conservation Commission conducting a vegetation survey in the forests of the southern Ozarks. The goal of the survey was to determine how much deer forage existed in several types of forest systems, the better to make decisions relating to population management of the region's most important game animal. A lot of Missourians enjoy walking through these exquisite wilderness forests on crisp autumn mornings blowing away the gentle herbivores and the state legislature has always looked after this constituency. A personal goal was to save enough money to buy my first car; the car I intended to drive to Florida that fall to begin graduate work at the University of Florida. True independence and manhood lay ahead.

I didn't make all that much money, but then cars didn't cost all that much either. The mid sixties were a time when American made automobiles were still the quality standard for the industry and middle America's principal choice was whether to purchase a Chevrolet or a Ford. Honda was a motorcycle manufacturer and Toyota didn't exist. The invasion of the laughable Volkswagen bug had only just begun and, with gasoline at 55 cents a gallon, it would be several years before concerns about gas mileage would make it a serious contender in the marketplace. So I plunked down $200 and drove away in a white, two door, six cylinder, 1962 Chevrolet Biscayne. It was the size of an aircraft carrier but had a slightly smaller turning radius and handled a little better. At least it was commodious enough to carry virtually all of my earthly belongings to my new home in the land of alligators and Spanish moss.

For many years thereafter, this white chariot served me well; it was a reliable source of transportation, both for me, and later Jordan, and an assortment of organisms, both plant and animal. I took full advantage of its spacious interior when transporting plants and became adept at maximizing my cargo. On some occasions, every square inch of interior space except the driver's seat was occupied by plants, making it appear to other motorists as though I had picked up a hitchhiking rain forest. Animals, especially raccoons, tended to be minimally respectful of seat upholstery but, with one exception never created a safety concern. That exception occurred one afternoon near the Archbold Biological Station near Lake Placid, Florida when I applied the brakes as I approached a red light. At least I tried to apply the brakes; regrettably, no braking occurred despite my depressing the brake pedal to the floor, or so I thought. The pedal was actually pressed tightly against the carapace of Fang, my wood turtle, who had settled in on the floorboard for a nap to while away the long trip. In my haste to regain control of the braking system, I manipulated my personable armored pet like a hockey puck and thereafter consigned him to the back seat.

Many other memories of wildlife pets have become intermingled with recollections of my venerable white buggy. And perhaps my fondest is of a band of tree frog troubadours on my steering wheel one balmy spring night. It was not uncommon for Jordan and me to park my esteemed Chevy adjacent to a favorite swamp or pond listening to frog choruses, a pastime that afforded us pleasure, instead of at the movies, or another more conventional dating venue. Of course, it is helpful that naturalists are cheap dates.

Following one such swamp fest, we pulled up to the drive—in window of a fast food restaurant where the young lady taking our order inquired about the contents of a cloth sack that was wiggling about on the front seat. We removed three barking tree frogs, beautifully marked and calm by nature, and placed them on the steering wheel where they clung, looking serenely about. Because we were both familiar with the breeding behavior of frogs, Jordan and I spontaneously and seamlessly concocted a story about a training program these frogs were undergoing to teach them to sing on cue. To demonstrate, I touched each of the newly caught frogs and each responded in turn by barking out a note or two of their distinctive vocalizations.

The waitress reacted as though she had seen Jesus walk across water; she was absolutely astounded. Her jaw dropped and she loudly called associates to the window to witness yet another flawless performance. We explained that what they were witnessing was the result of weeks of disciplined practice and that we intended to expand the range of their vocal repertoire until they could be coaxed to belt out recognizable tunes. They swallowed it hook, line and sinker; the eyes never lie.

There are two things we both knew that enabled us to perpetuate this preposterous ruse. The first is that these were all male frogs since they had been located by their vocalizations and only males call. The second, and the key to our subterfuge, is that male frogs call to attract individuals of the opposite gender and grab, then firmly embrace, anything that touches them on the assumption that it is a lovestruck female. But because male frogs are sometimes mistakenly grabbed by other males, they are equipped with a second vocalization, known as a release call, that is used only in such cases of mistaken identity to secure release from a misdirected amorous embrace. I initiated a release call from each male by touching its torso with two fingers, just behind each forearm, right where another male would embrace a potential mate. It was a predictable response to a specific stimulus.

Eventually, the ravages of time dulled the luster of my machine and inadvertently invited the attentions of other animals. On one occasion, the passenger side window slipped off its track making it impossible to raise or lower so, until I found occasion to have it repaired, I accepted a stuck position that I could live with and left it. A four inch opening between the top of the glass and the upper window frame was not sufficient to allow entry to much more than a tablespoon of rain water and I was careful to park under a tree or overhang of some sort. Regrettably, it was sufficient to allow purposeful entry by assorted vermin, the worst being cats. The car's tattered upholstery had acquired a hint of cat scent from our pet, Petercat, who was an occasional passenger and this initiated a trans-Hogtown battle for territorial supremacy among the community's seemingly innumerable cats and immeasurably complicated my attempt to schedule an appointment to have the window repaired.

It all began when we parked our faintly cat scented vehicle to attend a party, unaware that we had inadvertently challenged the neighborhood's dominant male cat by introducing the scent of another feline into a territory he had marked as his own. Fortunately, from his perspective, the opening through which his rival's scent wafted outward presented a readily negotiable passage to the source of the offending odor and an opportunity to fashion a rebuttal. Once inside, he trumped the intruder's territorial claim with a liberal atomized specimen of his own essence. The resulting bouquet transformed my noble Chevy into a mobile litter box and made it impossible to consider restoring the window to a fully closed position for fear of the sort of asphyxiation that would make emphysema seem preferable.

And so, we drove the catmobile home with all windows down in an attempt to rid the upholstery of an odor that must have been concocted in Hell itself. The fragrance seemed slightly less toxic by the time we arrived home so we parked the car under a large live oak with the windows open to complete, or at least continue, the airing out process at the risk of annihilating any overhanging Spanish moss. Needless to say, this represented an affront, nay, a challenge, to our cat; the sort of challenge that could only be answered in kind. His response then became the basis for yet another territorial challenge wherever I next parked my now malodorous car. For the next few weeks, when we departed from any venue, our approach to the desecrated Chevy would often prompt a dispersal of felines, mad leaps and scrambles from the ever more aromatic back seat through the barely open window. In the worst case, we beheld a full blown melee in the back seat, involving cats so engrossed in a battle for territorial supremacy that they took no notice of our horrified onlooking.

Ultimately, we found a way to curtail the aromatic cycle of revenge spraying and reclaim our esteemed Chevy. Since northern Florida is devoid of the sort of topographic relief that would afford me the option of an honorable "Thelma and Louise" style termination for my reekmobile, I elected to pursue a more moderate course of action. It entailed daytime stints with all windows open alternating with evening intervals when three windows were tightly closed and the inoperative fourth sealed with a sheet of plastic and tons of baking soda employed to dispel toxic fumes and any evil spirits that might have taken up residence. It also involved our enduring levels of discomfort comparable to heroin withdrawal.

Nor did the exterior of my vintage Chevy escape degradation. When we first began marketing plants, I recognized that what I really needed was a truck to transport soil, fertilizer and various equipment. Since we had no truck nor the resources to buy one, I elected to temporarily transform our clunker into one by removing the lid to our commodious trunk as occasion required to provide convenient access to what we dubbed the "Biscayne Bay." I learned soon enough that the advantage to having a trunk lid affixed to the car body, as opposed to lying on the ground behind it, is that you can't back over it, branding it with a permanent crease that thereafter renders it unserviceable as a hinged cover. Still, iron oxidation is such an obligingly slow process that I was confident of many more years of loyal service from my versatile vehicle.

Then one day, while I was at the wheel of our distinctive crease-trunked and cat-scented conveyance, I was stopped for speeding, driving 45 in a 35 mile per hour zone. At first, the episode seemed altogether unexceptional as I suffered the customary verbal abuse from a smiling patrolman on one side politely demeaning my character and Jordan on the other tersely reminding me that, because of my lead foot, we now had ice cream melting in the back seat. Then, things took a strange and unexpected turn. The officer asked me to get out of the car and, when I complied, to face the car and put my hands on it with arms outstretched. As he frisked me, all I could think to ask was, "How fast was I going anyway?"

He then informed me that his routine radio check had identified ours as a stolen car and that I might be in "a lot of trouble, buddy." I laughed almost convulsively. "If I was going to steal a car, " I told him, "I sure wouldn't steal this one. I've got better taste than that."

The officer found it difficult to believe that Jordan, despite her spirited demeanor, represented a serious flight risk, so he directed me to accompany him downtown and for her to follow us in the allegedly stolen vehicle. This she could do only with some difficulty since she is of Hobbit-stature and could just barely see over the dashboard. She reached into the back seat and retrieved the cushion with the barest hint of cat essence to provide the boost she needed as well as protection from the coils of wire that protruded from the raccoonized upholstery. By the time we arrived at the police station, the paperwork error had been corrected. With the stroke of a pen, my Chevy was pronounced unstolen and my felony commission expunged. To atone for a mistake that resulted in melted ice cream, the officer tore up the speeding ticket, in the process proving my mother wrong; sometimes two wrongs do make a right.

Due to the good fortune that sometimes derives from serendipity, we have significant photographic documentation of our catmobile turned truck. Having a large circle of friends, we came to be acquainted with Gary Branam, a New Orleans architect who came to Gainesville in pursuit of post baccalaureate work in the University of Florida's Fine Arts Department. As the focus of a course photography project, he set out to capture a slice of the life of a naturalist—me—and followed me relentlessly about for a few weeks during which he collected enough incriminating photographs to support a career as a professional blackmailer in case I ever amounted to anything, still an unlikely prospect even years after his untimely death. Among the many wonderful photographs generated by this consensual stalking are several of my venerable white coach. And whenever I look at them, I always think the same thing; with the hood and trunk lid up and the underlying spaces filled with soil and planted up, it would've made a great planter.

Instead, however, I gave it away, unknowingly initiating what thereafter became a family tradition. Both Alexis and Summer gave away their first automobiles to people who really had need of them. I could have made a few bucks selling it but not enough to explain away the distinctive trunk crease; and besides, it was in need of several repairs to remedy the toll of time and lackluster maintenance. As it lumbered out of my driveway one last time, and under the control of another, I felt a tinge of sadness at parting with a silent witness to so many adventures. In the engine's ragged murmur, I could barely discern the residual sounds of a chorus of barking tree frogs clinging to the steering wheel. Then again, maybe it was the fan belt slipping.

9

Devil's Dung by any Other Name Would Smell as Sweet.

There are far more species of plants and animals on the planet than there are names for them, at least "common names." Not taxonomic names, of course; scientists have in place a standardized system whereby any new life form is christened with a Latin epithet that is filed under existing systematic headings that convey to those trained to read them its relationship to all other life forms. The system's cold and dispassionate structure reflects the virtual impossibility of individually naming every one of the earth's countless plants and animals without applying doctrine that makes the Dewey Decimal System look as simplistic as Dr. Seuss. For the same reason, astronomers have developed an unromantic system that combines letters and numbers to identify heavenly bodies

Common names are another matter altogether. These designations, which may vary geographically, have been bestowed by the common man and conventionally reflect distinctive attributes that are obvious to all. Diamondback rattlesnakes, for instance, are snakes that bear diamond shaped markings along their backs and rattles at the end of their tails and the preferred habitat of timber rattlesnakes is forested areas.

In many cases though, the origin of a species' common name is not immediately obvious. Such is the case with *Comandra pallida*, an unassuming little native herb that, through no fault of its own, has been branded bastard toadflax. What transgressions could possibly account for such a slight? Well, flax is a name that refers to several members of the genus *Linum* and the best known of these is *Linum usitatissimum*, the source of flax fiber (linen) and linseed oil. Then there are plants belonging to the genus *Linaria* whose wholesale appearance is similar enough to flax that they were christened toadflax, a designation intended to acknowledge this superficial similarity while setting them apart from the true and virtuous herb that has been so serviceable to humanity. And finally, there is *Comandra pallida* which, despite superficial similarities is not even a true toadflax, much less a true flax, and a shameless root parasite as well: the lowly bastard toadflax.

Taxonomic illegitimacy is apparently quite rampant in the realm of horticulture as there are at least ten additional bastard plants. Still, it could be worse. The herb *Ferula foetida* is possessed of a special pungency that makes it both a favored ingredient in many Indian dishes and an amulet to ward off evil spirits; small wonder it is listed on ingredient labels as asafetida rather than its other vernacular designation, devil's dung.

Most plants, of course, take their common names from some conspicuous physical trait. And among the most interesting of these are many members of the family Araceae, commonly called aroids. While most people are unacquainted with this taxonomic designation, they are nonetheless familiar with many of its members, known mostly as house plants or floral specialties: *Philodendron, Spathephyllum* (Peace Lily), *Dieffenbachia* (dumb cane), *Zantedechia* (callas), *Anthurium,* and so on. What gives rise to some of the more interesting names is the trademark aroid inflorescence, comprised of two components: the spathe and the spadix. The spadix is usually a rod like structure bearing tiers of tiny petal-less flowers, both male and female, at its base. The upper portion of the spadix often serves as a wick that releases fragrances that attract pollinators. The spadix conventionally arises from the base of a membranous sheet of tissue called the spathe.

Sometimes the spathe is strikingly colorful-red in some *Anthurium,* white in some *Spathephyllum* and a great array of colors in callas-but often it is green and relatively inconspicuous. In one beloved wildflower native to the forests of eastern North America, the spathe is green and envelopes the spadix like an inverted wraparound skirt and shelters its summit like a canopy. Only the upper quarter of the spadix is visible; the remainder is wrapped in the spathe, like a minister in an old fashioned pulpit, hence the name Jack-in-the-pulpit. Why Jack? Well, why not? He is the versatile and generic protagonist of many a childhood tale—

beanstalk climber, candlestick jumper, plum thumber or crown breaker, and even nineteenth century London's infamous and anonymous serial killer—so why not the personified spadix peering out of its enveloping perch?

The common names of some aroids reflect an anthropocentric bias that sees human genitalia reflected in the stark contrast between the straight and sturdy spadix and the soft and membranous spathe. Hence we have lords and ladies as well as Adam and Eve, among others. It may seem surprising that such allusions are reflected in the Latin—not the common—names of many species with large, sometimes enormous spadixes belonging to the genus *Amorphophallus.* And the flowers of a legume that are suggestive of the female counterpart, genus *Clitoria*, are tastefully named butterfly pea. Nor are secondary sexual features immune from incorporation into the mantles plants must bear. The suggestive protuberances on the fruit of *Solanum mammosum* have, as the species name might hint, resulted in its being known universally as lady's nipples or tittyfruit. Not all naturalists are dirty minded however, and some see other anatomical similarities in the same inflorescence. Thus, *Amorphophallus konjac* is known as devil's tongue.

When the origin of a plant's name is not readily discernable, there is often a story to be told. One such tale relates an unlikely but true account of how a widespread plant got its name in colonial America. In 1676, exactly a century before the Revolutionary War, a young hothead named Nathaniel Bacon, Jr. undertook a series of increasingly serious (and aggravating) challenges to British authority, namely the colony's governor Sir William Berkeley, who also happened to be Bacon's elder cousin. Berkeley repeatedly yielded to Bacon's escalating challenges, apparently in the hope that each might represent the last. Finally, he dispatched British soldiers to the settlement at Jamestown to quell "Bacon's Rebellion," and restore the authority of the crown.

Some of the encamped British soldiers gathered the tender shoots of a locally common plant to be cooked and served as greens. The plant was unknown to them but its pungent bouquet held the promise of deliverance from the bland rations that provided little except sustenance in an unfamiliar land. Deliverance indeed! The distinctive pungence was a property imparted by natural selection that alerted more mindful species to the presence of several dangerously poisonous alkaloids that are also potent hallucinogens. While this is apparently sufficient to discourage experimental sampling by rabbits and voles, it was a subtlety lost on the warriors charged with restoring British control of Jamestown. Their decision to cook up a batch of the plant leaves was a most unfortunate decision that was to determine the course of their lives for the next eleven days and secure for them an inglorious notoriety in the annals of botanic folklore.

The account of an eyewitness to the ingestion of the greens, and the memorable aftermath, was recounted in Robert Beverly's History of Virginia: "The Effect of which was a very pleasant Comedy; for they turn'd natural Fools upon it for several days: One would blow up a Feather in the Air; another would dart Straws at it with much Fury; and another stark naked was sitting up in a Corner, like a Monkey, grinning and making Mows at them; a Fourth would fondly kiss, and paw his Companions and sneer in their Faces, with a Countenance more antick, than any in a Dutch Droll. In this frantick Condition they were confined, lest they should in their Folly destroy themselves; though it was observed, that all their Actions were full of Innocence and good Nature. Indeed, they were not very cleanly; for they would have wallow'd in their own Excrements, if they had not been prevented. A Thousand such simple Tricks they play'd, and after Eleven Days, return'd themselves again, not remembering any thing that had pass'd."

Thereafter, the little herb with the distinctive fragrance and pale lavender trumpet flowers became known as Jamestown Weed. Over the centuries, the name has been corrupted to its present form, Jimson Weed.

A commonly observed convention in assigning plant names is to honor the naturalist who discovered the species and this has given us such mundane titles as Wilson's spruce, Parry's lip fern and Stuart's desert pea; but then it sometimes yields memorable gems like Gromwell's pucoon and Hooker's evening primrose. Perhaps the most mortifying result of the collision of plant nomenclature with the human ego can be seen in the names given to varieties of roses, water lilies, camellias, daylilies and other plants that have been obsessively interbred or otherwise genetically manipulated. Perhaps this arises from the fact that the sheer volume of different variants exceeds the number of permutations of suitable combinations of descriptive terms. Whatever the cause, it is all too common to learn that a glorious rose or tulip has been saddled with a name like Col. Bathazar Dingleberry.

Many other plants are known by names that represent amalgams by virtue of the incorporation of nomenclature from life's other grand kingdom, the animals. The incorporation of anatomical components of animal species into plant names usually reflects an understandable reference to gross similarities such as the long bristly stamens on the flowers of cat's whiskers or the furry paw-like rhizomes of rabbit foot fern. But they are sometimes more obscure, the product of the sort of convoluted semantic path that yielded bastard toadflax. And so we have such wonderfully bizarre gems as blue rat's tail, fish puddle, mule fat, rough dog's tail grass, spotted cat's ear, sow's-teat blackberry, fairy elephant's feet and weasel's snout. And it seems our closest relations have been singled out for an inordinate number as well: monkey puzzle tree, Panama monkey hat, baboon's shoes, salmon bush monkey flower and wide-throated yellow monkey flower among others.

Floral transformations are also celebrated. Four o'clocks are so named because of the predictable late afternoon opening of their flowers and release of an intoxicating fragrance just as Johnny-go-to-bed-at-noon is remembered for closure of its flowers at mid day. The lovely flowers of *Brusfelsia australis* are remarkably chameleonic, fading from deep purple to white, a feature that accounts for its being known as yesterday-today-and-tomorrow as well as morning-noon-and-night. One plant even takes its name from a surprising lack of floral transformation; unlike the flowers of its kindred hibiscus, those of *Malviviscus arboreus* do not fully open, a feature that has given rise to a name that encapsulates a common ethnic characterization, Scotch purse.

Sometimes, it is characteristics of the leaves that account for a plant's vernacular name. The leaves of *Stachys linata* are covered with a thick matting of white fibers, a feature that has made it known universally as lamb's ears. And the feathery leaves of the prickly *Mimosa pudica* fold up with dramatic speed when they are touched, accounting for its being known as live-and-die as well as by one of the green kingdom's more enchanting appellations, bashful brier.

It is unfortunate that the carcinogenic effects of tobacco were discovered long after the name cancer weed had already been assigned to *Salvia lyrata*, perhaps better known as lyre-leaved sage. And it sometimes seems that the psychotropic effects of yet other plants might have been involved in machinations of the human imagination that have further enriched horticultural nomenclature with such wonderful epithets as blackbutt, mud midget, exploding cucumber, mushugushugu, Oregon foetid adder's tongue, Texas mud baby, wood vamp, stinkwort, nut-leaved screw tree, humped fig, frogfruit, catgut, sticky tail flower, putaputawheta, blue lilly pilly, busy Lizzy, biddy biddy, hairy darling pea, Darwin woolybutt, and Billy buttons. And, of course, what discussion of plant names would be complete without some reference to the venerable snottygobble?

When pondering the mental ruminations that might have generated such a vast and varied array of identifying handles, one must ultimately consider one of the most perplexing mysteries of the process: How can sensibilities of the human palate be sufficiently broad that some find improvement in the flavor of so many culinary creations by the addition of an herb that others find so disagreeably pungent as to be called devil's dung? Clearly, this is a subjective assessment; a question to be answered, not by the mind, but by the palate. Therefore, I offer an opportunity for personal resolution of the enigma: Jordan's highly coveted and heretofore secret recipe for lima beans with devil's dung:

Cover the bottom of a small sauce pan with a thin layer of olive oil and sprinkle in a teaspoon of black mustard seeds. Heat on medium high until the seeds begin to pop and reduce the heat. Stir in one half to one chopped onion, two or three shakes of asafetida powder (available at stores that carry Indian foods), one package of frozen lima beans, a teaspoon of chicken base (or bullion) and one half cup of water. Allow to simmer for 20 minutes stirring occasionally.

It does not require a particularly sensitive palate to discern the unusual and distinctive flavor imparted by the asafetida and most will count it an asset. Those who find it disagreeable will remember it thereafter as devil's dung. A friend of mine finds the unusual taste of asafetida mildly addictive and contends that its addition will improve the flavor or almost any non dessert food.

"This dip could use a bit of dung," he would comment casually as fellow party goers shared sideway glances and backed slowly away from the bowl of corn chips.

In his defense, it must be noted that others feel the same way about oregano and advocate its widespread use with enthusiasm that is comparable, if not as psychopathological. In any case, it is a damn sight better than adding a spring of jimson weed.

10

Pests in Paradise

Gardening is the ultimate folly. In attempting to reorder the gods' handiwork, we place ourselves in opposition to natural forces that, in time, will undo our noblest undertakings and obliterate the fruits of our labors. The pervasive and oft heralded order of nature is not the spatial order we so desire, but an order of form and function, and since the gods are regrettably devoid of gardeners' vision and judgment, they seem to abhor the juxtaposed monocultures that are the foundation of our landscapes. We might as well build sand castles at low tide.

To restore natural order, these gods employ the reproductive excesses that characterize plants and animals alike. The omnipresent seeds of plants we don't want in our gardens, weeds by definition, germinate to add unwelcome diversity to our landscapes. Meanwhile, the species we covet exercise their own reproductive prerogative and increase their domain by seeds, runners and rhizomes, well beyond the bounds we deem appropriate. And, as we weed, hoe, trim, dig and mulch to hold these forces in check, ravenous insect hordes and countless pathogens appear from nowhere to disfigure and further mock our handiwork.

Still, to all true gardeners, as with geese, every day is a new one. Past failures constitute nothing more than a basis for amended strategies. So, we rush headlong, back into the fray armed with indomitable confidence that a squirt of fungicide or an extra dollop of mulch will finally make us masters of our domains. In the grand scheme of things, it is probably advisable to be content with the pleasure we derive from our occasional victories, however fleeting, as its own reward. For these ephemeral successes must be tempered by the certain knowledge that the Virginia creeper we battled in our earthly gardens will one day recline victorious in a graceless heap on our tombstones.

And so gardeners everywhere, must derive enough satisfaction in the performance of their various enterprises to compensate for their impermanence. Finding fulfillment in the moment seems the most we can reasonably expect of life and few ventures provide more satisfaction than affairs of the garden. After a while, most seasoned gardeners give up delusions of altogether vanquishing weeds from their gardens, but they nonetheless persist in reordering things to rectify the gods' most obvious aesthetic shortcomings.

Sometimes, though, gardeners are confronted by a paradox that defies resolution. Neophyte butterfly gardeners, for instance, are often horrified to learn that the delicate and glorious creatures they celebrate are, in fact, the final phase of a metamorphic succession that begins with some of the most hideously gluttonous life forms in the galaxy. And, in order to succeed, aspirants must provide a safe harbor for both by cultivating not only plants with fragrant, colorful and nectar laden flowers beloved by butterflies, but also types that entice their corpulent caterpillar predecessors. Even worse, they must endure the sight of legions of paired mandibles shredding their handiwork as bloated caterpillars bloat themselves even more. For regrettably, the sustenance they take from this carnage is prerequisite to their transformation into the gossamer winged creatures gardeners seek. If ever one required evidence that the gods' sense of humor is perverse and corrupt, they need not look beyond the lepidopteran life cycle.

Insect pests in general and caterpillars in particular are among the gardener's most prominent adversaries and they come in many forms. In Kanapaha's hummingbird garden, the greatest offender is the long-tailed skipper butterfly, an unremarkable species whose capital offense is depositing its eggs inside the unfurling funnel of the canna's crown leaves. This is a routine lepidopteran enterprise that, in itself, is unexceptional and depressingly common. It is the hatchling caterpillars, however, whose unorthodox behavior causes gardeners such grief. Upon hatching, they clamber out over this central funnel of leaves and suture closed the unrfurling edges with several thin strands of silk. It is this dastardly touch that distinguishes the caterpillars of this species from numerous other garden variety leaf dismantlers that are readily controlled by applications of a commercially available bacterium that selectively kills caterpillars. In most cases, spores of the bacterium applied to affected vegetation are inadvertently devoured by grazing caterpillars whose intestines they subsequently colonize and paralyze.

Whether or not the resulting constipation is a cause of death or only a gratifying side effect, it is unquestionably an appropriate punishment for these gluttonous defoliators. Unfortunately, it is difficult to impose such a sentence on long-tail skipper caterpillars because they reside within the deep recesses of their green sanctuary where the spores cannot readily penetrate. In theory, they emerge for nocturnal gormandizing but in fact the principal casualties of their ravenous appetites are the unopened leaves that are both bed and breakfast. Trussed together by a sturdy and unbreakable silk straitjacket, the plants' thwarted attempt to unfurl and grow produces sadly deformed leaves.

There are systemic insecticides that can be applied to eliminate these pests but their mode of action makes them inappropriate for utilization here. These poisons soak into the plants' green tissues and are carried by their vascular systems throughout, and therefore reach even the remote quarters where topically applied spores cannot penetrate. Unfortunately, this pervasiveness insures their eventual appearance in the floral nectar that brings hummingbirds here in quest of a megametabolism-sustaining sugar fix. The expansive web of species interactions strikes again, in this case making a toxin sipper of the very bird we hope to attract by poisoning the caterpillars that degrade their hosts. Most probably, hummers would be doubly affected because their principal dietary staple is insects and they might reasonably be expected to consume insects hobbled by sublethal concentrations of pesticides when they frequent their nectar sipping haunts.

Our solution was to substantially reduce the extent of our canna domain to make mechanical removal practical and use a letter opener to unzip the silken sutures of affected leaves and seek out the offenders. A bonus of this modus operandi is that it confers the soul satisfying opportunity to directly confront the enemy and squash their bloated rubbery carcasses into guacamole.

And then there is an annually recurring reptilian ritual that often produces dishevelment in several of our ornamental plantings. The meadows of Kanapaha Botanical Gardens, it seems, are one of the principal nesting grounds for the turtles of Lake Kanapaha. The procession begins as early as February when both chicken turtles and striped mud turtles have been seen laying eggs, the former within a stone's throw of our entrance building. With a spring peak, turtle nesting continues until fall with several other species, including huge softshell turtles, joining in.

Exactly what makes egg laden turtles decide on the right nest site is worthy of some conjecture since they'll struggle across considerable expanses of meadow before settling down to the arduous task of nest excavation in a spot that looks like everywhere else they've been. Back in 1988, a large softshell turtle resisted more gentle attempts at dissuasion and had to be physically removed from her chosen nesting site in greatly compacted soil in the middle of our unpaved entry road fully 300 yards from the lake.

Unfortunately, these turtles often elect to dig in amongst our plantings, likely because our soil conditioning endeavors and regular watering create conditions conducive to the excavation of their nest cavities. Although none of our major gardens has been spared these attentions, the hummingbird garden and erstwhile pepper garden seemed to bear the brunt of their reproductive indulgences. One year, in fact, we ceded sovereignty of the pepper garden to the great assemblage of turtles that transformed it into a reptile sandbox for the duration of the summer.

Their extraordinary efforts seem often to be exercises in futility since raccoons and crows relentlessly plunder the nests. At least the raccoons have the decency to wait for the cover of darkness before undoing this reptilian handiwork. Crows, on the other hand, work the day shift. These wary birds keep an eye riveted to Kanapaha's visitors, but are not readily startled to flight as they patrol the grounds searching for caches of the succulent morsels. As turtles lay their eggs in fact, onlooking crows often stand impatiently nearby, noisily protesting the slow pace of the process and the resultant delay in securing an egg or two for lunch. By the time the turtles dutifully cover their nests, as instinct compels them, the cavities have sometimes been emptied altogether by crows gobbling down the eggs as fast as they emerge.

While we recognize these antics as part of nature's order, we nonetheless find it irresistible to intervene when possible on the turtles' behalf. This entails posting oneself close enough to a nesting turtle to intimidate attending crows without causing the turtle alarm and suffering a spirited tongue lashing from the outraged marauders; crows deeply resent such deprivations and never suffer in silence.

During the warm months, we often have a jar or two of turtle eggs incubating on the shelf and sometimes hold a lottery, awarding a membership to individuals who correctly guess the date of hatching. To leave one world and enter another, hatchlings employ a small "egg tooth" on their snouts to slice an escape slit in the thin husk of the little capsules that have sustained and sheltered them. Upon emerging they are released into Lake Kanapaha to face other dangers that lurk there in the form of herons, alligators and other predators. But at least our intervention affords some of our meadow's hatchlings the opportunity to try. The procreative commitment of the lake's turtles seems more than ample to provide resources for raccoons, crows and the lotteries of human interventionists.

While all of this excavation and reexcavation is doubtless good for soil aeration, it is devastating to any plant that gets in the way. Still, our response is measured and minimal; we relocate wayward turtles when we find them before they've settled in and have erected low drift fences here and there in an attempt to redirect them to sites we deem less objectionable. But otherwise, we respect their birthright (or hatchlingright) to indulge in the timeless ritual of nesting. They were turning the soil long before we were so we owe them that. The embrace of Kanapaha's natural beauty is grand enough to compensate for what seems a small and reasonable concession to natural order.

In confronting our garden pests, we have not been adverse to a bit of experimentation with biological control, especially when the attack comes from below. Florida gardeners are well acquainted with aesthetic damage caused by two burrowing mammals, pocket gophers and moles. Moles are a bit easier to abide since their damage to gardens is an indirect result of their quest for earthworms, insects and other animals that constitute the diet of these fierce carnivores. Because moles just muscle through the surface soil to make feeding tunnels, their passage is evidenced by long ridges of cracked earth that meander away from their deeper permanent residence tunnels. They tend to be more of an annoyance than genuine problem since these surface tunnels are short-lived and serve to aerate the soil.

The enterprises of pocket gophers, on the other hand, can reduce a gardener to sobbing despondency, an anguish attributable to both the animals' vegetarian diet and a commitment to excellence in the excavation of their distinctive subterranean burrows. For, while moles simply employ a back buckling maneuver to create a crawl space, gophers dig out the soil and must, therefore, find some place to unload it. And this is where they run seriously afoul of the fondness gardeners reserve for most of our fur bearing brethren. Gophers burrow to the surface every so often and discharge large caches of unwanted subsoil. While this neatly solves the gopher's problem, it can be the undoing of a gardener's handiwork as large mounds of yellow sand appear overnight—literally, for gophers do most of their dirty work while we sleep—like an archipelago of sandy mounds in a sea of garden and turf.

Summer Goodman and Leah McTigue pose with a large gopher snake prior to its release as part of Kanapaha Botanical Gardens' gopher eradication effort. Photo by author.

So what's a gardener to do? The commercial poison baits found at garden supply stores don't work any better than a good fist shaking rant and aren't nearly as soul satisfying. However, we discovered a biological control that does work, a native reptile that seeks them out and devours them where they live. The Florida pine snake, also known to many as the gopher snake, is a robust shovel-nosed snake that is seen infrequently enough to warrant its designation by the State of Florida as a "species of special concern." This means its population is not sufficiently diminished to cause concern (among herpophiles, who care about the welfare of snakes) for its continued existence, but enough to justify keeping an eye on.

We have been keeping an eye on them for years at Kanapaha Botanical Gardens and noticed that we often find them lying halfway out of a subterranean cavity into which they hastily retreat when disturbed. Furthermore, gopher mound building tends to diminish or cease altogether in sites where we see or relocate them. Accordingly, we adopted a gopher control policy built around the purposeful relocation of these snakes to gopher "hot spots." And it has worked! It appears that pocket gophers are pursued in preference to other prey when available, so we began relocating any pine snake we could lay our hands on to the eastern most gopher tunnel system at the Gardens. And, since forests devoid of gophers circumscribe our meadows to the east, north and south, the net effect has been to eradicate our problem gopher population from east to west. Within a few years, pocket gophers were gone altogether.

While reptiles tend not to gain notoriety, we picked up an exceptional pine snake during the years of the gopher bloodbath, one that gained international attention in 1986 because of a penchant for eating light bulbs. "G.E.," as he was subsequently named, was brought to Dr. Elliott Jacobson at the University of Florida College of Veterinary Medicine with two intractable prominences in its otherwise svelte torso. An x-ray revealed these to be light bulbs that had likely been mistaken for eggs, another favorite food of pine snakes, when the reptile came upon them in a hen house. The serpent's surgery and rehabilitation at the institution attracted the attention of the media and this alerted us to the need for a suitable relocation site. And so, on September 22, 1986, G.E. was released into a gopher burrow near the butterfly garden. Mound building activity ceased thereafter as our new recruit joined the crusade.

Dr. Elliot Jacobson of the University of Florida's College of Veterinary Medicine holds the x-ray of a gopher snake that clearly identifies the two objects protruding from its body as light bulbs. Note the relatively small mouth through which these light bulbs passed. Snakes are capable of disarticulating their jaw bones to swallow objects larger than their own heads. Photo reproduced with permission of The Gainesville Sun.

11

A High Man for High Office

I was still in my underwear when I received the call to political action. The phone rang one Sunday and Mark Foster, our neighbor, was on the line. Initially, I was surprised to receive a call from Mark because he doesn't have a phone. Or even a house. Mark was living as a squatter on wooded land just west of us in a teepee of sorts. The only other "structure" in his living area was fashioned from a sheet of clear plastic strung between tree trunks, posts and miscellaneous upright supports and it served as a canopy over a storage area where he kept a great miscellany of objects found or otherwise acquired, the most obvious being a great redundancy of empty two liter plastic bottles.

How Mark came to live there is a telling story. He was a world class hippie at a time when it was acceptably mainstream, at least in Gainesville, but declined to adopt certain elements of convention, selling out, as he put it, as vocational matriculation waned and the prospect of career choices loomed ever larger for flower children everywhere. Most of us sold out and moved on, but not Mark. I'm not sure he ever actually graduated, but we were students at the same time and were loosely acquainted through mutual friends. It was widely rumored that he had threatened the life of a dean over a contested grade, but it was never clear whether it was a serious threat or whether it was directly related to his ultimate abandonment of the system to become a nut-and berry-eating hermit.

Mark always had a weakness for drugs of any sort, consumed them with reckless disregard for his mental well being and, somewhere along the line, became a fervent vegetarian. His commitment to this dietary regimen was so uncompromisingly purist that he once refused to eat some of my tomatoes because they were grown too close to the septic tank of "flesh eaters."

Mark's singular claim to fame was his remarkable mastery of Hatha yoga, a practice he prefers to undertake, distressingly, in the nude. A friend once related a disturbing account of a nude Mark carrying on normal conversation while standing on his head with "his asshole winking at the sky" as he mastered the control of his sphincter muscles, an image that has scarred her for life. Mark taught yoga classes to those with enough persistence to find his woodland sanctuary and was able to make ends meet with the proceeds this generated and through a variety of odd jobs. He had a car, an old Chevy that could be coaxed to life with enough frequency to meet his modest transportation needs.

Originally, he intended to grow his own food, but that proved to be a difficult proposition in a sandy and shady wooded environment. Still, his lack of familiarity with the principles of agriculture was clearly offset by his inexhaustible optimism and enthusiasm for the venture. He once flung and outstretched arm toward a nearby live oak tree and declared, "soil that can grow a tree like this can grow anything." Regrettably, that is simply untrue; the vast bulk of any tree is actually composed of cellulose, derived from carbon dioxide and water, readily available, naturally occurring compounds. Unfortunately, cellulose is not even digestible to termites without metabolic assistance from their intestinal bacteria, whereas the production of nutritious food crops would require soil nutrients in the form of fertilizers and a dependable source of irrigation.

Jordan once encountered Mark in the produce section of a local supermarket just when plums were starting to appear on the shelves. He stood before a large produce display overflowing with various varieties of plums sampling those that struck his fancy, devouring the flesh and spitting the pits onto the floor at a pace that afforded him a clear palate between varieties. He was wearing only a tight fitting pair of extremely short jean cut offs and his hairy body was flecked with paint that had escaped his brush earlier in the day while he was working a gig as a painter. During the brief encounter and ensuing chat, she noticed a stock boy restocking bins immediately adjacent to this spectacle without taking any measure whatever to intervene or object, so intimidating was Mark. And a stooped, gray haired woman pushing a shopping cart looked up with a startled expression when a plum pit stopped a wheel of her cart, took in the menacing apparition, pivoted, and disappeared to seek refuge in the beverages aisle. Finally, Mark found a variety to his liking, put three in a plastic bag and exited via a check-out aisle where he was given wide berth.

Anyway, this is the wonderfully eccentric hermit on the other end of the phone, inviting Jordan and me to visit his humble abode a bit later in the day to personally receive some important news. Usually, when I got a call of such a cryptic nature, I assumed yet another Amway dealer had picked up the scent of our financial insecurity, as vultures sense carrion, and disengaged as quickly as possible, feigning death or imminent relocation abroad if necessary. But I knew Mark wasn't peddling soap and I was genuinely curious about the nature of his tidings.

So, Jordan and I bundled up our toddler, Summer, and made the brief jaunt through the woods. Mark welcomed us warmly and we chatted briefly about gardening, food storage, whether we were ready to begin taking his Hatha yoga lessons and other domestic topics as he rolled, lit and began smoking a very substantial joint. Then he motioned us into his teepee and dropped his bombshell: Mark had decided to run as an independent candidate for governor of Florida. Actually, it came as less of a shock than one might imagine because he had already run for political office a few years back, a state senate seat occupied by a career politico. He was branded a lost cause celebre by the mainstream media, but in Alachua County, Florida's hotbed of liberalism, he was sufficiently peculiar to attract enough disaffected hotheads and advocates of marijuana legalization, the central plank in his campaign platform, to come in second, admittedly a distant second, in a three man race.

In third place was a Bible thumping blowhard whose central thesis was that people like Mark should be beaten senseless and possibly executed. And many of his core constituency found it a compelling argument when embellished by the strictures of Leviticus and an eyeful of enlarged photographs of Mark's hairy body contorted into some bizarre yoga posture. Mark failed to see these images as liabilities and railed at the hypocrisy of a government that subsidized tobacco production while imprisoning dope smokers. His campaign flier flaunted a head and shoulders photograph of Mark that might have passed for Santa Claus's high school yearbook photo. All in all, it was one of the most animated and entertaining campaigns I can remember and the experience apparently convinced Mark that he was cut out for politics. To him, the obvious course of action when you've been defeated is to run for higher office. I assumed that a predictable failed campaign in the current gubernatorial election would be perceived as nothing less than a springboard to a run for the presidency.

Again, his central campaign theme would be the legalization of marijuana, a position for which there was little organized support outside Alachua County. In the course of Mark's rambling harangue, it became obvious that he perceived the governorship as a regional elective autocracy. Once in office, he would rule by fiat and his very first edict would be to legalize marijuana. It wasn't until we asked the identity of his choice of a running mate, a candidate for lieutenant governor, that we realized Mark wasn't aware he needed one, or even that Florida had an elected cabinet. He certainly knew a lot about vegetarianism, but he didn't know grits from granola about politics. Still, neither these revelations nor his lack of familiarity with Florida's elective process in general seemed to measurably dampen his enthusiasm and he continued to speak in grand but general terms about the enlightened governance he had in store for us all. The electorate had survived a circus grade clown named Claude Kirk*, so it sounded good to me.

We naturally assumed this was another of Mark's drug induced delusions that would die a quiet death once his hemoglobin resumed binding oxygen and some semblance of normal brain function was restored; an ephemeral scheme that would not survive the scrutiny of sobriety. But, we then learned otherwise as Mark produced a box filled with a very large number of petition cards, "only the beginning," he told us; others would be mailed to him. He needed to get these—and many more—signed by Florida voters in order to have his name listed on the ballot; otherwise, Floridians would continue to wander in the political wilderness. It didn't take long to figure out how we fit into his scheme; Mark needed petitioners to procure enough signatures from the electorate to compel the Secretary of State to list his name as a gubernatorial candidate. Is this a great country or what?

*A word or two of explanation are in order for those unfamiliar with Florida's rich history of gubernatorial ineptitude and, particularly, the colorful Claude Kirk era of government mismanagement. In 1968, he became Florida's first Republican governor since Reconstruction and embarked on a style of governance that reminded the electorate why this was the case. Even in a graying state where a pervasive ballot box Almostheimers syndrome generates repeat episodes of electoral idiocy that would be inexplicable elsewhere, Kirk's record was so abysmal that voters limited his hand at the helm to a single term. He is probably not better known nationally because he was upstaged in the media by neighboring Georgia's contemporary governor Lestor Maddox, whose rise to the statehouse came as an electoral reward for wielding an ax handle to chase blacks out of his fried chicken restaurant. It was truly an age of Southern clown colossuses. Supporters nonetheless insist that his use of a handshake buzzer was a singular and misunderstood incident that was intended to break the tension at a critical state dinner (and he apologized publicly for the resulting military actions) and that there is no conclusive evidence that he ever wore a squirt flower on the lapel of his customary plaid suit jacket.

We explained to Mark that we couldn't use the resources of the botanical garden to secure signatures since any such political activity would compromise its nonprofit status. And further, that we didn't have enough spare time to cruise parking lots accosting Winn Dixie shoppers or to otherwise be meaningfully involved in such an effort. Nonetheless, he entrusted us with a fistful of signature cards and encouraged us to do our best and return for more as necessary. Asked how many validated signature cards he needed and by when, Mark waved his hand dismissively; he needed only to secure a number of signatures equal to 7% of the number voting for the post in the last election, about 30,000 it turned out, and that we had until July to secure them. His throngs of supporters had only to thrust these cards before Florida's multitude of disillusioned voters and a groundswell of popular support would sweep him into office and his momentous reforms into public policy. Guests at his inauguration would be openly passing joints. A bold new era was at hand.

At least that's how Mark saw it. I had some reservations. First off, he didn't actually have hoards of supporters to badger registered voters into becoming signatories to such a bonehead scheme. Floridians have certainly bought their share of political snake oil but I had some reservations about the prospect of their anointing a nudist, dope smoking hairball as a candidate for governor. And then there were logistical concerns such as orchestrating a campaign without the benefit of a telephone, residential address or reliable source of transportation. Predictably, none of this fazed Mark, who acknowledged only a growing preoccupation with selecting from his acquaintances a running mate. We took this as a cue to depart posthaste and braved the spiny catbriers to return home to our native planet.

We set aside the candidate petition cards and might never have revisited the events of that bizarre exchange, but for yet another phone call from Mark. About 6 weeks had passed and he was checking in to find out how many completed cards we were holding for him. I was profoundly shocked to learn that he even remembered our chat, much less still aspired to high political office and, more distressingly, that he recalled enlisting my support for the effort. I grabbed a card from the stack that lay beside the phone where I had left it all of those weeks ago and began filling it out as we spoke.

"Well...uh...I have one right here and I think Jordan has filled hers out as well," I stammered. "We've been pretty busy."

The disappointment in his voice was palpable but fleeting. He had hoped we would have a better report, but nonetheless seemed somehow encouraged that the grand total of completed petition cards already numbered over one thousand! After all, there remained another 6 weeks to obtain the remaining 97% of the number required and he had a strategy to complete this phase of his bid, a scheme whose success rested, in part, with his newly anointed running mate. Since our consultation some weeks earlier, Mark had found a candidate for lieutenant governor, a colleague who not only enthusiastically endorsed Mark's drug legalization platform but who, in fact, appeared to possess considerable experience with drug related legal issues.

I conceded to Mark that it sounded as though he had found the ideal running mate. His strategy for procuring the additional signatures on his petition cards was to drive to Miami's Liberty City area and stage a 3 day street party during which residents would have the opportunity to fill out half the number of necessary cards amidst all the revelry. On the drive down, he would drop off his running mate in his hometown Orlando to get the remaining half of the cards completed by his associates and theirs. The only weakness with this plan, Mark conceded, was that the Florida Secretary of State had not yet sent him the additional crate or so of cards he would have to get signed to secure a spot on the ballot. And he needed them right away for distribution in Liberty City and Orlando. Inexplicably, the Secretary of State's office did not seem to grasp the urgency of transporting these documents and Mark professed to see the conspiratorial handiwork of shadowy political forces opposed to his bid for power. My sense of these circumstances was that state administrators didn't think it was worth cutting down the trees required to produce the paper they were printed on. Otherwise, everything was coming up roses. When the primary election selected, from a crowded field, gubernatorial candidates for the Democratic and Republican parties, Mark interlocked the fingers of his clasped hands and observed with satisfaction, "And now there are three."

I didn't hear from Mark again until the qualifying period had passed. Although the details were a bit sketchy, it seemed he had somehow failed to deliver to Tallahassee the required number of signed endorsements. In particular, the Liberty City street party had fallen somewhat short of expectations. It seems the party aspect succeeded beyond his expectations, but the card signing component was complicated by the fact that a good many residents were not actually U.S. citizens and virtually no one was a registered voter, though several people indicated their willingness to sign in exchange for a green card.

It became immediately clear to me, however, that the battle was far from over; he now intended to sue the State of Florida for failure to provide the necessary cards in a timely fashion. At the very least, the forces opposing his candidacy would be exposed and the playing field leveled for subsequent third party candidates. And, if the dominoes fell his way, the election results might be invalidated, giving Mark the chance to mount yet another campaign. Perhaps he would be appointed acting governor while it was all being sorted out.

I promised to hold our completed cards until Mark could plot a course of action but, within a month or so, his quest seemed largely devoid of the passion that had sustained it for so long. Mark retired to his former sedentary life, eating berries and grubs, practicing and teaching yoga and doing paid gigs as necessary to support his minimalist lifestyle. Eventually, I accepted the fact that I would not be living next door to the governor's tent, but took some measure of satisfaction at having been a part of the political process. Sometimes you have to content yourself with just being a patriot.

12

The Right Staff

While certainly not unique in the regard, gardening is a venture in which the practitioner's reach exceeds his grasp, except in cases of severely limited space or vision. This is because a garden is a living and ever changing entity. New weeds appear to replace those just plucked and the elimination of 99.9% of a garden's aphids just means the .1% that are superaphids remain to repopulate the place with a Malthusian vengeance. Mulch decomposes and must be replaced, lest weeds become insufferable, and pruning is absolutely necessary to keep things under control. When it doesn't rain, we must water, and the occasional fertilization required to keep things lush and colorful fortifies enemies as well as friends. It simply never ends. The only question is who does what.

While there is much to be said for being a big frog in a little pond, the reverse is also true. I have inside knowledge of that circumstance because I am a little frog in the big 62 acre pond that is Kanapaha Botanical Gardens. It might seem that being director of such an enterprise might afford big frog status but when everything is done by a small work force, everybody ends up being a little frog. At least that is how things have turned out at Kanapaha and it has proven to be a very good thing; I wouldn't want it any other way.

Marie Selby Botanical Garden in Sarasota, Florida is the opposite in terms of staffing. This wonderful and immaculately maintained facility is less than 10 acres in extent and employs more than 35 individuals full time, including four in a strictly research capacity. By contrast, 62 acre Kanapaha Botanical Gardens employs 3 full time and 6 part time workers. The difference relates to very different demographics and the existence of The Marie Selby Trust to cover many of that garden's expenses. The practical consequence of having a small staff to operate a large facility is that everybody, including the director, ends up pulling weeds, planting or whatever else must be done. This is very good news indeed, since it keeps me grounded, a small price to pay for sound sleep and a smile on your lips.

Of course, it is not practical to expect such a small staff to get everything done without the assistance of volunteers. And the world is truly filled with generous souls who have learned one of life's most treasured secrets; that giving freely to others brings spiritual rewards that are beyond measure. And like the flowers of a garden, each is unique.

For many years, Eda Prendes, a retired university librarian and consummate gardener, has volunteered at Kanapaha every Monday as our admissions attendant. In this capacity, she greets, orients and congenially shakes down visitors, answers the phone, transacts sales of plants, gifts and soft drinks, consoles spider traumatized brides and whatever else the day requires. She can communicate in English, German, Russian, Dutch or Latvian, among others, and with warmth that could melt an iceberg. She initiated and maintains a soft drink concession that keeps visitors hydrated and has thus far raised more than $10,000 for the purchase and installation of drinking fountains at various sites in the Gardens. She has contributed innumerable plants from her own gardens and established a crinum garden in memory of her mother, planted almost exclusively with her own plants and under her watchful eye. Over the past year or so, Eda has suffered from several health problems but still tries to put in half a day each week at her post, even if she has to outrun a tornado—as she once did—to get here. Eda volunteers because she loves gardening in general and Kanapaha in particular. This is the sort of devotion we couldn't buy even with the proceeds of a lottery win.

Two or three mornings a week, Clif Cullenberg, a dynamic gardener even in retirement, assists our gardening ventures wherever he is needed, often joined by another retiree, Peter Jennings, often while his wife tends the admission desk. Another volunteer couple, Barry and Kathy Davis, part ways upon entering Kanapaha, often several times weekly. As Kathy tends the admissions desk, Barry either heads for his adopted butterfly garden, or continues adding new specimens to Kanapaha's collection of pressed plant specimens, part of a cooperative project with the University of Florida that he helped initiate. Wayne Norton, a professional tree surgeon, contributes his invaluable skills whenever and wherever needed and with dexterity and agility that are so extraordinary as to confirm our kinship with the other primates. Additionally, he just completed his personal fund raising efforts to purchase and install a beautiful new sign that now graces the entrance to Kanapaha Botanical Gardens, a vast improvement on the old plywood and vinyl letter affair that had somehow seemed adequate but clearly was not. Dianne Walsh, formerly Summer's second grade teacher, orchestrates the publication of our quarterly newsletter and, in a thousand subtle ways, employs her considerable organizational skills and taste to push back the tide of disorder that would otherwise overwhelm our small cluttered admissions counter and adjacent storage areas.

It is the shocking orange color of Orin Fogle's bike, vest, hat and miscellaneous accessories that accounts for his notoriety as well as his survival in southwest Gainesville where University of Florida students, among others, flood roads made painfully inadequate by the unabated growth that continues to destroy the Sunshine State. Photo by author.

And so forth. It would not be possible to list all of the individuals who assist, or have assisted, Kanapaha Botanical Gardens and helped give substance to an erstwhile dream. But it would be equally impossible to get by without them or to accord them any tribute that comes close to expressing our indebtedness to them or the high regard in which we hold them.

And I count it a special blessing that an individual widely known in the Butler Plaza area and variously called The Orange Man or The Pumpkin Man was, for many years, a volunteer at Kanapaha Botanical Gardens and remains a cherished friend. Now in his eighties, Orin Fogle still relies on a bicycle to get from one port of call to the next. But how can a non-athletic eldercyclist survive on roadways dominated by some of the planet's most daring and inept drivers, a designation for which Hogtown is justly famous? By being bright orange! And in this he excels, peddling about in an orange hat, vest and pants on an orange bicycle.

And since the attacks of September 11, his conveyance has sported a bouquet of miniature American flags splayed out behind the seat so that, at a distance, he resembles a large orange turkey with a fan of red, white and blue tail feathers. On Earth Day, April 22, 2004, he was honored with a special "Uniquely Gainesville Award" at Gainesville's annual City Beautification Awards ceremony for "Contributing to the Unique Urban Character of Gainesville." What a town!

And then there is a second mainstay of unpaid workers whose assistance has been invaluable in developing and maintaining Kanapaha's gardens. These are community service workers, individuals whose lives have run afoul of society's conventions in some minor way and have been ordered by the courts to atone by providing some service that is of value to the community. Since the mid-eighties, Kanapaha Botanical Gardens has served as a work site for a great multitude of these scofflaws who performed useful work for us as a form of court sanctioned rehabilitation. In our first decade, the mainstay of our community service work force was a cadre of individuals charged with driving under the influence of alcohol (D.U.I.). Most of the remainder were charged with various petty drug offenses or a failure to cough up the legal tender necessary to keep some document, usually a drivers license or auto registration, current and their existence legitimate.

It was our good fortune to inaugurate this collaboration with the criminal element at the same time that Mothers Against Drunk Driving (M.A.D.D.) and others began campaigning to influence legislatures to rewrite D.U.I. legislation to mandate more severe penalties for drinking and driving. And during the years it took for this punitive attitude to become incorporated into the collective consciousness of Hogtown's youth, a great number of students pulled weeds, mulched or dug irrigation trenches to atone for their crimes. The average sentence, in addition to hefty fiscal penalties, was 40 hours of community service work.

Very often, especially in the early years of this new societal standard, community service workers complained of the program's unfairness or heavy handedness and some even saw themselves as victims of some sort of malicious entrapment. Of course, their recollection of events was often rendered less than wholly objective by insobriety. In any case, we didn't involve ourselves too deeply in the particulars of perceived societal injustice and endeavored to assure them that we were independent of the court's machinery and just needed a bit of assistance keeping weeds under control. The vast majority of those who have come through the gates of Kanapaha responded to our summons and contributed substantially to the furtherance of our various undertakings. But not surprisingly, they usually differed substantially from our volunteers in terms of both commitment and knowledge of gardening.

Occasionally, we suffered the attentions of truly inept bunglers but invariably learned something from the interactions and acquired interesting stories to tell. In one instance, I learned that the bounds of tolerance for bodily comfort are broader than I had imagined, for some at least. This insight dawned during a routine check on the progress of a mulching project when I found the assigned worker curled soundly asleep in a metal wheelbarrow, hardly a comfortable or form fitting accommodation. It was satisfying to discover that even a situation of such egregious dereliction of duty could be rectified with a judicious nudge.

Another remarkably unproductive jackass inspired me to expand my range of literary expression by affording me the occasion to fashion my first, and, to date only, triple negative to provide a truthful evaluation of his merit. The occasion was the completion of his community service work, a corner I was happy to turn since he had botched most of his assignments. He was given the traditional handshake, an expression of thanks, his discharge papers—a time sheet and a compliance form—and counsel to sin no more. Upon examining his paperwork, he loudly observed that I had failed to provide an optional evaluation narrative that would give testament to his motivation, attitude and productivity. This was actually a purposeful omission since my mother taught me to say nothing if I couldn't say something nice. I observed her advice a second time by explaining that I didn't generally bother to complete those three lines since it was both unnecessary and unlikely to have any effect whatever on the course of his life, kinder, I thought, than telling him what a waste of space he was. Still, he persisted in an attempt to coax me into providing a written characterization of his discharge of the community service obligation

Preferring to be truthful, I wrote that it was my observation that community service workers tend not to be unproductive, but that he was truly an exception. For a moment, he pondered the critique with a look of bewilderment as he struggled to grasp its gist. Then his face lit up. Being portrayed as "exceptional" in matters of productivity seemed to provide the satisfaction he sought as he vigorously shook my hand a second time and departed clutching the insult while grinning from ear to ear.

Because the availability of community service workers varies through time, there is no guarantee that they will be able to meet our needs for specific projects, so we very often end up performing routine maintenance work ourselves. And many of the more disagreeable jobs we simply take on ourselves since, after all, we are getting paid. Usually, these just involve cleaning up after a raccoon party in our picnic area, but sometimes, they can be genuinely bizarre, as in the following situation.

In addition to the familiar sinkholes that dot the region, limestone solution features sometimes occur as cylindrical "chimneys" that connect the surface with subterranean chambers or caverns, much like the narrow neck of a flask. At Kanapaha Botanical Gardens, one such chimney lies in the center of a little grove of trees near the palm hammock. Because the sides of these cavities are hard and sheer, they offer little hope of ascent to the various creatures that occasionally tumble into them. Ours, at least, has a large box elder tree root snaking downward and branching out against the vertical wall for the fifteen foot descent into a large cavern that is nearly filled with centuries of accumulated soil and debris. Many snakes, species accustomed to climbing, can cling to this sinuous network of roots to escape entombment, as can small nimble footed creatures like mice and lizards. Turtles, on the other hand, have no hope of escaping the shadowy netherworld without the assistance of tender hearted ladder bearing Kanapaha gardeners.

Over the years, we have rescued countless creatures, mostly turtles, as part of our policy that can be loosely expressed, "what goes down must come up," at least as relates to vertebrates with sorrowful eyes. Because these rescues are perceived, perhaps reasonably, as a hazardous duty affair, they often fall beyond the limits of what community service workers will suffer to set things right with the Alachua County Court system. One exceptional rescue involved a creature whose entrapment was discovered by visitors who leaned over the railing to identify the four species of ferns that, according to a sign, clung to the sheer rock face only to find the pleading eyes of a stout white dog staring back at them.

Clearly, this would be a difficult rescue; so I contacted the Alachua County Department of Animal Control. They dispatched an officer and the two of us descended on an extension ladder into the cavern bearing a nylon hammock, borrowed from our caretaker, in which to wrap the dog and hoist it out. The problem was in capturing the terrified animal without getting bitten; at least that's the problem I foresaw. This was not, however, the foremost concern of my partner, who had brought along a pole-noose to capture the dog without serious risk of bloodletting. His concern involved another matter that he wisely chose not to trouble me with until our rescue operation was well underway.

The chimney extended upward from the roof of a cavern that was of undeterminable dimensions since it was filled almost to the ceiling with centuries of deposited soil and miscellaneous debris and rubble. It was possible to stand upright only in the chimney shaft itself. To move outward in any direction necessitated stooping under the cavern's roof and walking, then crawling, and finally wriggling to the point where the rubble floor converged with the roof, about 30 or 40 feet in any direction. The dog clearly enjoyed the advantage in these confined quarters, leaping nimbly about and bolting away from near capture time and again as we scooted clumsily along on our bellies like sea turtles on a sandy beach.

Suddenly, I got a whiff of something so monstrously malodorous it could have dropped a vulture in mid flight. Believing I had inadvertently crawled near or even through something our elusive canine had left behind, I instinctively aimed my flashlight beam at the soles of my shoes and then my other clothing to locate the source of the stench. I gave voice to my concern, but it elicited nothing more than a grumble of acknowledgment from my colleague, and, in any case, I could not find any physical evidence to support my suspicion.

We continued our pursuit in the hot cramped cavern, occasionally banging our heads against the harsh stone that seemed present at every turn. Just when I began to think things couldn't get any worse, I was assaulted again by the wretchedly bad odor that seemed to hang like a curtain in the stale air. That is when my companion, in a matter of fact tone, informed me that dogs often become flatulent when frightened and confined, good news, he said, since it meant the canine effluvium we were experiencing was limited to a gaseous state. I had never heard canine flatulence characterized as a positive phenomenon and reckoned animal control work to be more thankless than I had imagined. I might have believed I had been consigned to Hell except that the scent of brimstone would have seemed like a veritable bouquet of lilacs.

And so our pursuit through the underworld continued, with the two of us scuttling like crabs breaking our skulls in pursuit of a sprightly dog ahead of us breaking wind. Where had my career path taken such a disagreeable turn? And if limestone is so porous, why wasn't it better at absorbing odors? Finally, my companion managed to get the noose around the neck of our long winded quarry and we wrapped him in the hammock netting and hoisted him out of the little hellhole, making sure to pull from above and not push from below. This was one animal I did not want to ever again be behind.

On the one hand, retaining "little frog" status at a place where there's so much to do means being regularly engaged in the most mundane of tasks, weeding, digging and planting, irrigation repair and maintenance, watering and such; even chasing flatulent pooches through the underworld. And, in recent years, I have found myself slowing just a bit or at least showing somewhat diminished enthusiasm for some gardening chores, especially during Florida's hellish summers, an ebb I share with my orange octogenarian friend. But there are benefits as well and they are more than compensatory. There is an unquantifiable, but very real, connection to the natural world that can be maintained and nurtured only through intimate engagement. An academic appreciation for the grandeur of nature is commendable and rewarding, but nothing can eclipse the satisfaction that comes from enterprises that leave dirt under your fingernails.

13

Secrets of Victoria

With Hogtown's glorious December days warming into the sunny seventies, it's not difficult to extrapolate to hellishly muggy August days in the nineties. That's when most folks rush from one air conditioned refuge to another and shrink like vampires from the sun's unrelenting scowl. And as they wilt and mildew away, natives invariably complain at some point that it has never been so hot, that this August is the worst ever. But the truth is, Augusts in northern Florida are always this hot and assertions to the contrary reflect a selective amnesia that enables us to accept our lot, to remember the good parts and forget about the bad. Otherwise, nobody would hang around Hogtown for yet another August, just as no woman delivered from one 'blessed event' would contemplate another. Still, August is not altogether without merit. Its long fiery days are essential to the nurture one of Kanapaha's signature plants and one of the planet's most majestic life forms, the incomparable giant Victoria.

The first time I saw Victoria was in the summer of 1964. I was one of three college students working for the Missouri Conservation Commission providing care for a collection of native wildlife that was to be displayed at various county fairs and eventually, at summer's end, the Missouri State Fair in Sedalia. In fact, we lived in quarters upstairs from the state fair's interior display space in pretty plush accommodations built to accommodate the state's governor, as necessary, when he visited Sedalia. In retrospect, it possibly was the cushiest job I ever had. I landed the position because I was a snake hunter and that's what was needed to ensure that the six display cages that housed poisonous snakes had at least one specimen each of Missouri's six poisonous snakes. The Commission didn't seem to have the organizational will to keep alive over winter the minimum six specimens required for this display and so the three man crew always included at least one herpetologically inclined individual who could fill any gaps in their offerings with freshly collected specimens.

In particular, pigmy rattlesnakes, also called ground rattlers, are high strung pugnacious little scamps that frequently refuse to feed, or for whom suitable food wasn't always readily available, the result being that we generally started the season without one. Finding and capturing pigmy rattlesnakes in my old Poplar Bluff snake hunting haunts was a cinch for me, far easier than happening upon a Massasauga Rattlesnake to the north or rousting a canebrake rattlesnake from the marshes of the Mingo Wildlife Preserve near the state's southeastern "Bootheel," my boyhood home. And, in truth, the canebrake is actually just a subspecies of the same snake called the timber rattlesnake farther north, but whoever was responsible for the design of the poisonous snake display allowed matters of aesthetic balance to trump taxonomic dogma.

Two tiers of three cages each, six in all, were required to counterbalance another six bearing non-venomous species and separated from them by a central colonnade bearing the words "Snakes of Missouri." The glass front of each cage fit into one of twelve symmetrically ordered openings in a masonite facade. They were maintained from behind; each opened at the top and could be slid out for cleaning. When the display was open to the public, a great crush of people was constantly pressed against the glass panes awaiting the opportunity to ignore our ceaseless mantra—"please don't tap on the glass"—and attempt to elicit a response from snakes numbed unconscious by relentless harassment.

Finding at least one of all six venomous snakes required a lot of work and a fair measure of luck. But there are so many non poisonous species to choose from that I usually collected them just prior to our first on-the-road exhibit at Springfield or Missoula. In a pinch, water snakes, racers or rat snakes could be rousted from any of a number of sites.

Beside the Conservation Commission's exhibit was a beautifully landscaped display called Highway Gardens. It was maintained by the Missouri Highway Department, possibly to atone for the environmental devastation they perpetrated everywhere else in the state. Beyond a railing, down an immaculately manicured Zoysia grass slope in a small pond was their prize offering, the water platter. This stunning water lily is so called because its perfectly round leaves turn upward for an inch or so around their entire margins to present the appearance of green floating platters surrounding a majestic ivory flower. This is *Victoria cruziana*, known to many as the Santa Cruz water lily or simply Victoria. It is one of only two *Victoria* species and both are residents of the steamy backwaters of Amazonia.

Because I was versed in reptiles and not in plants, I was unaware that these two species are unusual in more ways than their mere possession of pie pan leaves. To begin with, the two species of Victoria are the world's largest water lilies. The leaves of *Victoria amazonica* may grow to a diameter of seven feet or more and those of the Santa Cruz water lily only slightly smaller. I would never have guessed as much while admiring the Sedalia plants whose leaves attained a diameter of perhaps 24 inches. But this is a consequence of their circumstances. The climate of northern Missouri is notably unAmazonish, featuring cooler nights and a short growing season. Rather than growing for years on end in warm tropical waters, these plants are grown as annuals, propagated from seeds each year. And since they never really grow with abandon until the days are long and hot, a maximum leaf diameter of a couple of feet is the most they could muster.

Victorias are unusual for another reason, too. Their petioles, flower stalks and leaf undersurfaces are covered by fierce spines making it impossible to handle them without wearing leather gloves. I was not only unaware of this armament, but didn't learn of its function until many years later when I first attempted to grow one at Kanapaha Botanical Gardens. We had taken advantage of access to a dry lake bed, all that a severe drought had left of 250 acre Lake Kanapaha, to construct a hundred foot boardwalk into what would be a shallow lakeside cove once an inevitable rainy season restored the lake. When, in a short while, this came to pass, we planted all sorts of aquatic and emergent plants in our maiden venture into water gardening, and the fairest of them all, of course, was a giant Victoria water lily. We purchased one for $25 from a mail order pond supply business based in Winter Haven, Florida. When it arrived, our Victoria had only three spiny leaves each perhaps 15 inches in diameter and flat, not yet sporting the upturned rims that give them their trademark platter shape. Bare handed, I carried it gingerly into the water and, amid exclamations of "ouch! ouch!! ouch!!!," scooped out a handful of black mud from the pond's bottom and nestled the root system into place.

The next morning, it was gone! Or so I first thought. Upon closer examination, however, it seemed that much of the plant was still around, but in pieces floating here and there. All three petioles had been severed and what remained of the leaves was badly torn and disheveled. What could have done such a thing? And why was my precious Victoria singled out for such abuse? Nothing else seemed to have been touched.

I ordered another Victoria right away, cognizant of the fact that the window of seasonal availability was closing fast; in another few weeks, these plants would be too big and spiny to handle and ship. It arrived soon enough and I amended the planting process in only one respect; I held the plant overnight and planted it on the morning of the day after it arrived so I could check in on it periodically during its first eight or ten hours of residence to hopefully see what was going on. It didn't take long. When I first checked in on my new baby perhaps an hour after planting, one petiole had been severed and the leaf blade was being ineptly dismembered by a cooter, a native turtle, bumping it around the pond with its snout as it paddled behind nipping out small chunks. It showed no interest in any of the other water lilies I had planted and, in fact, was so absorbed in chasing this bit of green flotsam that it was unaware of my presence to the point that I slowly waded in and very nearly caught it.

On that day, I learned something very central to successful cultivation of Victorias in natural bodies of water. They are a delicacy to herbivorous turtles, and fish like koi and carp, who will devour them in preference to anything else available. And ever since that day, I have installed turtleproof fences constructed of chicken wire or nylon netting around newly planted Victorias until they are producing leaves 30 inches or more in diameter, a size that bears spines substantial enough to repulse their adversaries. In fact, their savory taste is doubtless what has necessitated the evolution of this unique armament.

It is quite a remarkable thing to witness the unfurling of a new Victoria leaf. The spiny petiole is attached to the center of the leaf blade's spiny undersurface which is itself curled inward so that its main radiating veins appear like fingers of a hand tightly clenched palm up in a prickly glove. As much as anything, it looks like a turgid green hedgehog on a spiny leash. There is simply no way to nibble on the leaf without first confronting the arsenal of fierce bristles radiating outward. At the water surface, the leaf unrolls outward in all directions like a round carpet, exposing row after row of spines pointing outward, then downward, but leaving the outermost strip upright with its spines pointing outward parallel with the water surface.

Never in the unfurling process does it leave its delicious leaf tissue vulnerable to assault from below. Only airborne creatures can access the leaf's upper surface and, in fact, young leaves are sometimes chewed up by caterpillars of the China mark moth. But more often, any disfigurement of the buoyant leaves is attributable to scratch marks left by the feet of small herons utilizing them as fishing platforms and I have, on two occasions, seen small alligators, seemingly immune to the Victoria armament, basking half out of the water on a green platter.

Over the years, we have learned much about growing water platters. Initially, all we could get our hand on was the Santa Cruz water lily, *Victoria cruziana*, even though it does not grow quite as large as the Amazon water platter, *Victoria amazonica*. In an industry, and culture, that generally equates bigger with better, this seemed peculiar. It turns out, however, that Amazon is a finicky plant whereas anyone with a large pond devoid of herbivorous turtles or fish can succeed with the robust Santa Cruz. Amazon's seeds don't germinate well, for instance, in water that is cooler than 90 degrees F; make that 80 for Santa Cruz. After germination, Amazon seedlings don't show the vigor of Santa Cruz and are less likely to survive the predations of China mark caterpillars. And once they are finally planted out, Amazon water platters don't show the initial explosive growth that is characteristic of Santa Cruz and, at Kanapaha Botanical Gardens, seem to be just reaching their prime when the cool nights of October bring the Victoria season to a halt. These are, after all, tropical plants that are only truly happy in the still waters of the sweltering tropics.

There is another reason besides stature, though, that makes the Amazon water platter worth a second look. The undersurface of its leaves is wine red. And since an inch or two of the leaf's periphery is upturned, this means that the outside of the pie tin leaf's rim is, astonishingly, red. I believe firmly in the doctrine of natural selection and have no doubt whatever that this stunningly beautiful feature confers some survival value to this plant. But the visual impact of a flotilla of perfectly round gigantic vibrantly green leaves with upturned red margins moored around a stately central ivory flower confers, at least to me, the impression of a magnificent but alien life form. I love and appreciate many many plants, but only a very few project an aura of such transcendent majesty. It is on a par with the Venus' flytrap and that is high praise indeed.

In late afternoon, a Victoria looks quite different, because the white flower is no longer white; it was pink at noon and is now maroon. The Victoria is not alone in its production of chameleonic flowers, Confederate rose does so, and also yesterday, today and tomorrow among others, but it is a rare capability and only adds to the allure of an already charismatic plant. Then the flower sinks below the surface to set seeds in a swollen burr-like ovary.

Presented with such disparate species profiles, any knowledgeable plant breeder would unhesitatingly recommend the obvious: hybridization of the two Victoria species to produce an intermediate form. With any luck, some, at least, might show hybrid vigor, combining the best qualities of both species. And, in fact, that is exactly what was done at Longwood Gardens, one of America's premier gardens, in 1962. The Longwood hybrid, as it is known, is a gardener's dream come true, at least a gardener with a very large pond. It exhibits the ease of germination and vigorous growth characteristic of the Santa Cruz species while flaunting the Amazon's red leaf rim.

For many years, Longwood Gardens distributed seeds of the hybrid, newly hybridized each year, to botanical gardens until the demand proved burdensome to Longwood's staff. During those years, Kanapaha Botanical Gardens always received a few seeds of the Longwood hybrid as well as its parent species. Since Longwood has discontinued its distribution program, private collectors have stepped forward to do so. Consequently, our water gardens have, almost since their conception, displayed both the hybrid and/or the Santa Cruz as signature plants. The Amazon has lived up to the reputation that precedes it; germination success is low, growth is disappointingly slow, and it shows a general failure to thrive. But what does it matter? We have the Longwood hybrid which is wonderful consolation.

I'm not sure who first had the idea to photograph someone standing or sitting on a Victoria leaf, but it's probably the sort of notion that arose independently in many quarters. It is common, after all, to see other life forms, most notably frogs, squatting on water lily pads and it takes just a small leap of the imagination to invision gigantic leaves of Victoria supporting the weight of a human body. In the black and white plant photo book, Exotica, there is a photograph of a girl of indeterminate age seemingly kneeling on the leaf of a Santa Cruz Victoria, though it's not possible to see the leaf condition at the point of contact as that is concealed from view by the high rim in the edge-on photograph.

According to some unconfirmed but persistent accounts, somebody in a Tarzan movie once floated down a jungle stream on a Victoria leaf. I'm less concerned about the inconsistency an Amazonian plant being pressed into such unlikely service in an African jungle than the prospect that I somehow missed a Tarzan movie during a childhood that accorded a high priority to watching jungle adventure shows or those showcasing monsters. I routinely accepted the appearance of plants and animals from the New World tropics in Tarzan's African jungle as the price of viewing images of wonderful wild creatures at all. Those were, after all, the days before the onset of high quality nature documentaries that now routinely bring the wild into our living rooms. But if somebody commandeered a Victoria kayak, I missed it.

Necessarily, I decided to stage a photograph myself so I consulted our original Santa Cruz supplier, Peter Slocum. He told me that Victoria leaves are actually quite fragile and that their capacity for supporting weight is greatly exaggerated. When such photographs are taken, therefore, the ballast rests on a thin green plywood disk that more evenly distributes its weight across the entire leaf. Since plywood sheets are unwaveringly sold in four by eight foot panels, the largest circle I could cut from one would be four feet in diameter. And so, back in 1989, I waited until my Santa Cruz first began producing leaves of that size and cut such a disk from a 1/4 inch sheet of plywood. I covered it with paint that was computer matched to the color of some Victoria leaf tissue I entrusted to a perplexed paint clerk and slipped it onto the leaf surface encircled by the upright rim. Although the color match was good, I fretted that my faux leaf lacked the texture, sheen and reticulate venation of the genuine article. I knew from experience, though, that if I captured the image I sought, nobody would recognize these trifling inaccuracies while transfixed by so remarkable a spectacle.

Audrey Dickinson rests on the giant leaf of the Santa Curz Water Platter, Victoria cruziana. Actually, between Audrey and the leaf surface is a circular panel of thin plywood that distributes her weight across the entire surface. Photo by author.

My model for what was to become one of Kanapaha's most celebrated photographs (and, ultimately, postcards) was Audrey Dickinson, the 3 year old daughter of two of Kanapaha's veteran volunteers, John and Laura Dickinson. Under Laura's watchful eye, I carefully lifted bathing suit clad Audrey from the deck of our boardwalk and waded perhaps 10 feet to my plywood-reinforced Victoria leaf and plopped her down in the direct center of the leaf. To my immense delight, the leaf's buoyancy was equal to the task; no water rushed in and I was able to coax several shots from sweet Audrey who looked as adorable as only a 3 year old frog girl on a water lily pad could. In three minutes, she was back in her mother's arms. Audrey is now in college and will doubtless accomplish things that will eclipse her brief stint as a Victoria pixie, but to me, that brief convergence endures as a magic moment. And as I sort through slides selecting images to provide viewers with a fleeting glimpse of our planet's botanic treasures, one of the Audrey-on-Victoria shots always seems to end up in the final cut.

The warm and rich waters that nurture these magnificent plants are also home to many other species of plants and animals and, over the years, I have come to know many of them intimately well. Tiny floating plants called duckweed and water meal grow and coalesce into a green film at the water surface as spring yields to summer, creating what many unflatteringly denounce as pond scum. It certainly is preferable to see Victoria leaves against the black mirror of Kanapaha's coffee colored water than pea soup, but eradicating, or at least controlling, these plants is more easily said than done. The approach I've always employed for dealing with floating offenders entails wading in and manually removing them. Duckweed and water meal must be screened out with a fine mesh net, whereas larger plants, like water hyacinths and water lettuce, can be tossed out a handful at a time.

There are two problems with this approach. The first is that all of this wading about constantly stirs up the rich bottom sediments adding nutrients into the water and fostering an explosive regrowth of the offending vegetation. The second is that wading about and grabbing fistfuls of green jetsam occasionally puts you on speaking terms with an assortment of swamp creatures. Mostly, these are aquatic salamanders, small snakes, turtles and varied insects, spiders and other arthropods. And while many might consider this an unholy mix of vermin, I find it preferable to interacting socially with the cross section of humanity that comprises so much of the work day of so many non naturalists.

Over the years, I have encountered hundreds of visitors to Kanapaha who observe me splashing about in our display ponds and want to know, first, what I'm doing and, second, if I am aware that there may be snakes and alligators about. Because there is so much misguided vilification of these reptiles, I've always considered it part of our educational mission to take the time to share information about their natural history and behavior and help, in small measure, reduce the unfortunate estrangement humanity has with so many wild things. In fact, I assure them, my chief fear is being assaulted by a biting bug variously called the hot bug or the gator flea. These nondescript little hemipterans have a piercing bite far worse than they look like they should, a bite that feels like an intensely painful sting. They unleash this venomous bite whenever they feel trapped and may do so repeatedly, so I always wear a bathing suit when swamping to make sure one doesn't find itself in the throes of claustrophobia between my leg and pants. The pain of their bite is more than sufficient to vanquish all but the most ardent commitments to modesty and reduce its victims to ripping away all confining garments; I know because I've done it.

Because they grow large and occasionally attack people, alligators do present some risk and it's best to avoid them at close quarters. My first experience with a substantial alligator occurred in the summer of 1990 when an eight foot female began construction of a nest on the bank of our water lily pond not 25 feet from our boardwalk. Only our regular addition of water to the pond had forestalled its consumption by one of the region's trademark droughts that was daily reducing the domain of Lake Kanapaha. Apparently, the huge reptile had cast her lot with us in a backhanded tribute to our ability to maintain a stable water level in a time of drought. Not surprisingly, I learned that compliments of this sort are not always interspecific as some observers were more horrified than flattered by her endorsement of our environmental stewardship.

It was easy enough to understand their distress and I had a few reservations as well. Alligators use their great bulk to deepen the reservoirs they fancy by wallowing them out into 'gator holes' that, in the wild, tend to retain water and a microcosmic sampling of its aquatic denizens that will repopulate the area when rains replenish it—Noah's Ark in reverse. While all of this is ecologically gratifying, it constitutes a horticultural nightmare in which pond bottom mud, laden with our precious Victoria seeds and seedlings, is heaped up, trampled down and generally defiled. By comparison, our disputes with gophers and caterpillars seem like a frolic in the Bahamas.

Our initial response was naivety incarnate. We redistributed the mud and encircled our colony of young Victoria seedlings with an expanded version of the fencing that had proved successful in repulsing the attentions of marauding turtles. This effort ended in failure, however as the barricade lacked the integrity to break her stride, much less her spirit.

Thereafter, turtles happened onto the breaches in our failed bastion and entered our new crocodilian playpen to devour the succulent fledgling Victorias. We now had turtles inside our "turtle proof" enclosure. Other increasingly desperate measures were taken following this grievous episode and preceding our ultimate capitulation.

Along this path of delusion and insufficiency, we were counseled more than once that our gator's actions qualified her for 'nuisance gator' status with the Florida Game and Freshwater Fish Commission, nominal justification for tossing her into somebody else's swamp. But we rejected this counsel on the grounds that alligators preceded humanity in colonizing Lake Kanapaha and that it is humans, not alligators, that are interfering with natural order. So we accepted for the season a diminution in the glory of the 1990 episode of our annual Victoria spectacle. Eventually the tenacity and perseverance of our toothsome matriarch bore fruit as legions of baby dragons issued forth from her mounded nest and followed her back to the retreating waters of Lake Kanapaha. In her wake, she left a disheveled water lily pond turned gator hole, the tattered spoils of a battle won.

The passage of time healed these wounds and our little pond flaunted its majestic Victorias in other summers. Such skirmishes are the price we pay in our quest for a modicum of balance in the natural world we have so badly damaged. And not all of our encounters with alligators have been so benign; but that's another story.

14

Phytoamericana: The Ben Franklin Tree

The thing that endears many plants to those who grow them is the sensory delights provided by their flowers. The beauty and fragrance of a rose defies characterization, but both qualities, indescribable though they are, are exalted by all who have personally experienced their glories. Nothing could differ from a rose more than an orchid—or a passion flower or a tiger lily or a bougainvillea—and yet each is uniquely wonderful and aptly celebrated.

In many other plants, it is ornamental foliage that is revered by those who pamper them. Crotons produce flowers, but who can bring to mind an image of one? We admire them instead for their decorative leaves. And ferns do not even produce flowers, but many are adorned by soft feathery fronds so sumptuous that they are more than compensatory.

And then there are plants that are captivating, not so much for how they look, but rather because the machinations of the human memory have given them a place in history. The legacy of Socrates forever cast hemlock as a portal to the dark realm, an estate it shares with the deadly nightshades. Acanthus has been immortalized by Corinthian columns and papyrus is remembered both as the original source of paper and as the Egyptian bulrushes that figured so prominently in the Biblical tale of Moses. History is punctuated by accounts of plants that have assumed prominence in our recollections of momentous events or extraordinary people.

One such plant is an unassuming little tree whose story is pure Americana. The year was 1776. Colonists opposed to British rule met in Philadelphia to draft a document that would forever change the world and whose eloquent prose gave voice to the radical notion that ordinary men possess inherent rights, beyond those conferred by government.

Not all of the individuals who streamed into Philadelphia that year were motivated primarily by political concerns, however. Of particular interest was the return to the city of a young naturalist named William Bartram. At this politically tumultuous moment, the gentle Quaker returned from a remarkable three year expedition to the wilds of what was to become the southeastern United States. His mission was to collect botanical specimens for the British Museum and record observations on the region's flora, fauna and human inhabitants. Over the course of those years, his travels had taken him to realms that have long since disappeared, and which we know only through the detailed and eloquent account he recorded on his remarkable journey.

He related accounts of his interactions with Indians, merchants and slaves as well as his encounters with huge rattlesnakes and alligators. He documented the existence of plants and animals in places where they no longer occur—royal palms on the St. Johns River and wolves on The Great Alachua Savannah, now Paynes Prairie State Preserve. But his place in the chronicles of botanical exploration was secured forever by his discovery of a flowering tree that exists today only because he undertook his incredible expedition.

On the banks of the Altamaha River, in what today is southeast Georgia, Bartram paused to revisit a grove of shrubs and small trees that he had seen once before, when he accompanied his father, John Bartram, on a botanizing trip in 1765. Here, in the Georgia wilderness, was a thicket of plants that he believed to be new to science. On his previous trip, the small trees were devoid of flowers so it was not possible to classify them taxonomically; but his return visit found numerous flowers that were a "snow white colour, and ornamented with a crown or tassel of gold coloured refulgent stamina in their centre." Their flowers revealed that they clearly belonged to the tea family, Theaceae, that includes in its ranks camellias and tea, among others. The flowers were similar to those of the native loblolly bay, *Gordonia lasianthus*, and he was tempted to put it into the same genus. But, he then "found striking characteristics abundantly sufficient to separate it from that genus, and to establish it the head of a new tribe." Accordingly, he assigned the new plant a genus that would honor an old family friend, Benjamin Franklin and a species denoting the place of its discovery. Thereafter, the little tree would be known to science as *Franklinia alatamaha* and to gardeners everywhere as the Ben Franklin tree.

Bartram collected seeds from the plants and took them with him back to Philadelphia where he cultivated them in his garden. And it is good that he did, for this tale of discovery is only the beginning of a great mystery. It now seems likely that the little thicket of Ben Franklin trees discovered by the Bartrams was the only population in existence anywhere. Bartram himself wrote in his journal, "We never saw it grow in any other place, nor have I since seen it growing wild, in all my travels, from Pennsylvania to Point Coupe, on the banks of the Mississippi, which must be allowed a very singular and unaccountable circumstance; at this place there are two or three acres of ground where it grows plentifully." Nor has anyone since surveyed what Bartram beheld on the banks of the Altamaha River. In fact, a search for *Franklinia* in 1790 located only a single tree and it has not been seen in the wild since 1803, the year of the Louisiana Purchase.

Apparently, the Ben Franklin tree was teetering on the brink of extinction when John and William Bartram chanced upon the little colony that likely represented its last stand. Today, the species is available to gardeners solely because William Bartram stuffed a few seeds into his saddle pack on that long ago summer day when *Franklinia* still enjoyed a most tenuous grasp on existence in a world whose changes were extinguishing its flame. But what changes? And why was its native range even then so stiflingly small? The answers are unknown and Bartram's accounts provide the sum of our knowledge about the Ben Franklin tree in the wild.

One thing that is known with certainty is that most Florida gardeners find this plant difficult to grow. That certainly has been our experience at Kanapaha Botanical Gardens. I planted my first *Franklinia* in the summer of 1985, much as I would a native oak or pine; I shoveled aside a couple of scoops of soil, firmed the root ball into place and watered. Its decline appeared to commence the moment it came out of the pot. The leaves withered and, within a matter of days, it whimpered and died. Its demise was so precipitous that there remained no doubt whatever that some special accommodation would have to be made if visitors to Kanapaha were ever to see the celebrated Ben Franklin tree. We had experienced this phenomenon before with a Chinese species called the dove tree, so called because, when flowering, its branches appear as though they are filled with white doves. But the climate of its native habitat was cooler and it probably found Florida summers unbearable. However, the Ben Franklin tree's only known habitat is just a bit north of the Georgia-Florida line, so it seems as though it should thrive here or, at the very least, not curl up its toes and die.

Since it originally grew adjacent to the Altamaha River, perhaps *Franklinia* was actually a wetland plant and would thrive in more moist circumstances. Reasoning thus, I acquired a second plant and planted it in the rich alluvial soil of Lake Kanapaha's shoreline. Unlike my first tree, which was placed in full sun, this one was planted in a carefully selected site that would provide a mottling of sun and shade, most probably the light regime that would be familiar to a diminutive tree. Regrettably, its decline was as abrupt as the first. Over the next several years, I attempted to succeed with *Franklinia*, not with feverish determination, but with sporadic efforts mixed into a full and varied gardening schedule. Speculation on the cause of the ensuing successive failures tended to focus on soil problems, particularly Florida's abundance of soil nematodes and pathogenic fungi.

After some failures, I bellowed to all within earshot my disgust with the whole futile affair, vowing to abandon the venture altogether, though I have since come to recognize that these resolutions were simple expressions of frustration and not to be taken seriously. At least I never really succeeded in divesting myself of the obsession with growing *Franklinia*. Gardeners eventually learn that the undoing of the resolve that leads to such rash pronouncements comes in the form of colorful and alluring plant sales catalogs that appear in the mailbox each autumn to sustain them through the dark abyss of winter. And there, I would always succumb to another promise of deliverance, a siren song of praise for the charismatic and historically alluring Ben Franklin tree, and place an order for yet another doomed specimen

Finally, I went back to the sole source of information regarding the species' natural habitat. And there, among the very few written references to *Franklinia*, appeared a clue. One of Bartram's conventions when penning entries about plants into his journal was to record other plant species found in association with it. While it did lead to a mind numbing repetition of plants with broad environmental tolerances—like Virginia creeper—or species of which he was particularly fond—like southern magnolia—it did provide a record of significance in the quest for *Franklinia's* habitat preference. Among its associates was another small tree with very narrow environmental tolerance, at least for soil. The fever tree (*Pinckneya pubens*), so named for its medicinal properties, including the treatment of fevers, is another tree that we have found impossible to grow, presumably because its preferred habitat is seepage bogs, circumstances where the soil is highly acidic and where tea colored water seeps from the soil surface, at least during most non-drought situations.

This is an important clue in two regards. Kanapaha's soils are nearly uniformly alkaline as evidenced by exposed limestone boulders and limerock. And the survival of *Franklinia* plants while potted and awaiting transplantation could be attributable to the peat that is a major component of virtually all commercial potting mixes; it would tend to keep the medium both moist and acidic. We have plenty of water at Kanapaha; it flows down the stream in our water gardens at a rate of 50-100 gallons per minute; our problem is a dearth of peaty acidic soil. And so we decided to test our conjecture that acidic wet soil was the key to growing *Franklinia* by creating our own acid bog. Actually, it was a peat wick. We bought eight cubic yards of peat that was dug from a peat mine in the little nearby community of Florahome and had it dumped down the embankment of our little stream to create a small peninsula of peat. Since peat soaks up water like a sponge, it seemed clear that a Ben Franklin tree planted on the peninsula would have a close equivalent of an acid seepage bog. Some months earlier, junkie that I am, I had acquired yet another *Franklinia*; and once again, a smack on the pot bottom with the heel of my hand brought the sacrificial sapling out of its plastic sanctuary and onto the world stage, in this case, the peaty bog we had fashioned beside our little stream. Whether this situation was similar enough to the environment William Bartram surveyed two centuries earlier on the banks of the Altamaha River remained to be seen, and in time we learned the answer. As you shall. But that is part of a larger story.

15

Green Treasures

Many things we value for their utility. Malleable metals are valued highly enough to justify the considerable effort involved in extracting their ore from the earth's crust and putting it through elaborate refinement processes. Thereafter, they have served humanity as ploughs, weapons, automobiles, typewriters, printing presses and in innumerable other forms. Crude oil is similarly extracted for its potential to serve humanity as a source of both fuel and plastic. So great is its assigned value that it has afforded geopolitical clout to some unlikely players and caused significant tumult across the planet. And so it is with most things, from apples to horses; the value we ascribe to them is a function of their utility to humanity.

But what of precious metals, like gold and silver? It is true that they are valued for their malleability, but far more than iron which, in most cases would serve as well or better. They are precious, rather, because they possess intangible qualities that we greatly revere—scarcity and unique beauty. It is not utility alone that confers their value, but also the collective aesthetic judgment of humankind. And as we pass through our lives, we ascribe to certain things a value that far exceeds their simple utility. This is as true in the realm of gardening as any other field of human endeavor; we value the rose as well as the potato.

Examples abound. Back in 1969, the collective imagination of our race was focused on the moon. Humanity has always revered the diminutive satellite as a source of inspiration, an intoxicant of the lovelorn and for the reflected light it sends our way. But in that year, we were trying to reach it physically as astronauts blasted off from the Florida coast on a mission that seemed so impossible just a few years earlier. And within a few brief years, the journey became almost routine as Apollo crafts ferried three man crews to the moon with nearly flawless perfection. The one exception, of course, was Apollo 13, which came perilously close to ending in disaster while most of humanity's 4 billion prayed as one for the safe return of the only three humans who were in great peril far from the earth and trapped with their fears in the cold black void of space.

The very next mission, Apollo 14, took yet another trio to explore our barren satellite. As was the convention, two of them, Alan Shepard and Edgar Mitchell, descended to the moon's surface in a lunar lander while Stuart Roosa manned the Apollo 14 command module orbiting above. With him in the cabin of the Apollo craft, were several other living organisms, a batch of seeds that Roosa had brought along. These had come from a variety of trees that were selected as important American natives—redwood, Douglas fir, sycamore, loblolly pine, slash pine and sweet gum. Upon their return to earth, these seeds were given to the U.S. Forest Service where they were germinated and grown to determine the effects, if any, of weightlessness and proximity to the lunar surface. Exactly how this was supposed to advance the renown of humanity was all a bit sketchy, but those were exhilarating times when optimism held sway in the public arena, NASA had more money than it knew what to do with and anything seemed possible. Apparently, they did it just for the hell of it; our tax dollars at work.

Today, the trees that have grown from those seeds have become national treasures. Their value to the citizenry far exceeds the market price of comparable specimens because they grew from seeds that had been to the moon; they're called moon trees and are a source of pride for any community that is fortunate enough to have one. But just getting a moon tree did not always confer celebrity upon its recipient community as Hogtown residents learned. The Forest Service gave the University of Florida three seedling trees—two pines and a sycamore. They were grown out in pots of commercial potting soil and planted out a few years later on the UF campus. Because of their notoriety, location of the planting sites, even acknowledgment that they had been planted, was withheld from the public due to fears of theft or their being loved to death. The secrecy worked a bit too well. The two pines were so uncelebrated that they were unceremoniously mowed down by a maintenance worker who was not only unaware of their celebrity but of their presence in the path of his mower as well. However meager, minimum wage always seems ample to purchase a level of industriousness that is capable of neutralizing the most expensive technological ventures.

Regrettably, pines do not sprout from the stump as many hardwoods do, and so this decapitation spelled the demise of two invaluable and irreplaceable moon trees. The third tree, a sycamore, has grew into a fine specimen and years later, its existence and location were finally revealed to the long suffering taxpayers who had footed the bill for the whole affair. It still stands on the UF campus on the northeast corner of the intersection of Museum Road and North-South Drive. An area tree nursery even began propagating and selling moon trees grown from cuttings taken from the tree or, later, from cuttings of the second generation it had established, a practice that is widely emulated elsewhere.

Institutional memory, unfortunately, is not always as keen as one might hope, and in a few years, many folks had forgotten about the sycamore's erstwhile celebrity. Thus it was one sunny afternoon that I observed, to my horror, that a sizeable chunk of the moon sycamore's imposing trunk had been gouged by a backhoe that was idling beside a work crew, which was also idling, that had been contracted to frame and pour a sidewalk parallel to the north curb of Museum Road. Furthermore, a substantial pile of soil had been piled beside the tree in violation of a widely accepted horticultural taboo since it could result in damage to the root system either through oxygen deprivation or mechanical injury as the soil was scooped up in a backhoe bucket.

Even back then, there was no reasonable prospect of finding a legal parking space on campus (and the University's vigilant contingent of enforcement storm troopers are notoriously unsympathetic and fast with a tire boot), so I raced to the nearest phone booth to call Noel Lake, the campus' head of landscape design. Noel always fretted over the smallest detail of campus landscaping and it seemed inconceivable that such a thing could happen on his watch. As, in fact, it hadn't. I was informed that Noel had recently retired and discerned very quickly that his successor had not inherited a knowledge of the existence of a moon tree on campus. When enlightened, however, he did what needed to be done. The next day a barricade was erected around the tree and the offending soil pile had disappeared. Happily, the tree recovered completely.

Gardeners everywhere have plants that are special to them by virtue of one thing or another, and there are many that come to mind in my own experience. But there is one whose value to me far exceeds its worth for any conceivable purpose to anyone else. It is a specimen of one of many cultivars of the Chinese juniper, *Juniperus chinensis* and was acquired in the very early years of Kanapaha Botanical Gardens' existence.

In those days, I didn't decline many offers of free plants. There were many acres of pasture and woodland to be transformed and a place could be found for almost anything of ornamental value. Thus it was that I responded affirmatively to an invitation to drive down to Greenbrier Nursery near Ocala to look over a variety of nursery stock that was being discarded for one reason or another. I made the journey in a commodious Ford pickup and, in short order, had its bed loaded to the gills with potbound shrubs and trees that had been destined for the Marion County landfill.

In the course of sorting through the bounty, proprietor Bill Reese asked me if I would like to have a flat of *sylvertris* liners. Not wishing to confess that I didn't know what either *sylverstris* or liners were, I enthusiastically accepted, whereupon he picked up a plastic tray molded into rows of small cylindrical receptacles—liners—each bearing a seedling tree that was recognizable as a conifer of some sort, and flung it onto the substantial heap of fellow disheveled discards in my truck bed. It was clearly of little value for my purposes so I didn't bother to nestle it in among the many pots to spare it wind damage on the trip back. My intention from the outset was to discard the entire flat yet a second time when I had returned.

My daughter, Summer, was 5 years old at the time. I held her aloft and showed her my truckload of acquisitions and identified them as best I could to her steady refrain, "What's that?" She was especially taken with the little forest of spiny *sylvestris* liners and wanted to plant them in our yard, at this time a barely improved blackberry thicket. So I outfitted her with a hand trowel and coached her as she pulled four of the seedlings from their receptacles and planted each as carefully as a child of five might in the sandy soil of our lawn to be.

Sharing with her the transplantation of the little trees was for me nothing more than another of the myriad endeavors parents undertake daily to spend time with their little ones and keep them amused. It held no more significance than reading Summer a story or bouncing her on my knee to elicit the squeals of delight that allow us to fleetingly share in the wonder and joy they seem to find at every turn.

For the next dozen or so years, Summer and her younger sister, Alexis, knew Kanapaha Botanical Gardens as an after school playground and watched it evolve year by year, much as they themselves did. They knew all of the good climbing trees and found special excitement and freedom driving around (under vigilant adult supervision) the golf car that was a work horse for the rest of us. Where there were sensitive mimosas or Venus' fly traps to be harassed, they were always equal to the challenge. They both loved fruits of the palm hammock's jelly palms, which I found a bit too tart, and sported purple hands when the mulberries were ripe, a passion we shared. One of our fence lines still sports a buckled fence post that is testament to 15 year old Summer's steep learning curve in distinguishing between my clunker's brake and accelerator.

It was a wonderful place to grow up and they truly made the most of it as was abundantly documented photographically in our periodic newsletter, Bulletin of the North Florida Botanical Society. Despite the staid and sober title, this little publication was actually quite unpretentious and served not only to document the development of Kanapaha and to offer articles of interest to gardeners, but also to chronicle the childhoods of the two original children of Kanapaha. There was Summer, with her friend Leah holding a muscular gopher snake in a picture accompanying an article that celebrated the effectiveness of these reptiles in controlling pocket gophers, a curse of Florida's gardeners. Or Alexis, with her friend Kristen posing with a specimen of the world's largest seed, the spectacular "double coconut" from a Seychelles Islands palm, and a case of mounted butterfly specimens collected at Kanapaha by a neighbor. Whatever happened at Kanapaha, they were in the thick of it. And Kanapaha was always an important part of their lives for they knew it from the inside as only they could.

In May, 1995, Summer graduated from high school. She was dually enrolled in the local Santa Fe Community College and planned to continue there before transferring to a university. She moved out, but not far away. She set up house in Kanapaha Botanical Gardens as its caretaker in a mobile home that had served as the residence of two caretakers before her. It was a special treat to be invited over to a dinner prepared by Summer and her boyfriend, Jess. It all seemed so natural for this child of Kanapaha to strengthen, rather than sever, her bond with her erstwhile playground. And, of course, it gave me a chance to mingle with her and her friends to a greater degree than is usually the lot of parents that are banished by their former charges once hormones begin to percolate.

The following July fourth began uneventfully. Summer and Jess had left late the previous afternoon to drive to New Orleans to visit his grandmother. So it was just Jordan, Alexis and me to sort out how to spend the day. We had talked about possibly taking in one of the area's fireworks displays later that evening, but had planned nothing definite. And then the phone rang and Jordan answered. She was visibly shaken by word from a neighbor that a sheriff's patrol car had stopped to ask them for directions to our house. Her fear was not of concern for any wrongdoing, but the concern of a mother for her first born, a fear that something had happened to Summer and that the officers were bearers of terrible tidings. She had worked in the medical community long enough to know that this is how it sometimes happens. I, on the other hand, could not accept that, if the visit concerned news of Summer at all, and this I thought unlikely, anything other than minor injury in an auto mishap at worst could be expected. Alexis was immediately cognizant of the concern in our voices as we asked a young neighborhood playmate if she would please depart for home while we dealt with our swelling dread.

Jordan immediately called Jess' mother to learn whether she could shed any light on the impending visit from a sheriff's patrol car. Then she dissolved into sobs. Summer and Jess had both been killed in a collision just outside Mobile, Alabama. Apparently Jess had fallen asleep at the wheel, crossed the median and crashed head on into another car whose driver, thankfully, was not killed. In that moment, the life we had known was gone forever. Thereafter our standard for measuring time became "before or after."

So difficult is it to speak of this unfathomable loss, that, even nine years later, it has taken me more than six months to complete this paragraph. Three lines into the account, I was so stricken with the dread of revisiting the sheer life ravaging horror of that day that I set it aside and only returned to the keyboard after the passage of many months. Some find it cathartic to speak openly about loss, but I am not one of them. Losing Summer has validated the truth of the oft repeated adage that losing a child is the most tragically painful of all human losses and I have no desire to employ discourse to relive those dark days; it is an unimaginably horrific tragedy pure and simple. Those who have not lost a child cannot know how deep a gash anguish can leave on the soul and I envy them that good fortune. Mine is gone forever. I have yet to discern a shimmer of any silver lining that might attend this dark cloud that has visited so much pain on our lives. Except perhaps a far deeper sense of compassion for other survivors of loved ones taken tragically before their time. And yet affairs of the larger world continued undiminished and unaffected by the collapse of our own. It is truly remarkable how many distinct personal worlds we humans can simultaneously inhabit as we live out our uniquely separate lives.

In the days and months, and then years, that followed, raw grief surrendered to a grim acceptance that is necessary to regaining a diminished sense of equilibrium that allowed some joy back into our shattered lives. After all, we still had our Alexis, now sisterless, to cherish and her grief was a matter that concerned us greatly. And so we set out to do what we could to restore her spirit as well as our own.

In taking account of the impact of Summer's life, we found some comfort. She had friends who loved and admired her and had brought much happiness into our lives and those of others. She was a liberal firebrand, an animal rights advocate who picketed McDonald's and supplemented a vegetarian diet with cheese only when her weight began to drop. She was concerned about the homeless and often visited a group she called "the dumpster people," because they lived behind one, and helped them as best she could. On one occasion, she gave the $20 in her possession to a stranded hitchhiker and, on another, gave away her little red car; or more accurately, she traded it for drumming lessons. She wrote poetry, loved Mozart, Nine Inch Nails and The Beatles and laughed easily and heartily. She loved life and lived it well. We were justly proud of her.

Five days after her passage, we held a memorial service in the embrace of a venerable Kanapaha live oak whose canopy had, over the years, provided shade for many happier occasions—weddings, birthday gatherings and especially our annual Easter brunches. As I walked to the site, consumed by heartache, I beheld something perhaps a hundred yards to my west. It was white, most probably a white flower, set against a mosaic of coalesced earthtones, but not where I had seen its like before. I took a brisk detour to confirm a growing suspicion that a long elusive quest had been realized. There on the outstretched branches of my Ben Franklin Tree, were three lovely flowers. They appeared as William Bartram had described them two centuries earlier; each bore five white petals radiating from a central hub that was obscured by a great circular mass of golden stamens. Thus, at my life's nadir, did I experience the great triumph of coaxing this rare and finicky tree into producing flowers that seemed, more than anything, like a natural tribute to my precious lost Summer and a hollow victory indeed. Still, it seems as though this was but the ephemeral extravagance of a species committed to a path of extinction; for the following spring, its bare branches produced no green flush, having inexplicably died during the cold months. Our singular and fleeting triumph with the enigmatic Ben Franklin tree.

Shortly after Summer's death, I spied one of the Chinese junipers she had rescued from my trunk bed all of those years ago when Kanapaha was still a dream devoid of substance and she was little more than a baby. I had dug them up, potted them and moved them to Kanapaha where they had been endlessly shuffled about since I never really knew what to do with a plant possessed of so little charm. Suddenly I looked at these homely little waifs differently. They were tangible evidence of Summer's meteoric passage through our lives; they would not even exist had Summer not intervened to save them from the dumpster all those years earlier. Thus were they transmuted at that instant from a horticultural commodity to exalted memorial of inestimable value. I selected a spot in our developing arboretum and relocated one of the junipers; it would henceforth be on public display as our representative of *Jupeperis chinensis 'sylvestris'* and a private memorial to my beloved daughter.

As I walk through Kanapaha today, I can see everywhere the impact of time's passage. Where there was once a field of broomsedge and prickly pear cacti, torrents of water now pour over waterfalls and roses bloom in profusion. Statuesque palms from a dozen Edens have transformed an erstwhile pasture into a splendid oasis and stately bamboos confer the essence of the East. At every turn, there is a special plant whose unique form reflects the twists and turns of an evolutionary path that differs from all others, and each comes with a story. And though I often stop to admire them and contemplate the import of their singular beauty, there is only one that I always pause to kiss. Its prickly branches are a balm for a wounded heart.

16

Summer of the Dragon

While floating the Ichetucknee River, one commonly finds fossil evidence of Florida's past protruding from the sandy stream bed. Fossils of both marine and terrestrial origin have long been trophies of those with the fortitude to fight their way back upstream to retrieve items of interest they've just been swept past by the river's cold swift current. Fossilized bones and teeth of long extinct mammals like mastodons, giant ground sloths and native camels lie mixed with the teeth of giant sharks and dung (coprolites) passed by alligators thousands of years ago.

Notably absent are the remains of dinosaurs of any type. At the time these magnificent creatures were tromping about North America, Florida was completely submerged, accumulating the gastropod shells, coral skeletons and other calcareous marine deposits that would become the peninsula's limestone bedrock. When sea levels subsequently subsided to expose a vast appendix at the continent's southeast corner, dinosaurs had long since been consigned to a bygone world that mankind never knew. Florida does, however, count among its varied fauna a large and fearsome primitive reptile that coexisted with its dinosaur brethren, a species that probably edges out oranges as a symbol of the Sunshine State: the alligator.

In the mid sixties, when I moved to Florida, sighting a wild alligator was an unusual and noteworthy occurrence. These magnificent creatures had been hunted to near extinction and those still living in the wild carried an extreme wariness of humans. In the late fifties, "Orange" Orin Fogle and his wife spent two years paddling around the backwaters of the Everglades filming birds and other wildlife; and during that time they saw many mounds of alligator bones left by poachers but only two live alligators. In perhaps the best alligator habitat in the world—two! For decades, baby alligators were collected from the wild and sold to tourists who unwittingly contributed to the species' decline by resigning untold thousands of their living Florida souvenirs to the abuse of slow starvation in aquaria and bath tubs or release into inhospitably cold waters of the North.

There were only two places in Gainesville where one could always see these toothsome reptiles, but neither could be considered remotely wild. On the University of Florida campus in the shadow of the Century Tower was a small cage housing the latest in a succession of alligators that served as UF's in-the-flesh mascot, Albert. In fact, there is a 50% probability that Albert was a female, as the gender of an alligator is very difficult to determine, and no one ever volunteered to conduct the sort of examination that would settle the matter. The current Albert was about seven feet long, fat (as captive gators tend to be), bored and ceaselessly teased by students hoping to elicit a growl or hiss. To my knowledge, Albert never obliged or even moved, resulting in the minority opinion that he was stuffed.

It wasn't much of a life, even for a comatose reptile and the first local stirrings of what would become the animal rights movement emerged as an appeal to the UF administration to release Albert into the campus' Lake Alice where he could find fulfillment and companionship, or at least respite from harassment. In a tumultuous era when the liberal entreaties of most students ran afoul of the sensitivities of a university administration that tended to be politically paleoarchaic, the appeal for Albert's release nonetheless fell on sympathetic ears. And thus, on a fine summer day, Albert gained his freedom.

It was not long after Albert's release, that one of Hogtown's many colorful eccentrics, Curtis Reid, brought additional attention to Albert and his reptilian colleagues and, in the process, acquired the title of Gatorman. For a brief period before University police intervened, Gatorman demonstrated his penchant for swimming in Lake Alice with the former mascott and numerous other alligators and, on occasion, even riding on their backs! It later turned out that Reid's true calling was standing immobile for hours at a time as a living mannequin, an act he took on the road, even to Europe, supporting himself with money left by passersby. People tended to give him wide berth in either persona lest they be struck by a loose screw.

Lake Alice was the second site that always sported alligators and watching them there was a more exciting venture. There were quite a few gators living in the lake and they could usually be observed basking on the banks or swimming about, at least during the warm months. They were accustomed to human presence and were often fed by students and others oblivious to the obvious risk inherent in enticing large predators to come closer. The prevailing opinion of the student body was that alligators loved marshmallows, and marshmallow toting gator watchers were usually in evidence on the lake's bank. While wieners were doubtless preferred by the reptiles, these sank upon splashing, denying their tossers the opportunity to witness the action. Marshmallows, on the other hand, float and are prominently white, insuring that perpetrators can incite a toothy and electrifying lunge, always the outcome desired by those who feed or harass alligators. And alligators do, in fact, ingest marshmallows with considerable enthusiasm, so it is possible to buy a lot of excitement for the price of a bag of marshmallows.

Except for these two clearly artificial situations, alligators could not reliably be observed in Alachua County, at least by the public at large. The best chance one might have of glimpsing a truly wild alligator would result from surveying the open expanses of The Great Alachua Savannah (now Paynes Prairie State Preserve) at night with a powerful flashlight. Any glowing red spots would be light reflected from the eyes of alligators and even a single sighting was cause for excitement and worthy of recounting.

But that was forty years ago. With the passage of the federal Endangered Species Act, alligators were afforded full protection from hunting and exploitation and their numbers rebounded remarkably in perhaps the greatest success story to emerge from the program. In the early years, alligator eggs were removed from wild nests, incubated and hatched in research facilities and released into the wild. In a few short years, alligators were everywhere, wandering into waterfront neighborhoods and pools, hanging around fishing piers for handouts and generally making nuisances of themselves. Not that it was their fault; a great many swamps and wet places they used to call home have been drained, filled and developed, leaving far less suitable habitat and often forcing them to be our neighbors.

Regrettably, new generations of gators had no aversion to the presence of humans and, in fact, came to associate our kind with mealtime as fishermen and assorted gator watchers tossed them snacks just to hear their forceful jaws slam shut. In a few decades, we had created a realm in which large, potentially dangerous predatory animals were living in close association with human populations.

Usually, the casualties of interspecific misunderstandings were dogs that strayed too close to the shorelines of lakes, canals, ponds or other bodies of water where splashing and frolicking in the shallows became a dinner bell to its large resident alligators. And then, occasionally, it was humans that suffered the attentions of hungry gators; usually they escaped with a few cuts and abrasions or a lost limb; but sometimes they were killed. Predictably, laws were enacted to effect a peaceful coexistence between people and alligators. It became illegal statewide to feed alligators, perhaps the behavior that directly or indirectly generated most attacks on humans. And a program was established to remove "nuisance alligators" from bodies of water where their human neighbors reported behavior they deemed a threat to themselves or their pets.

Alligator trappers, many of whom, ironically, were former poachers, were licensed by the state of Florida to remove nuisance gators. For small animals, three feet or less, removal could simply mean relocation to another site. For larger individuals, though, the involvement of gator trappers was a death sentence. In exchange for providing this public service, trappers are entitled to the revenues generated by the sale of the hide and meat. And so legally procured meat began to appear on menus of restaurants throughout the South as "gator tail."

The alligator's population rebound has been so successful that the state now annually sanctions a regulated hunt to remove 'surplus' animals from the reptile's burgeoning population. This is the bittersweet consequence of a well executed program that rescued a species that was teetering on the brink of extinction and restored its numbers to a level where the concept of a surplus was unthinkable a short time ago. The size and number of animals to be removed during each annual 'harvest' varies from one water body to another depending on a number of factors including proximity to human populations and the number of complaints generated by this often uneasy coexistence. The number of gator harvesting permits issued each year is far exceeded by the number of hunters seeking them, resulting in the state's resort to a lottery procedure to award the privilege of blowing away marked individuals of Florida's trademark animal. Hunts begin at nightfall when reflected eye shines betray the size and location of potential harvestees and when they are most easily approached.

Our first occasion to report a nuisance alligator at Kanapaha Botanical Gardens came more than a decade after work was begun, despite our proximity to 250 acre Lake Kanapaha. While there was no doubt that this lake harbored a healthy alligator population, we never even saw one for a number of years. This is attributable to the fact the Lake Kanapaha is not always a lake bounded by an unambiguous shoreline that is auspicious for gator spotting; much of the time it exists as what, in Florida, is called a prairie. Lake Kanapaha was once fed by a small spring, called Split Rock, at its northern edge and otherwise received water only from what fell as rain or flowed in from Hogtown Creek. Its sole outlet, Haile Sink, is a sinkhole that drains into the deep caverns and passageways of Florida's limestone lattice, the Floridan Aquifer. Split Rock never delivered more than a trickle into the lake and the flow ceased altogether when the construction of nearby Interstate 75 apparently caused the collapse of the subterranean rivulet that carried water to this diminutive discharge point.

During dry periods, Haile Sink drains virtually all of the water flowing in from Hogtown Creek and Lake Kanapaha becomes a wet prairie. With some notable exceptions, this has been the condition of Lake Kanapaha during the past few decades. We never doubted that these dinosaur contemporaries inhabited the vast expanse beyond the dog fennel, dewberry and sagittaria we knew as the prairie edge. But, until the summer of 1990, when we lost the battle for possession of our Victoria pond to a nesting female, we never saw one.

All of this changed a few years later when we collaborated with Gainesville Regional Utilities, Gainesville's public water and electric utility provider, to construct an extensive water garden utilizing reclaimed water from nearby Kanapaha Wastewater Treatment Plant. A simulated "spring-to-sink" system was installed to demonstrate the pathway by which much of Florida's surface water flows into the aquifer; in the process, we became possessed of the means to display a substantial assemblage of aquatic and wetland plants including, of course, our beloved Victoria. Further good news was our entitlement to utilize this water source—free, under high pressure and bearing an understandingly elevated nitrogen content—for irrigation purposes. We disconnected our existing irrigation system from an aging well, reconnected it to our newly acquired source and commenced planning substantial expansions. It was truly a gardener's dream come true.

The first element of our reclaimed water garden is an artificial spring, artificial in the sense that water emanated, not from labyrinthine subterranean passages, but from a 10 inch PVC pipe whose origin was a wastewater treatment plant a quarter of a mile to our north. After filling the spring basin, this clear water spills over a six foot high ledge created by landscape designer Bruce Morgan's seamless amalgamation of native limestone boulders to become one of the highest waterfalls on the Florida peninsula. It is then received by a narrow channel which it ushers downstream over two smaller waterfalls before cascading over a fourth into a large terminal pond.

The system was designed without any sort of confining layer; evaporation, infiltration and plant transpiration would be the only sources of loss. These would be balanced by a continuous flow of new "spring" water so an equilibrium would be maintained. Unfortunately, a subsurface layer of clay reduced infiltration to so minimal a volume that little more than a trickle of replacement flow was required at the "spring," a feature that made the waterfalls look unacceptably feeble. So, two recycling pumps were installed in the lower pond to recycle a large volume of water by pumping it to the first waterfall where it would visually augment the whole system. The pumps were controlled by a timer which turned them on during visiting hours, a feature that resulted in the transformation every 8:30 a.m. of a tranquil trickle of clear water flowing over the head waterfall to a startlingly massive gush of greenish pond water, an occurrence both inexplicable and astounding to early visitors.

Even before the water garden construction was fully complete, a Lake Kanapaha alligator had migrated and settled into our new swamp. Alligators are among the few reptiles to broadcast a vocalization of any type and, unlike frogs, both genders engage in the practice to attract a mate or advertise territorial claims. In what later seemed an ominous portent, our new resident bellowed menacingly during Gainesville Regional Utilities' ceremony dedicating the new garden. But, portentous or not, this "growl," as gator vocalizations are called hereabouts, was but the first of many to reach our ears over the next several years as a succession of the reptiles moved back and forth between our little watery microcosm and the larger lake that was their true home. These ranged in size from 10 inch hatchlings to an eight foot long female, Gertrude, who became our only long term resident.

We were aware of Gertrude's gender only because she built and guarded a nest during three successive summers. In 2000, she built her first nest, a mound of sticks, leaves and other plant material that would release heat as it decomposed and hasten the blessed day when a score of hatchlings would trundle out to make their way in the world. This created a bit of difficulty for us because she sited it in a most inconvenient location about three feet away from the sidewalk that parallels our water garden's stream. Many gardeners are real troopers and are used to dealing with a great multitude of pests, plagues and problems, but we were not sure their tolerance of nature's adversities was sufficiently broad as to abide a growling alligator along the garden path.

Gertrude's nesting behavior reduced the likelihood of that prospect and did little to promote interspecific tolerance. Guarding her cache of eggs entailed raising her body up on her forelimbs, hissing and, if necessary, advancing menacingly toward her adversary with mouth agape and teeth prominent. And to Gertrude, every passerby was an adversary. In order to protect our guests as well as Gertrude's nest, Gabe Duclos (a young "old hand" at Kanapaha) and I erected a chain link fence around Gertrude and her coveted mound, taking great care to have an erect metal post between ourselves and the vigilant hissing reptile throughout the process. The enclosure extended from the water's edge, past her nest to a point across the sidewalk, turned 90 degrees and ran for fifteen feet or so past her nest and parallel to the sidewalk before cornering, recrossing the pavement, repassing her nest yet again and terminating at the water's edge. Gertrude's nest was essentially centered in the enclosure which was fenced on three sides and allowed her free access to water on the fourth.

Bypassing Kanapaha's alligator corral required visitors to detour off the sidewalk onto the turf and around the enclosure, but the experience more than compensated for any inconvenience by providing a glimpse of nature in the raw. Almost universally, the experience proved to be exhilarating and was always on the lips of visitors returning from the water gardens. We considered it a triumph since the concerns of all parties were addressed in a fashion that offered a thrill and hopefully fostered an enlightened tolerance for our fellow creatures.

In 2001, Gertrude nested again, this time hidden from view by a massive live oak's drooping branch and its curtain of vines. People could walk within 10 feet or so of Gertrude, as, in fact, they regularly did, without suspecting there was a gator in residence; for her part, Gertrude ignored the nearby foot traffic since it invariably bypassed her and her procreative venture. Kanapaha's water garden had made alligators a part of the Kanapaha Botanical Gardens experience and it seemed everyone was richer for it. We posted our "Dogs on Leash" signs more prominently to insure against misunderstandings and other signs cautioning of the prospect of seeing one of the beasts and to never approach them. Everyone was satisfied.

Well, almost everyone. We found that a few of our guests had misgivings about fraternizing with alligators under any circumstances that did not include their confinement by concrete and steel. Even in the absence of aggressive behavior—or any behavior whatever—on Gertrude's part, some visitors reported extraordinary tales of peril and narrow escapes. One of the most imaginative was related by a young man who bolted into Summer House one morning, breathless and near collapse, to recount, between gasps, the account of his miraculous deliverance from the jaws of an alligator that he reckoned to be at least ten feet in length. I listened intently to every word, immensely concerned that all of my assumptions had somehow been erroneous and that we had created, not a natural showcase, but a death trap. When he reached the conclusion of his gripping account, however, I realized that I had not actually grasped the part where Gertrude had threatened him. And so I asked him to tell it all again, feigning a fascination with his near escape, all the while professing not to understand how our Gertrude could be party to an unprovoked attack.

When he completed his retelling, again devoid of any hint of misbehavior on Gertrude's part, I realized that nothing had actually happened. He had apparently come upon Gertrude by surprise lying at the water's edge obscured by a tangle of vegetation and was startled to find himself in the near vicinity of an "enormous" (and undoubtedly sleeping) alligator. Pivoting to flee, he slipped in the moist grass and fell, then hurried to regain his footing and raced away, never looking back until he reached Summer House. This was a distance of perhaps a thousand feet, so I understood his breathless entry. He was convinced that he heard Gertrude hiss when he fell, which is possible since that would be her response to being awakened and scared witless, and that she was in hot pursuit, which is nonsense. In his account, luckily, he outpaced her. But for his hysteric tone, I would have offered the old cliche that Gertrude was probably more scared than he was, but I doubted that was possible. He returned the following day, camera in hand, to collect photographic evidence of the beast responsible for his brush with death and possibly material for memoirs of a life lived on the edge.

Our alligator situation changed dramatically with the advent of spring in the following year. On the ides of March, the morning of March 15, 2002, we discovered that we had four more alligators in residence. These animals had simultaneously migrated overnight from drought ravaged "Lake" Kanapaha to the water garden's large pond. We immediately recognized that one of the quartet was an order of magnitude larger than anything we had ever seen, a true dragon. A few days thereafter, we received a disturbing report from two of a score of artists who were participating in a five day "paint out," an event wherein portions of Kanapaha were transferred to canvas, that while painting in the water gardens, they watched our dragon kill and devour one of his lesser brethren. Alligators will, in fact, eat virtually anything when they're hungry, as these drought- and winter-weary stragglers doubtless were. But I assumed this account was an exaggeration of what was probably little more than a spirited skirmish. I was wrong. Within a few days, the three foot long front half of a second alligator, bitten clear through, was floating belly up in the pond.

Our dragon, it seems, was a monster as well. A day or two later, when I could visually confirm the whereabouts of our new giant reptile in seclusion elsewhere, I waded waist deep into our pond to remove the half carcass so as not to startle or horrify visitors. I dragged it about 40 yards and deposited it under the canopy of a huge live oak where it lay obscured by the curtain of catbrier and grape vines draped from the sweep of its outstretched boughs very near Gertrude's previous nest site. My intention was to follow the course of its decomposition and, at the opportune moment, claim the skull for a friend who needed one to give his life meaning. When I first returned after a few days, however, I discerned from its absence that the dragon had followed the scent trail, as gators will, to reclaim his prize. The only other creature hereabouts that could have removed the remains intact is a human and few would have braved the putrid bouquet for any reason.

We figured our monster had to be about 12 feet long in order to dispatch a six foot alligator in that way and it looked every inch of it. Few alligators reach such a length and it's rare to see or hear of anything larger. The growth of alligators, and reptiles generally, is indeterminate i.e. they continue to grow throughout their lives. Unlike mammals and birds, which attain their adult size and cease to grow, alligators increase in length and bulk, though at a diminished rate, with every passing year. This means that very old alligators may be very large as well.

For millennia, adult alligators have had no predators other than man and in times long past, when hunters employed weapons fashioned from wood and stone, there must have been some true giants. In modern times, the longest alligator ever recorded was an individual from Lousiana measuring 19 feet, 2 inches long. Florida's record is 17 feet 5 inches. I remember that some establishment has a billboard south of here on Interstate 75 that advertises a 13 foot alligator and the St. Augustine Alligator Farm's largest animal is supposedly just over 14 feet. But these are exceptionally large alligators that have been corralled over the years and funneled into public exhibitions precisely because their size is exceptional. By any standard, ours was a true giant and its aggressive nature concerned me.

To determine whether or not I had a problem on my hands, I needed more information about alligator behavior. Fortunately, Gainesville has no shortage of knowledgeable authorities on just about anything. I first came to fully appreciate this when I called the University Department of Environmental Horticulture several years ago to seek advice on cycad seed germination and was immediately connected to their resident cycad seed germination specialist who matter of factly laid out my options in some detail.

Of the many people here who know a lot about alligators, one of the foremost researchers is Dr. Kent Vleit, who unhesitatingly pronounced gender for our giant beast. This sort of mayhem is classic behavior for a mature male, or "bull," gator staking out a territorial claim, behavior that, in this case, entailed eliminating competitors and breaking a long winter fast in the bargain. Despite the alarming carnage, however, Vleit said there was no reason to think any of this suggested a likelihood of aggression toward humans. Dr. Vleit was familiar with the layout of Kanapaha's water garden and suggested that we increase our signage alerting visitors to the possibility of seeing alligators and to construct barriers around sites where a dearth of shoreline vegetation facilitated their egress for basking.

We followed Dr. Vleit's recommendations fully by constructing bamboo corrals around patches of lawn likely to serve as basking spots to keep visitors and their dogs from getting too close. We also increased our signage and modified the text of some to stress the fact that steering clear of alligators and keeping dogs on their leashes were related concerns. Alligators do virtually all of their feeding, and are therefore most dangerous, when they are in the water and we could not conceive of a situation in which one of our visitors might find himself in such circumstances. However, many dogs enjoy taking a dip or having a wet frolic in just such places. The greatest likelihood for a calamity would result from a dog owner getting wrapped up in an altercation between his pet and our alligator indulging the species' well known penchant for snacking on poodles. We hoped that taking these measures would enable us to accommodate both visitors and their dogs while offering the thrill of seeing an enormous wild Florida alligator.

Our sensational new resident was not only visually imposing, but somewhat oddly shaped as well. At least he presented a very distinctive profile at the water surface; he was hump-backed. When alligators swim, they typically expose the tip of their nose, the crest of their head, a sliver of their back and the serrated top edge of a tail that sweeps slowly from side to side as it propels the body forward. Our dragon's back protruded as a pronounced bulge rather than a sliver. Inevitably, this distinguishing feature figured prominently in our bid to name our dragon and so "Quasimodo," Notre Dame's disfigured but celebrated bell ringer, came readily to mind. I somehow missed the internal Kanapaha radio chatter that resulted in the abbreviated "Modo," which I misheard as "Mojo," a name that somehow stuck.

It was not his arched back that I found most notable, however, but his steely leer. Early in his tenure at Kanapaha, I thought Mojo might be missing an eye, as it was difficult to make one out on the left side. Or was it the right? Subsequent investigation ascertained the presence of two windows to the world, but they seemed proportionately small and their metallic pupils mere slivers. Recessed below massive ledges of chain mail, they were disturbingly sinister, not at all like Gertrude's benign orbs.

Mojo was a great celebrity all of that spring and summer. His location and behavior figured prominently in our daily radio communications and visitors endlessly and excitedly recounted sightings. He was relentlessly photographed and the subject of several paintings as well. We deemed it a microcosmic glimpse of the excitement that must have pervaded the Barnum and Bailey domain when they boasted the towering Jumbo as crown jewel of their sawdust empire. For our part, we continually monitored Mojo's whereabouts to make sure our efforts to insure responsible behavior by our enthralled onlookers were sufficient to keep them apart.

There was only one Mojo-related incident that occurred during the summer of his residency, though it turned out to be a non-incident akin to Gertrude' non-attack on the young man whose velocity was exceeded only by his imagination. In a pennywise/pound foolish bid to cut Kanapaha's mowing costs, I briefly engaged the services of an upstart and under equipped mowing company and one of its employees reported narrowly escaping the giant alligator as it attacked him and his mower when he rode past. This distressing tale was offered to justify the shredding of a newly planted eucalyptus tree—clearly, he said, an unavoidable consequence if his harrowing escape. Later, he related to one of our workers a less stirring account of the affair in which he came upon Mojo unexpectedly and, in his sudden change of course to avoid the reptile, mowed our tree to smithereens. In his third and final telling on the same day, he was distracted by the basking alligator and ran over the eucalyptus because he wasn't watching where he was going. I shudder to think how often other creatures are held responsible for the negative consequences of asinine human behavior.

Mojo moved about mostly at night and tended to spend his days in the near vicinity of wherever we found him each morning. And so we checked on our resident dragon each morning before throwing open the gates to make sure he was properly sited. In one case, this surveillance resulted in my witnessing an early morning tryst with Gertrude, an awkward boarding that resulted in her near constant submergence until she carried the affair to the pond's shallows where she could catch her breath. We never doubted the paternity of that season's clutch of eggs.

This photo of Mojo was taken in the summer of 2002 by photographer Jim Castner at Kanapaha Botanical Gardens. The attack occurred a few months later less than 100 feet downstream. Photo reproduced with permission of Jim Castner.

On another occasion, we learned the importance of proceeding slowly when awakening our sleeping giant when it was necessary to effect his relocation away from the path of foot traffic. Upon discovering a slumbering Mojo one morning half on the sidewalk, half in a thick stand of horsetail, a bamboo-like reed, I administered a poke to his tail using a shovel handle. He responded with violent thrashing to gain traction in the wet vegetation and reduced our stream side horsetail bed to something reminiscent of aerial photographs of the formerly forested slopes of Mt. St. Helen after its violent eruption.

On another occasion, I surrendered to a growing preoccupation with determining Mojo's length. Riding in a golf car, I approached him slowly and silently, bearing two of the wire and plastic surveyor flags that we used for a multitude of purposes, primarily marking planting sites. From the cart, I thrust one of the flags into the ground as close to the tip of Mojo's snout as I dared to approach and then tiptoed to jab the other into the soil at the tip of his tail. Later, after his departure, I returned with a roll of flagging tape and stretched it between the two points trying as faithfully as possible to reproduce the slight curve of his midline while in repose. Ideally, I would have preferred his lying perfectly straight, but I didn't feel I was in a position to press the issue and elected to introduce an element of subjectivity instead. When I measured the length of the flagging tape laid straight along the baseboard in my office, I arrived at a disappointing 10 feet, 10 inches. It would be months before circumstances allowed an accurate determination of Mojo's length that would confirm my conviction he had been under-measured.

Regardless of length, however, Mojo's bulk was imposing. Hatchling alligators are little more than lizards; and until the length of about four feet, they tend to maintain the same profile. Then, they begin to bulk up as every increase in length is accompanied by a disproportionately great augmentation in bulk. We had no doubt that eleven or so foot Mojo would outweigh eight foot Gertrude not by a proportionate 40% but by perhaps 250%. It was his imposing bulk that gave him majesty and convinced many of our visitors that he was twenty feet long.

Over the course of that summer, we observed our resident dragon devour a number of other creatures. I watched in astonishment as he crunched through the thick bony shell of a large cooter (a native turtle) much as I might munch corn chips and watched him swallow an adult opossum in a single gulp. Despite his immense size, Mojo was quite nimble and capable of swift movements whenever the occasion required, especially when pursuing prey. It did not seem possible, though, that the caloric needs of such a large animal could be satisfied by the turtles, snakes and other denizens of our little water gardens.

I figured hunger would eventually compel him to lumber back to Lake Kanapaha. Even though we had never felt at all threatened by any of the alligators that called Kanapaha home over the years, we were nonetheless concerned about working in the near vicinity of an alligator of Mojo's proportions, both because animate beings as large as an adult human might, by his reckoning, still qualify as foodstuffs and also because even an interaction resulting from misjudgment or misunderstanding could still result in death or serious injury. And so we vowed never to work in any body of water when he was in residence.

This vow was not adequate to meet Jordan's growing concerns about having such a beast at Kanapaha. Even with the precautions we took and the visitors we thrilled, she continued to advocate the dragon's removal, lest unforeseen circumstance result in injury to a dog or human. Given our common experience with wild critters, I was perplexed by her fearful attitude, especially since it seemed to swell, rather than diminish, with the passage of time. Except for a few instances, usually involving poisonous snakes, we tended to see eye to eye on matters of animal husbandry and I thought her apprehensions were out of character. And Mojo had become such a celebrity that having him purposefully removed—killed—was not a prospect I fancied. After all, he would likely return to Lake Kanapaha soon enough.

The access to reclaimed water that allowed us to accommodate alligators and water lilies was a godsend, but it came at a price. Under the glare of the Florida sun, this nutrient rich water warms and begins to green with the growth of algae and other aquatic vegetation. Eventually, this excessive growth must be removed. And so it was our regular practice to venture forth into our ponds and streams to remove this surplus with dip nets. Actually, I used just the net portion detached from the handle. Wading thigh to waist deep, I would sweep the net back and forth until it was brimming with the algae, then empty it on the bank near the water's edge. Thereafter, it could be used as a durable mulch around trees and other plantings.

September 23, 2002 was one of those days when the need

to remove surplus aquatic vegetation from our water garden weighed heavily. Our large lower pond was awash with haggard dark mats of a particularly unbecoming gray-green algae that snagged on the spiny edged leaves of our giant Victoria water platters, still in their summer glory despite summer's passage. A relatively small amount of these unsightly algae could be dispersed into a gloomy shroud across the entire surface. On the other hand, a brisk west wind could consolidate it all into a thick crescent at the pond's east end where easy access enabled an individual working net in hand to remove the entire mess in a few hours. Mojo was lying in repose upstream from the pond above the waterfall that separated the two, so I seized the opportunity to remove the offending stratum while it was consolidated into a single dense mat. I worked for perhaps two hours, sweeping up mats of the algae, carrying them to the shore, where I added them to a growing mound, and waded back for more. I then broke for lunch confident that another hour of work would see the project to completion.

After a quick bite of lunch, I returned to the task, wading into the same part of the pond I'd been working earlier. The sun was intensely hot and it felt good to be moving about in the water. Suddenly, there was an explosive swirl in the water immediately before me as Mojo erupted to the surface. I could see his left eye clearly, sinister and metallic, and it was trained firmly on me. His head was less than a yard in front of me and his body was curved in an imposing arc to my left. Before I had time to react in any way, Mojo jerked forcefully backward and I went with him, flying face forward into the water. It was only then that I realized Mojo was holding my right forearm in his jaws. As he pulled me down, I instinctively thrust my left arm forward to catch myself and landed as a tripod, on my knees and left arm with my torso at the water surface and my right arm extending straight out into the dragon's mouth.

Inexplicably, I felt no pain. I managed to pull myself to my feet where I could now see that my right arm disappeared into Mojo's snout just below the elbow. My only thought was to escape those terrible jaws. Even though I was gravely concerned, I was not terrified, as I was possessed of a naive certainty that I would be able to wrest free. After all, as a seasoned naturalist, I had sustained bites from countless creatures and always managed to free myself. This was doubtless the worst of them, but I thought I could escape with only a nasty bite. My assumption of deliverance was naive indeed.

I delivered a sharp blow to the hard bony bridge of his snout and raised my arm to deliver another. Again Mojo yanked back with irresistible force and I sailed forward, this time submerging completely and taking in a mouthful of the warm muddy water. Again, I managed to pull myself onto my feet. For the first time, I realized that I might not get Mojo to release my arm and that death was a very real possibility if not imminent. In a split second, I imagined being pulled under one last time and losing consciousness as my lungs filled with the water I could still taste, and in the same split second, found comfort in the knowledge that it would be over very quickly. How dramatically my life had changed in a few seconds! I turned my head toward the Butterfly Garden, where a colleague, Barbara, and a community service worker were gardening, and managed to get out two words, "Barbara! Alligator," the only sound I made during the struggle with Mojo. Barbara turned toward me and an expression of sheer horror came over her face.

At that moment, the water before me began to churn violently and Mojo disappeared in the froth and spray. Still in shock, my first thought was that Mojo was shaking his head back and forth; then I realized that I wasn't moving with him and remembered with horror that alligators didn't tear food that way. They spin their bodies to detach a morsel. *Mojo was twisting off my arm!* I was powerless to do anything that could affect the course of events; he held all of the cards. The churning stopped and I looked down to see that only a smooth white cord of tissue, likely a tendon, protruded below my elbow and into Mojo's mouth where the rest of my detached arm had disappeared. With one more lunge, he could grab my upper arm and withdraw into the pond consigning me to a certain death. And so I pulled upward forcefully with what remained of my arm and snapped the white cord to finally separate us, pivoted and slogged the twenty feet to shore hoping he wasn't in pursuit but not taking the time to look back. As I slogged, I wrapped the end of my remaining upper arm with the tail of my tee shirt to make a crude tourniquet. There was remarkably little blood.

"He got my arm," I told Barbara and her companion who met me on a golf car as I emerged from the water and made my way up the bank.

Her co-worker removed his shirt to improve on my tourniquet and Barbara hustled me to a waiting golf car as she radioed to our volunteer at the front desk to call an ambulance. I was greatly concerned that our volunteer, an elderly lady who tended to get things mixed up, would inadvertently dispatch an emergency vehicle to nearby Kanapaha Park, a county facility with which we were now regularly confused. I was fully alert and slid over into the driver's seat to operate the golf car while Barbara jumped off to open a service gate en route back to the building. I then sat in the little vehicle in our parking lot awaiting the arrival of an ambulance whose barely audible siren was soon shrieking up our driveway—not, thankfully, to Kanapaha Park.

As I waited, Gabe broached the prospect of employing his ever ready 9 mm handgun to retrieve my arm for possible reattachment, the first time I had considered the prospect. I wasn't especially hopeful because this was not the clean slice of a shark's razor sharp cutlery. My arm had been most indelicately twisted off in a manner that had doubtless caused tremendous tissue damage. Nonetheless, even the remotest possibility of reattachment offered both hope and a welcome distraction. I cautioned Gabe to be careful and to first report the incident to the Florida Fish and Wildlife Conservation Commission so they could dispatch a gator trapper with the more powerful weaponry that would be required to slay a monster like Mojo.

As I sat awaiting the ambulance, I began to feel a burning pain in my missing right forearm and, especially, my hand; I was experiencing phantom limb pain, the phenomenon I had dispassionately described countless times to biology students to demonstrate that the brain is the seat of all sensation. I could feel every finger of the hand that had served me for 59 years and which now lay in the belly of an alligator 200 yards away. And they all hurt! I told a concerned colleague about the pain and requested a couple of ibuprofen tablets from the bottle in my desk, but predictably,he couldn't find it.

No matter; the ambulance arrived and I was on my way. I had asked Barbara to inform Jordan and Alexis of what had transpired and Jordan had immediately made several calls to facilitate my entry into the red brick monolith that Summer, as an infant, used to call "the big building," Shands Hospital. I was asked my weight so many times by so many people that I began to wish someone would put the information on a slip of paper and tie it around my neck, or at least write it down. I wasn't sure what I weighed now but reported that prior to losing my arm, my weight was 165 pounds. Because my spouse is a health care practitioner, I was acutely aware of the sorts of cabaret that routinely pass for medical care and considered it to be in my best interest to maintain consciousness as long as possible. And so, with a resolve derived from self interest, I resisted the temptation to succumb to an insistent drowsiness.

As I was carried from the ambulance, I asked one of Jordan's colleagues to be sure to tell her that she was right about the alligator. In response to her expression of perplexity, I added simply that Jordan would know what I meant. It was my first serving of the crow that I would surely be eating for a long time to come and I figured I might as well get started while I at least enjoyed her sympathy. In the operating room, I finally surrendered consciousness and cast off my worries for another time, fully aware that it would not be long in coming.

17

Living Single-handed

My tussle with Mojo introduced me to much besides clip on ties and half price manicures. And one of the most exhilarating was morphine. When I regained consciousness and enough lucidity to discern the source of my cheerful demeanor and deliverance from pain, I vowed to stop squandering my life and become a devout heroin addict. Like heroin, morphine is a delightful opium derivative; it smooths the jagged edges of pain, makes an anguished spirit blithe and transmutes mundane notions into profound insights. At least they seemed profound as long I pushed the button that kept it dripping into my bloodstream. Since the medical establishment restricts the availability of this exhilarant, I would necessarily have to resort to substituting Afghani heroin, the form readily available to civilians.

Morphine also greatly affected my perception of time, even to the point of questioning its existence. It enabled me to fit a two hour nap into a two minute time slot and transformed my three days at Shands Hospital into a delightfully lighthearted and pain free month. Regrettably, it was not especially memorable, for despite my apparent lucidity, positive deportment and talkative nature, I remembered little of the experience.

I was aware, of course, that my right arm ended at the elbow where there was now a bulky wad of gauze and tape. I knew too that my days as a right hander had come to a sudden end. But for the moment, my spirits were soaring; after all, I was born with a spare; who needed two arms anyway? With or without my right forearm, I was still here, at least mostly; for my family foremost, but also for my friends, for Kanapaha and for myself. I had much healing to do, physical and emotional, and much to learn but at least I was alive to heal and learn.

Mojo had not fared as well. An alligator trapper and an assortment of law enforcement officials converged upon Kanapaha shortly after the attack. Mojo had the advantage of bulk, strength and innate armament, but he was on his own. I, on the other hand, hold membership in a social species; an organized throng that doesn't take kindly to having its members eaten or roughed up by predators, whether bears, mountain lions or alligators. What we lack in physical strength or prowess, we make up for with organization, weapons and the wherewithal to use them, factors that clearly put the advantage in our court. And so, our side dispatched a team of trained thugs to settle the score.

Usually, such affairs are postponed until the cover of darkness allows the employment of a spotlight to pinpoint a gator's location. A beam of light projected across the water surface will transform the dull gaze of a gator's eye into a glowing red ember that could be mistaken for nothing else. In this instance however, waiting for darkness was not an option since a potentially reattachable arm was lodged in Mojo's gut and its timely retrieval was the utmost concern. And so with grim determination and (reportedly) little grace, a bid to retrieve a severed forearm was undertaken on my behalf. Mojo was already tremendously agitated when the confrontation commenced. Gabe had gallantly leapt into the swamp armed with a 9 mm handgun which he emptied in short order, but with little effect, as he felt about on the pond bottom for an arm that he hoped Mojo might have dropped. But all evidence suggested that my arm now resided in the belly of the dragon.

Gabe recounted the official recovery effort which was apparently executed with all the finesse of FEMA's mobilization in the wake of Hurricane Katrina. Gabe, who understood the necessity of prompt action, was prepared to act but he lacked the weaponry to kill Mojo and was unable to secure the timely cooperation of those bearing sufficient armament to do so. At the peak of the spectacle, nearly 30 individuals were on site, with the Alachua County Sheriff's Office most conspicuously represented but also with officials from the Florida Fish and Wildlife Conservation Commission and Emergency Medical Services. Still, they took no action despite Gabe's increasingly desperate pleas, deciding instead to await the arrival of a gator trapper.

Collective officialdom expressed concern that shooting at Mojo might cause him to flee the site before the trapper could arrive; Gabe assured them it was a closed system, a pond, from which unmonitored escape was impossible. Then perhaps, they offered, a wounded Mojo might disappear under the thick shoreline vegetation where he would be difficult to relocate; Gabe countered that the pond's edge was shallow, only a foot deep—he knew because he had just been wading in it—not deep enough to conceal an animal of such bulk. He was incredulous to hear the further pretext for inaction that they perhaps lacked the authority to kill an alligator; so he took it upon himself to contact the Lake City office of the Florida Fish and Wildlife Conservation Commission to secure that permission from a similarly incredulous official who asked, "What are you waiting for? Shoot the damn thing!"

Still, they waited for the trapper. The entire time those assembled stood at the pond's edge, only a single shot was fired, by someone unknown and with no effect on the situation. For much of the time the assembled throng awaited the trapper's arrival, a clearly agitated Mojo glared at them from the same spot where the attack occurred, perhaps fifteen feet from the shoreline. Gabe, whose swelling pain and frustration were palpable, was stung by a dawning awareness that he was being perceived as a nuisance by most members of the alleged rescue team. I can only assume that the fear of reptiles, even when unfounded, is primal; and, in this case, fear clearly was justified. Despite their armament, it appeared those assembled were simply too fearful to act.

Finally, the trapper arrived, teenage son in tow, and initiated his services with time consuming preliminaries that were altogether inappropriate for an agitated bull gator like Mojo, casting out a hook on 100 pound test line and spattering the shoreline waters with a branch to emulate the splashing of a small animal. Mojo, who had been shot and pursued by Gabe shortly after the attack, was clearly not naive enough to respond to such chicanery; he was distressed and fully aware that the situation was adversarial. Finally, trapper and son slid a small flat-bottom boat into the water. Within a few minutes, they were able to pierce the animal's tough hide with their harpoon and the real battle began. At one point, the trapper was unceremoniously yanked from the small boat and sent splashing by the beast at the other end of his rope. Preferring not to share the same confined space with a wounded and furious dragon, he rose out of the water with legs spinning like a basilisk and did not stop until he reached the bank.

Most of the crowd of rescuers, meanwhile, stood along the shoreline providing commentary that was at least redundant, if not helpful. In the end, whether it be credited to vaudevillian fluke or to skill, Mojo was dispatched. Only when the time came to haul out and shoot the thrashing monster did the rescue team realize that nobody had thought to bring a rope, at least one equal to the task. It was Gabe who produced a stout and conveniently knotted rope that he used at Kanapaha for tree work to reel the monster in. He was then able to join four other men in pulling the reptile ashore where it was killed with a single 12 gauge shot to the head. Finally, the erstwhile fearsome dragon lay dead. He measured 11 feet 4 inches in length and weighed 393 pounds.

Within a few hours of the attack, Mojo was dead and my arm had been surgically removed from his stomach for potential reattachment, which was deemed impractical. Photo reproduced by permission of the Gainesville Sun.

Mojo was relieved of his recent repast which was rushed to Shands Hospital where the rest of me lay unconscious but intact. Reattachment was deemed impractical, in large part because my arm was severely mangled. Whether it might have been otherwise if first responders had killed Mojo right away as Gabe had urged, medical personnel could not say with certainty. But it was now clear that if I was henceforth to possess anything beyond my elbow, it would be a synthetic prosthesis.

The reaction to my experience was nothing short of phenomenal. Even in a morphine induced stupor, I was aware that news of my plight had attained prominence nationwide, not just as tabloid fodder but fare for the mainstream media as well. Exactly why this should be the case I wasn't sure and, in fact, don't understand to this day. Perhaps it was the novelty of a large predator attacking a human in this day and age. A cave bear attack on a Neanderthal probably wouldn't merit a sketch on a cave wall but my ordeal apparently was newsworthy enough to stop the presses in twenty-first century America.

And not just America; Armand Kuris, a colleague doing field work in Tasmania read about it in the local press and an account was carried by the New China News Agency (which, like many accounts, reported the victim to be Dan Goodman, a cousin with whom I was regularly confused throughout my school days). I received a request for a live radio interview from a chatty Colombian deejay and a member of Germany's wild and crazy media requested a photograph of the severed arm. When I checked out of Shands Hospital, I was given a list of media phone calls to return that included associates of Connie Chung, John Walsh, The Today Show, etc. It was now official. In a nation whose media celebrate idiocy, I was the uncontested bonehead of the week.

It was a week or so before I felt like returning any of these calls and it was immediately obvious that any residual notoriety that still clung to me was rapidly dissipating. On the day that Connie Chung's minions were scheduled to descend on Gainesville to record an interview, I was informed by a perky communications director that the networks had just received word that President Bush had hurriedly scheduled yet another major address to the nation about Iraq that would compete for the same broadcast time slot.

"So I guess you'll have to reschedule Bush then, huh?" I goaded.

"Well, actually...uh..."

I interrupted her in mid-stammer to assure her that I was only joking, that I understood the relative merits of the two matters and was sadly aware of the public's fleeting attention span. It was obvious that, by the time they got around to rescheduling my interview, the bonehead mantle would have passed to someone who'd been pecked to death by pigeons or electrocuted by fireflies. My Warholian fifteen minutes of celebrity had abruptly ended, yet another casualty of Bush's Iraq policy.

The only positive consequence of my newfound notoriety was that it warranted my being relocated to a private hospital room. Entry to this inner sanctum could be gained only by those uttering an appropriately botanical password ("roses"); all others would be wrestled to the floor and cast out. Chief among the keepers of this semantic key were Jordan and Alexis who were ruthlessly frugal in meting it out to keep visitation minimal, a measure I appreciated, especially when I realized that, under the jumble of assorted bedding, I was nude.

As is my convention when battling aquatic weeds in hotbug infested waters, I was minimally attired—swim trunks, tee shirt and wading shoes—when Mojo tried to eat me and my shoes disappeared in the scuffle. With my express permission, the ambulance crew scissored away the rest to attend to my wounds. I was greatly impressed that they exercised the courtesy to ask since, at that point, I looked like I had just executed a cannonball into a septic tank. Jordan hounds me regularly to discard beloved and vintage articles of clothing—especially tee shirts, a key element of Kanapaha's uniform—simply because, while completely serviceable, they are worn, stained and tattered and have resulted, on several occasions, in my being mistaken for a homeless person. I was wearing such venerated but low thread-count garments when Mojo attacked and I felt a tinge of vindication that health care professionals felt it necessary to seek my consent at a time of such gravity before peeling them away piecemeal and then asking whether I wished to have them saved for future service. For the record, I declined that offer, reasoning that having the hospital launder them would cost at least $1,000.

Now, a day or so later, I lay naked under some rumpled bedding and minus half an arm babbling spiritedly. In time, I would cast aside the bedding and prattle, but the arm-and-a-half condition would remain, a permanent reminder that I should have heeded Jordan's entreaties to remove the monster. I had naively hoped that our dragon and the gardens of Kanapaha could peacefully coexist. In the end, it was a vain hope.

Many times, I have reviewed the events of that fateful day. I saw clearly that, whatever experiential differences may separate this life from the hereafter, the gulf between the two is exceedingly slim. Why was I able to step back from a chasm that daily claims so many, often unaccountably, forever separating them from their lives and loved ones? It was an intensely surreal—not a religious—experience; I never felt the presence of any consciousness or will beyond what Mojo and I brought to the struggle. But how improbable it was that Mojo would have migrated to my exact work site during the same brief period I was away for lunch. And more remarkable, how I survived an attack by a monster more than twice my weight in a watery morass where he held every advantage. I have no doubt whatever that my forceful resistance averted a seemingly inevitable death by frustrating Mojo's two attempts to drag me away and persuading him to settle instead for a portion of his intended meal. Nor is there any doubt that adrenaline facilitated my unlikely transformation into a serious opponent to a beast that was clearly used to having his way.

I also found it nothing short of remarkable how differently the same event can be perceived by two individuals. Several well wishers told me that God must have been looking out for me since I survived the alligator attack when it could as easily be argued that God was asleep or acted with malicious intent since, after all, I started the day with two arms and ended with one. The basic evidence advanced for intervention into human affairs by a benevolently watchful God often seems to boil down to the fact that things could be worse, when it could be noted with equal veracity that things could also be better. For my part, I much prefer having two arms, but, given the circumstances, was glad to have the opportunity to walk away with one. I still have taped to my office door—beside two alligator-themed *Far Side* cartoons and an amputee-themed *Doonesbury* cartoon—a get well card from Chris Clark that asks, "Do you ever think your guardian angel stepped out for a smoke?" I didn't see evidence of divine involvement one way or the other. Even among friends, there was great disparity in how the event was perceived. A minority opinion held tha I am somehow a hero—though in a way that is apparently unfathomable since nobody can put their finger on it—but I feel that Tom Patton hit closer to the mark when he told me "I always thought you were smarter than that."

In any case, I lost more than an appendage; I forfeited my credibility as an apologist for creatures like Mojo and instead inadvertently became a poster boy for the "blow 'em away" crowd to whom the only good alligator is a dead alligator. But the fact is that my error was not in underestimating the potential threat of this fearsome predator because I never doubted Mojo's capacity to unleash such havoc. My error, rather, was an assumption that he was elsewhere; and I paid dearly for that mistaken assumption. Still, to many that distinction is of no consequence; what matters is that an alligator bit off my arm and circumstances be damned. Mojo, on the other hand, didn't make a mistake; he was busy being an alligator and a damn good one. If fault must be assigned, it would fall squarely on the shoulders of the combatant bearing a specimen of nature's most advanced brain, crammed with a PhD's worth of knowledge about animals and not a primitive reptile instinctively following the directives of a walnut sized brain.

Within a couple of weeks, I met with a prosthetist and got an assessment of my prospects for regaining some function via an artificial forearm and hand. It was a major misfortune that Mojo's attack and subsequent surgery had taken everything below my elbow. If anything had remained there, it could be fitted with an extension and capped with a hand that could be positioned with precision wherever its grasping function was needed. As it was, my prosthesis would be fitted over my upper arm and would be equipped with an artificial hinge that would serve as the elbow. Since the electrode-operated motor controlled only the hand (which opened and closed) and wrist (which rotated in either direction), it would be necessary for me to swing my forearm to bring my plastic hand into my best approximation of the target site and lock it there with a shoulder-buckling motion.

For weeks, I practiced before a computer monitor connected to electrodes taped to the biceps and triceps muscles of my upper arm while a custom fitted prosthesis was being manufactured to replace parts missing below. A mild steady contraction of my biceps would cause the hand image on the screen to close; a strong spike of the same muscle would cause the wrist to rotate in one direction. A mild contraction of the triceps would cause the hand to open and a spike would rotate the wrist in the opposite direction. By using combinations of these contractions, I could, in theory, grasp and manipulate objects to regain some function.

Regrettably, it didn't work out that way. The prosthetic arm was fashioned from hard plastic. A sleeve, with imbedded electrodes positioned to contact my biceps and triceps, was fitted over my remaining upper arm and held in place by a shoulder strap. Additional straps traversed my chest and back to unite and encircle my left shoulder, a truss that was as uncomfortable as it sounds. At the age of 59, I got an inkling of what it must be like to wear a bra.

Because the electrodes have to be pressed tightly against the muscles of the upper arm to detect muscular contraction, the hard plastic sleeve had to fit very tightly over my upper arm; so tightly, in fact, that I found it necessary to apply a lubricant to the stump before it could be forced into place. It was not until I had purchased gallons of a popular brand of lubricating jelly that I was apprised of its more conventional use in facilitating sexual union. At least this insight better explained the whispers that followed my passage through Publix check-out lanes. I can only assume those who scanned my purchases concluded that the loss of one member was compensated by increased activity of another.

In any case, the tight, hot and slippery fit and uncomfortable trussing harness did not endear the prosthesis to me. But I would probably have persisted in using it if it wasn't "in the shop" for repairs more than a chain saw. Or, if its operation had truly, as promised, become second nature rather than a matter of constant thoughtful exertion. In most cases, the problem was that my mechanical hand was unresponsive to muscular contractions in my upper arm—or maybe that I couldn't generate the right contractions—but once, while I was gesturing during a conversation with The Gainesville Sun's gardening editor, my hand fell off. That was one of the defining moments in the mental ruminations that led to my decision to live with an arm and a half. In any case, within a few months, I found I was wearing the apparatus less and less; and finally, not at all. These days, my principal interaction with the device is to gasp and bolt backwards at the sight of an outstretched arm arising from the floor of my bedroom closet. With no prospect of regaining the function or appearance of a two hander, I have bid farewell to my twin retirement goals: I'm too asymmetrical to succeed as an Olympic downhill skier and too recognizable to be a gentleman bank robber.

And so, I have adapted to life with one arm. Or, more accurately, an arm and a half. That extra half arm, my right upper arm, makes an enormous difference in my capabilities. I can carry a newspaper, or the equivalent, tucked under it and employ it as a point of opposition for my left hand, allowing me to pick up and carry a basket of laundry and to manipulate objects more effectively. It can be used to depress the arm of a pair of nail clippers that have been carefully positioned on the edge of a sink or counter to trim my nails, operate a manual can opener, push and pull, flip light switches, close doors, hold objects in place and much more. I can hang an umbrella or plastic produce bag on my abbreviated limb, held straight out, without becoming fatigued, since there is no weight beyond the elbow. And, of course, I quickly learned which other opposable body parts could be used in concert with my left hand to compensate for the loss of my right. Holding a wine bottle between my knees, I can operate a corkscrew; and clenched teeth can be employed to oppose clasped fingers in opening a zip-lock bag.

While these innovations enable me to perform a myriad of everyday operations, they come at the expense of speed, convenience, and precision. And, of course, it is difficult or impossible to use many "two-handed" tools, like wheel barrows and hedge trimmers, or to perform "two-handed" functions, like tying a tie, removing childproof lids, attaching a paper clip, operating a pepper grinder or separating stuck pages in a book or newspaper. It is my most fervent hope that the increasingly en vogue rock salt grinders don't displace the ever dependable salt shaker since salt, unlike pepper corns, is of identical constitution and freshness throughout regardless of particle size; sodium chloride is sodium chloride. And, I can report that an occupational difficulty for single-handed gardeners is the removal of splinters or cactus spines from that single hand.

I was surprised that I found "stump" to be a disagreeable term of reference to what remained of my right arm. It is the word conventionally used for such circumstances and is altogether appropriate since is the anatomic equivalent of that portion of basal trunk that is left behind when the branching body of a tree is removed. So I have come to accept it, disagreeable or not, as a term that is both a universal allusion to a truncated limb and more succinct than saying "my remaining right upper arm." While I elected not to suffer the discomfort of a prosthesis, I have nonetheless chosen to wear a fashionable black sock over my stump. It serves not only to spare onlookers the sight of the unsightly but also to provide a welcome cushion at a point where surgery has left little natural buffer between skin and bone.

I learn on a daily basis how many routine functions are enabled or at least facilitated by paired hands. Because we write from left to right, it is necessary to hold the left edge of a sheet as we do; otherwise the friction of the pen tip would pull the paper along to the right. And while it is not as convenient for lefties, even they can be two places at once to hold the paper in place. Without a second hand, however, I would regularly, and helplessly, watch an unrestrained invoice slide across a counter without the generous assistance of sales clerks who seem to instinctively perceive the problem and kindly intervene to hold the paper in place as I crudely affix my signature. Even my domestic obligations have changed, and now extend beyond leaving the toilet seat down; I must now remember to move the mouse back to the right side of the keyboard after using the computer.

Some of the most painful dispossessions are the simplest of pleasures. Offering the tribute of applause is not as satisfying—or audible—when accomplished by slapping the palm of my hand against a thigh instead of another palm; and the spontaneity of roughhousing with children is forfeited to the necessity of anticipating and constantly recalculating the logistics of supporting a squealing and writhing tyke one-handed without inflicting injury. A lifetime exemption from hedge trimming hardly seems compensatory.

The transfer of ingrained single-hand functions from the dominant to the subordinate hand can be difficult in operations requiring precision, like writing, using chopsticks or shifting gears in a vehicle with manual transmission (which I prefer). Prior to my accident, I could type 45 words per minute; now, if I carefully eye my fingers working the keyboard, I can manage perhaps twenty. And I came to realize that for me, like many of my generation, having pen in hand between my brain and a legal pad was imperative to the creative writing process itself. It has taken time to neurally retool so that I can now employ a keyboard instead of a ball point to cogitate and refine rather than simply record.

For months after Mojo's attempted homicide, I confronted these problems on a daily basis, finding new approaches to performing the mundane tasks I had woven like threads into the fabric of my life. But day by day, thread by thread, I was able to mend the frays and tatters to create a new fabric, slightly coarser, but whole and seamless. It takes more trips to carry groceries in from our car, but I have learned to leave the front door ajar an imperceptible sliver so my second entry can be achieved with a nudge rather than the cumbersome routine of setting down cargo to free my lone hand for service as door knob turner. That is unless Katie, our ever helpful Jack Rascal, leaps against the door's interior side, closing it with a characteristic thud, to announce her availability to escort me on my return trip to the car. Still, I have not yet learned how to routinely apply the amount of force that will cause a door to regularly swing shut with a mere click and not sometimes a bang.

Probably the most recurring frustration attributable to this sudden lopsidedness is a systemic clumsiness in the performance of many routine tasks. I was unaware how often we rely on a second hand to compensate for imprecise operations of the first; to catch a listing glass, a slipping package or make a grab to arrest a slip and fall. Only when you lack this compensatory appendage do you realize how essential it is to our conventional poise.

As a matter of principle, I try to be as independent as possible and to rely on others only when necessary or when an inordinately great effort is required on my part to achieve what a factory equipped mortal could effect easily. There are some itches that are difficult to scratch, or impossible if they're on my phantom forearm, but I can usually find a way to scratch them, even if I sometimes feel like a horse rubbing the sides of its stall. Although I haven't consciously amended my shaving schedule, I have learned that any sandpapery stubble can be employed as a scratching surface as well. And, mercifully, it turns out that the human forearm-wrist articulation, mine, at least, provides enough flexibility to facilitate the application of deodorant to my left underarm as well as my right. It is nothing short of astonishing what you can do with one hand when you have to. And I have come to recognize that my handicap is no greater than the one voluntarily borne by so many of our fashionable youths who keep one hand permanently occupied holding up their pants. If the planet's largest land animal can get by with a single manipulable appendage, a nose, at that, I should be able to manage.

Still, coping with the loss of something so central to the human condition is not without its difficulties. Mine is a very unusual condition outside a VA hospital and my unconventional appearance draws attention. Most adults have been so thoroughly bludgeoned by the strictures of political correctness that they respond minimally, if at all, to my appearance, as though I had left home in such a rush that I had departed with uncombed hair and only one arm. And I am genuinely grateful for this convention since no amount of discussion can alter my situation and it spares me the necessity of retelling once more the tale of my struggle with the beast.

Young children, on the other hand, respond with an expression of such innocent astonishment that I can seldom suppress a smile. How wonderfully genuine they are, so devoid of pretense, with eyes bulging and mouths agape! And, if curiosity is allowed to run its course before attending adults intervene to squelch it, their response generally includes a stubby finger pointing my way and a broadcast of the obvious: "That man only has one arm!" Some seem perfectly willing to accept a one sentence explanation that an alligator bit it off as a complete account since, after all, theirs is a world of orcs, ogres and other villainous brutes. To other wide eyed tykes, however, this would be little more than the opening volley in a long lopsided dialogue highlighted by their offers of seasoned advice. "You should have hit him real hard and maked him turn loose!"

But, above and beyond dealing with the responses of others, I have had to cope with a nearly incomprehensible loss that continually impacts my life. Having been a two-hander for almost 59 years, I face the daunting prospect of living out the remainder of my life with the constant limitations that attend my situation. I am regularly reminded that many are worse off than me, an obvious truth that is reinforced daily by experience and media accounts. Still, the greater suffering of others doesn't really diminish my own.

Losing an arm is a great rarity in the chronicles of human misfortune and certainly something I never thought would befall me. I still haven't fully incorporated it into my self image as I still am occasionally startled by a glimpse of my form in a mirror or upon awakening from a dream in which I am still a two-hander. Sometimes, as I return to my own reality after enjoying an engrossing book or movie, I remember my loss anew. And, of course, I endure the constant sensation of having a nearly paralyzed right hand where none exists, the particularly cruel "phantom limb" sensation experienced by approximately 80% of amputees. I can still feel every finger of my phantom hand but under great pressure—not bilateral, as if caught in a vice, but omnidirectional, as though held in an iron glove one size too small—overlain by the sort of numbness that comes when a limb "falls asleep," though multiplied in intensity by a factor of ten.

With considerable conscious effort, I can move my phantom arm and fingers, but generally don't bother on the assumption that generating activity on these neural pathways might be misconstrued by my brain as reinforcement of its misguided conviction that these parts are still there. My hope is that the brain center responsible for sensation in these missing elements will eventually cease to function for want of neural traffic. Because, as always, things could be worse, I am told with some frequency that "God was watching out for you." In fact, however, any claim of divine involvement would be tantamount to a clear admission that God's sense of humor is truly perverse. After all, any omnipotent being that would remove an arm and then make it hurt may possess a refined capacity for dispensing irony but certainly has a limited faculty for compassion.

The phantom sensations themselves, nonetheless, are truly fascinating phenomena. My phantom forearm's "resting position" is perpendicular to my upper arm as though I were a waiter carrying a towel on his forearm or someone inserting a key into a door lock. When this becomes annoying or uncomfortable, I can straighten my phantom arm in one of two ways. If I use a concerted conscious will, I can unbend my elbow but it will revert to the resting position as soon as my focus wanes, as if it were possessed by a steel spring. The simpler way is to hold my arm against something impenetrable, like a wall or door jamb. The arm will then be automatically straightened against the surface by a brain that cannot abide the impossibility of a forearm, even a nonexistent one, extending into a solid surface. How I wish constant visual confirmation of my forearm's absence could similarly convince my brain that it is no longer there! Early on, this false perception of a perpendicularly oriented forearm occasionally resulted in involuntary droppage of items I carried sandwiched between my upper arm and torso. This resulted from a subconscious loosening of my grip to forfeit support of those items to a forearm that wasn't there.

Several months following the attack, Jordan and I attended an opening at The Ice House Gallery in the rustic little community of McIntosh south of Gainesville. Entering a small room in the gallery, I was astounded to find myself again in the presence of the giant alligator that had figured so prominently in my life. There hung a painting of Mojo—clearly distinguishable from a generic alligator by his humpback—that had been painted by artist Sean Sexton, one of several artists who participated in a paint out the preceding March when Mojo first appeared at Kanapaha Botanical Gardens. Image reproduced with permission from Sean Sexton.

The phenomenon apparently derives from the brain's reluctance to modify a strongly held perception of the body's form. Small children who lose a limb usually do not experience these sensations, suggesting this perception is not innate but develops early in life. And its coverage is comprehensive; women who have had mastectomies report experiencing hardening of non existent nipples during sexual arousal.

Because phantom limb pain results from a conversation the brain is having with itself, it is very difficult to find a way to interrupt the dialogue to interject an element of pain relief. Acupuncture, so effective in treating other types of pain, proved to be ineffective because the body part that hurts is unavailable for puncturing. Many types of limb pain can be effectively treated with the injection of chemicals that block nerve transmission somewhere between the pain site and the brain; but these are ineffective in the treatment of phantom limb pain because there is no anatomical pathway to interrupt. The pain is produced and felt within the brain.

Because the phenomenon is confined to the brain, I hoped that hypnotherapy might be effective in interjecting subconscious suggestions that might influence the brain's perception. But, unfortunately, this also proved to be a blind alley. At the present time, a relatively low dosage of a synthetic opiate taken sublingually twice daily is the only thing that has affected my brain's perception of pain in my non existent right forearm and hand, a pale reflection of the opium habit my morphine-crazed brain had in mind.

All of this said, I still consider myself extremely fortunate because the standard of measure by which I gauge my misfortune does not involve one-versus two-handedness so much as alive versus dead. This was one of the profound lessons I learned from losing Summer. I am still here, most of me anyway, to love and be loved and to continue life's journey. Even minus a hand, I can still experience life's joys and to look out for those I love. These are possessions of the living. And I still am alive!

18

Interacting with Alligators; The Rules of Engagement have Changed

After a hot and exhausting day of landscape maintenance work, 41 year old Kevin Murray decided to cool off with a dip in the canal that bordered a yard he had been tending. It was his habit to refresh himself with a swim whenever he worked at this Port Charlotte residence and the mid July day had been a scorcher. There was a full hour of daylight left when he abandoned his equipment and plunged into the water. Like the water in Florida's hundreds of miles of drainage canals, this was by no means cool in the sweltering summer months, but was at least below body temperature and afforded an invigorating respite from the sun's unrelenting glare.

Suddenly, backyard neighbor Rich Clinkhammer heard Murray's frantic screams for help and looked just in time to see him disappear below the water's surface in the jaws of an enormous alligator. Murray fought his way to the surface only to be dragged under again, this time for good. In a matter of seconds, he had become the most recent casualty of the increasingly assertive demeanor of Florida's ancient dragons. Thus in 2005 did he become the seventeenth fatality from alligator attack since record-keeping began in 1948, the fifth in three years.

And then, in the span of a single week in May of 2006, three women lost their lives to alligator attacks to become victims 18, 19 and 20. I learned about the first two attacks from a local television newsman who called me to arrange an interview with a survivor of an alligator attack. I had to decline the request because I was unable to find the time that Friday to drive to the television station for a live in-studio evening news interview and assumed that was the end of it. But on Monday, I was an even hotter media commodity because yet another attack over the weekend had claimed the life of the third victim.

For the next few weeks, an alligator frenzy swept the state and I was among a handful of people who were relentlessly interviewed and quoted ad nauseam to quench a seemingly boundless public fascination with the notion that latter day humans can still be killed by reptilian predators in the United States. The one positive outcome of this second fleeting spate of notoriety was that it restored my tarnished credibility as a proponent of coexistence with alligators. After all, if one who lost an arm, and very nearly a life, to an alligator attack can profess an appreciation for the toothsome dragons, then it becomes more difficult to make the case for a more vengeful approach to dealing with them

. In the years before the American alligator was afforded federal protection, the species had been hunted to near extinction. Alligators justifiably feared the presence of human beings because of their association with pain, noise and death. Thus it was when I moved to Gainesville to pursue graduate work; spotting a gator in the wild was a rare event and a cause for excitement. Even those animals bold enough to remain in the near vicinity were extremely wary and quick to submerge. These qualities were the product of long enduring hunting and exploitation, traits that enabled them to survive man's relentless quest for trophies, hides and meat.

They were not always so wary and retiring, however. British naturalist William Bartram described a more fearsome and formidable creature just a few centuries ago, when their principal adversaries used weapons fashioned from wood and stone, a circumstance that leveled the field of combat considerably. While exploring the St. Johns River, he stopped one night and set up a camp on the highest ground he could find, "a matter of no trivial consideration...having good reason to dread the subtle attacks of the alligators who were crouding about my harbour."

Bartram had gathered a good quantity of firewood with which to prepare his evening meal, but found his provisions meager. He decided, therefore, to set out again in his canoe to fish in a promising lagoon he had passed about a hundred yards up the river. For fear of losing his gun to the river, he took along only a club for protection from the numerous alligators and set out. His subsequent journal entries detail his experience among these fearsome dragons:

"...penetrating the first line of those which surrounded my harbour, they gave way; but being pursued by several very large ones, I kept strictly on the watch, and paddled with all my might towards the entrance of the lagoon, hoping to be sheltered there from the multitude of my assailants; but ere I had half-way reached the place, I was attacked on all sides, several endeavoring to overset my canoe. My situation now became precarious to the last degree: two very large ones attacked me closely, at the same instant, rushing up with their heads and part of their bodies above the water, roaring terribly and belching floods of water over me. They struck their jaws together so close to my ears, as almost to stun me, and I expected every moment to be dragged out of the boat and instantly devoured, but I applied my weapons so effectually about me, though at random, that I was so successful as to beat them off a little; when, finding that they designed to renew the battle, I made for the shore, as the only means left me for my preservation, for, by keeping close to it, I should have my enemies on one side of me only, whereas before I was surrounded by them, and there was a probability, if pushed to the last extremity, of saving myself, by jumping out of the canoe on shore, as it is easy to outwalk them on land, although as comparatively as swift as lightening in the water."

After catching fish sufficient for his needs, Bartram returned to his camp hugging the shoreline in his canoe, where he was again "pursued near my landing (though not closely attacked) particularly by an old daring one, about twelve feet in length, who kept close after me, and when I stopped on shore and turned about, in order to draw up my canoe, he rushed up near my feet and lay there for some time, looking me in the face, his head and shoulders out of the water."

Bartram returned to his encampment to retrieve his gun, returned and dispatched the threatening alligator and began to scale his fish "when, raising my head, I saw before me, through the clear water, the head and shoulders of a very large alligator, moving slowly towards me; I instantly stepped back, when, with a sweep of his tail, he brushed off several of my fish. It was certainly most providential that I looked up at that instant, as the monster would probably, in less than a minute, have seized and dragged me into the river."

While it is unequivocally true that Bartram was not above resorting to an occasional embellishment to render a tale more compelling, it is also beyond question that his accounts, on the whole, are credible and represent the closest approximation to accurate and objective descriptions of the behavior of alligators before their exposure to humans bearing firearms. Clearly, the reticence that characterized these dragons during the next two centuries was learned behavior that was reinforced generation after generation by the negative consequences associated with the sight of man and the sound of gunfire. Now, it seems, after a half century of serious protection, they have, as a species, forgotten those lessons. The rules of engagement have changed; or rather, they have reverted back to their original state where it is humans who need to beware.

This is one of the lessons I learned from Mojo. The alligator I knew in the sixties no longer exists. I thought I had been attacked by mistake and was convinced that a few sharp blows on the snout would secure my release and send him packing. I had learned too late, and at great cost, that I didn't know as much as I thought. If I had, from the start, treated Mojo as a Bartram era alligator, he would have been returned to Lake Kanapaha and I would be intact. I have long and loudly decried the pervasive and unreasonable fear and revulsion most people have for spiders, reptiles, especially snakes, and other creatures that offend them. And while I remain confident that most of these fears result from uninformed prejudice, I must readily concede that my altercation with Mojo initially reduced my credibility as a champion of interspecific tolerance.

Today, alligator attacks regularly occur in Florida though they rarely result in death. Only a few months after my skirmish with Mojo, an elderly woman, a resident in the Fiddlers Green condominium complex in Englewood, Florida, lost an arm to a six foot, three inch alligator despite being assisted by neighbors who responded promptly to her cries for help. One grabbed her ankles and pulled to prevent her being dragged into the water while another gouged the beast's eyes with hastily gathered palmetto fronds. In the end, though, the alligator detached her arm and escaped, only to be killed shortly thereafter by a licensed alligator trapper.

Such altercations, especially involving dogs, but increasingly, humans as well, occur with disturbing frequency not only because the true nature of our resident dragon has resurfaced, but also due to the greatly increased contact caused by human expansion into, and frequently destruction of, alligator habitat. Residences built on the shoreline of lakes, rivers and canals insure the regular mingling of the two species. And, despite state laws outlawing the practice, many people still toss fish scraps and other edibles to the seemingly docile and appreciative reptiles. When a gator's behavior becomes too threatening or unsettling however, it is designated a "problem animal" and a call to the Florida Fish and Wildlife Conservation Commission will result in its removal and, unless it is less than 3 feet in length, execution. Release into another wild system isn't deemed practical even if they were not guilty of "problem" behavior because there just isn't suitable habitat remaining that isn't already teeming with them.

I learned all of this shortly after my release from Shands Hospital. While I lay recuperating, the same alligator trapper who dispatched Mojo had returned to Kanapaha to finish the liquidation of its other resident gators for good measure. Under cover of darkness, the single remaining animal of the quartet that appeared simultaneously the preceding March, a ten foot male, was located in the water gardens' "spring" and executed. I understood the necessity of killing Mojo, both because his stomach contained my arm and because he obviously represented a threat to other humans. But this alligator, ten feet or not, had always been a retiring animal, silently submerging and disappearing whenever approached; its demise was unfortunate and altogether unnecessary. I was very concerned for Gertrude's well being and was pleased to learn that she had laid low and escaped detection on that fateful evening. But it was unlikely that officialdom would allow any sizeable gator to remain at a public site where such mayhem had ensued. It was only a matter of time before they would return for her.

I consulted with officers from the Florida Fish and Wildlife Conservation Commission to request that Gertrude be relocated to another suitable habitat rather than killed. Unfortunately, it seems that the "trappers" of nuisance alligators are paid, not with public dollars, but with proceeds from the sale of the meat and hides. These dollars are the funding source for the entire program and nobody was going to capture, transport and release a live thrashing eight foot alligator without some recompense. Fair enough. So I asked whether I would be allowed to pay the trapper the equivalent of Gertrude's market value to secure her relocation, only to confront yet another hurdle. Florida's rivers and lakes are already stocked to the gills with alligators and the FFWCC officials were not about to dump in another just because my heart had a soft spot for her. No, the relocation scheme could only proceed if the trapper agreed to live relocation and if I was able to find a suitable relocation site. And they made it clear that this was a favor. It was only because of the unique and extraordinary circumstances of this case that I was offered this opportunity to spare Gertrude the fate typically dispensed to 'nuisance' animals.

I found it hard to believe that finding someone to take a fine strapping alligator could be too difficult; I would've given my right arm to have one when I was a boy. So, I called The St. Augustine Alligator Farm, one of Florida's oldest wildlife attractions, to learn whether they would accept a healthy eight foot female alligator as a gift. They too, it seems, were up to their eyebrows in crocodilians and didn't need another. On my next call, however, I succeeded. Gatorland, another Florida alligator farm located near Orlando, agreed to give Gertrude a home and three squares a day for life. The trapper was apparently touched by our concern for our toothsome lady and reduced his regular fee of $800-$100 per foot-by $200. And so, a few weeks later, we bade farewell to Gertrude, trussed up securely in the trapper's truck for transport to a safe refuge to live out her days in the company of other dragons in a sunny Florida swamp.

It is this uneasy peace that exists today. In perhaps the greatest success of the Endangered Species Act, federal protection has restored the alligator, in both numbers and temperament. In essence, our tax dollars have bought Floridians a scaled down version of Jurassic Park, the opportunity to live amongst dragons that regularly try to eat them. And to be truthful, I think it is wonderful. It implies that we value other species, even large predators, as unique natural treasures that enrich the quality of our life on Earth. My heart beat still quickens at the sight of a large alligator, not just because one tried to eat me, but because it is truly an awesome and magnificent life form, a primitive armored beast whose form harkens to a bygone era when real dragons walked the earth.

19

The Search for Noah's Ark...and Truth

During my days in graduate school, I fielded a classic question while at Newnans Lake east of Gainesville collecting brown water snakes as part of my doctoral research. As I loaded a bit of equipment onto my boat, a fisherman struck up a conversation in an apparent attempt to discern the object of my setting out on a renowned fishing lake when so conspicuously devoid of fishing gear. I was sparing with the details of my mission because I've learned that most civilians are utterly perplexed by the concept of research that is not intended to promote the physical betterment of humanity, at least indirectly. It was clear to me that, to this individual, the minimal expectation of any research that involved snake handling would be a comprehensive cure for cancer. When informed of the particulars of my mission, he had one query: "Moccasins or vipers?" Apparently, his world is world is inhabited by only two types of snakes: bad and worse. More recently, a young man who appeared at Kanapaha's doorstep to commence his community service laid bare his principal apprehension about doing penance at an outdoor venue: "Killed any snakes lately?" The unspoken assumption, of course, was that any snake we encountered in the course of our work would be immediately slaughtered. Both of these young men clearly knew nothing about snakes and yet they feared and detested them. Why?

Certainly, our differences in perceptions arise, in part, from innate predispositions that seem inexplicable except, perhaps, to Buddhists who would see these inborn tendencies as nothing more than traits carried over from a succession of lifetimes lived, knowledge gained and karma accrued. But regardless of origin, these predilections clearly flavor our perception of the world into which we've been born. Experience, too, is an important determinant of our discernment. Jordan—otherwise fearless of the natural world—concedes a fear of certain types of beetles dating back to a specific terrifying childhood incident in which she panicked at her inability to readily detach a beetle that had grasped her finger with its pinchers and refused to turn loose.

Fortunately, there is a third component to our perception—beyond innate predisposition and and experience—that is under our conscious control: knowledge. The simple laws of probability guarantee that the interaction of these three components would make each individual's perception unique, even in a world of 6 billion people. Even so, the common body of knowledge shared by practitioners of a specific discipline will tend to impart to them a common view of those aspects of life; so astronomers, for instance, might share a common grasp of our circumstances in the cosmos better than the rest of humanity. We have a capability that is unique among all of the earth's animals to learn about the true nature of our world by assimilating into our world view the cumulative wisdom gained from our ancestors. This means we have the capacity to transcend ignorance and conquer unfounded fears, even the irrational fear of snakes, precisely because it is irrational.

Naturalists know much about the nature of the organic world and can bring a uniquely objective perspective to understanding the world and our place in it. Looking at our world through the lens of biological accuracy can separate fact from fiction in realms as varied as science, art and even religion. Necessarily, these perspectives set naturalists apart from most of humanity and impart a unique flavor to their taste of life. The principal advantage of possessing a working knowledge of the natural world is that it provides endless venues for pleasure while demystifying an otherwise immeasurably complex world, making it at once less threatening and more orderly without diminishing its grandeur and the sense of wonder it engenders.

While naturalists may know a world that is less frightening and more interesting, they can also be killjoys, as in their insistence on accuracy in the media's portrayal of the natural world. Movie directors often play a bit loose with the facts, justifiably confident that their audience won't know the difference. But scientists of all stripes tend to offer criticisms of their work based on the degree to which the presentation is at variance with reality. Truly, it can be a curious experience to hear a movie reviewed by a group of naturalists who pick apart an otherwise superb film because it fails the test of biological accuracy.

What are South American boas doing in a Tarzan movie supposedly set in Africa? And while Australian kookaburras are cackling in the treetops as well? Similarly, herpetologists across the globe rolled their eyes and groaned audibly in unison when confronted with the image of a huge assemblage of snakes in the underground crypt portrayed in Raiders of the Lost Ark. Firstly, snakes would have no way to enter a buried crypt and absolutely no reason to do so since they are not social animals and only congregate when utilizing a resource in short supply, such as suitable hibernation den sites or concentrated food sources. Certainly deserts are notoriously sterile and barren ecosystems that could never yield enough food in one place to support such numbers and the reptiles certainly weren't hibernating. Also, any herpetologist would immediately recognize the reptiles as something other than asps; many, in fact, appeared not even to be snakes, but rather legless lizards, a taxonomically significant distinction. "Who cares?" you say. Naturalists! That's who! On the desks of directors everywhere there are piles of smoldering letters of outrage to prove it.

On the other hand, it is attention to details of biological correctness, not a compelling storyline, that endears other movies to those of us who study the natural world. As one who had to content my boyhood self with movies in which dinosaurs were portrayed by embellished rubber lizards, I was mesmerized by the frighteningly real images of these long extinct monsters stomping about in Jurassic Park. Here, in fact, it was clearly the resurrected dinosaurs (and particularly their ingestion of a lawyer) that compensated for a weak story line and moronic characters to make viewing it a memorable and exhilarating experience. Thereafter, I didn't have to content myself with Fantasia's fanciful animation to witness the raw ferocity of a Tyrannosaurus.

None of the foregoing should be interpreted to suggest that naturalists are necessarily exceptionably bright individuals but rather that they possess of a specific body of knowledge, a distinction that is readily demonstrable. Where the path of reason diverges from that of faith based belief, in fact, intelligent judgment often takes a back seat. Apollo 15 astronaut Jim Irwin, for instance, was very obviously an intelligent, and courageous, explorer, one of an elite corps of humans to take temporary leave of our planet to pay a call on our lunar neighbor. While hurling through the cold dark void, Irwin had a transcendent experience which he interpreted as perceiving the presence of God. So far, so good; this happens to people all the time and the trigger is often far more mundane like the scent of a flower, or the splendor of a sunset or even psychotropic pharmaceuticals. But when Irwin returned to Earth, he inexplicably embarked on a quest that illustrates clearly the need to keep faith based belief—however empowering or exhilarating—apart from what we know to be true through direct experience or the experience of others. He undertook a quest to locate remains of Noah's Ark, somehow equating a personal validation of God's presence with confirmation of the literal truth of Biblical scripture, two completely different things. Intelligence constrained by faith limited by knowledge.

Naturalists everywhere—in fact, anyone possessing a knowledge of the natural world—grimaced in concert at the word of this Quixotic quest, recognizing it from the outset as a doomed mission. Because of shared elements in their perception of reality, they knew the tale of Noah and the flood is fraught with as many impossibilities and errors of logic and biology as the story of Dorothy and the Wizard of Oz. Still, Irwin's undertaking demonstrates a condition that is common, if not the norm, in a species gifted with reason; uncritical adherence to the edicts of religious dogma, set out eons ago by unknown individuals whose words are taken as universal truths solely on the unquestioned basis of their alleged infallibility. If we had some bacon, we could have bacon and eggs...if we had some eggs.

To maintain control and cohesion, all armies rely upon the mindless submission of their recruits; as do many religions. Thus are religions distinguished by geography as easily as philosophy; for despite our endowment with a capacity for analysis and reason, the vast majority of us put infinitely more critical thought into the selection of a laxative than a God to unquestioningly worship. How disappointed with us God must be!

To demonstrate the problems that can result from the assumption of truth that has not been validated by experiential knowledge, let's briefly examine the Biblical account of Noah from the perspective of biological accuracy. A story that is divinely scripted should not bear the earmarks of inaccuracy common to Hollywood productions. Unfortunately, whatever its purpose, the account of Noah reflects the limited knowledge base one might reasonably expect of a mortal living in that era, clearly not the omniscience of a Creator who knew the true nature and extent of His handiwork. The author didn't know, for instance, that the world was so large; that there were other continents with thousands of species of mammals and birds—kangaroos, polar bears, llamas, penguins, platypuses, armadillos, roadrunners—that could not be gathered into his ark but which would nonetheless drown in the worldwide flood depicted in Genesis. And while a boat of the Ark's dimensions might be sufficient to hold all of the animals known to the writer, it could not possibly begin to accommodate two of all of the millions of species we now know inhabit the world.

The Ark described in Genesis would have 2.32 acres of deck space and approximately 4 acres of lumber surface overall. Assuming this was planking of 2 inch thickness, that would amount to 348,480 board feet, or enough lumber to build nearly 22 two-thousand square foot homes. That is a big boat and a lot to expect of anybody, especially since the undertaking predated by millennia the advent of home improvement stores and would necessarily involve felling the trees and milling the lumber by hand before the construction could begin; and, of course, Noah was 600 years old at the time. This structure was supposed to house two individuals of all animal species and enough food to sustain them for a very long time—ultimately a year and ten days between embarkation and disembarkation onto a sterile planet devoid of food.

While 2.32 acres of deck might be a shuffle board player's dream come true, it would not accommodate two each of all of the earth's animals. Not by a very long shot! In times past, it would have been difficult to make a definitive judgment about the possibility of such a boat accommodating such a cargo because our knowledge of the earth's fauna was too limited. Today, however, we have compiled a fair approximation of the planet's animate constitution; and in the age where capitalism is ascendant, the profit motive has been applied to yield figures for the greatest possible crowding of animals, a circumstance comparable to what would have prevailed on Noah's noisy and smelly vessel.

These latter day commercial animal concentration camps are

called beef feed lots, and the sort most closely approximating Ark-style lodging are confinement buildings with slatted floors. These buildings hold cattle for fattening before they are slaughtered and, since space is money, animals are held in extremely— many would argue inhumanely— crowded conditions. Cattle are allotted 25 square feet each in crowded pens serviced by drive through feed alleys. In such an arrangement, 2.32 acres of deck space could accommodate perhaps 3,600 animals, or 1,800 pairs. But since the quantity of food necessary to sustain an animal (as Noah was directed by God to stockpile aboard the Ark) for over a year would certainly consume at least as much space as the animal itself, the figure would certainly not exceed 900 pairs.

But there are many more than 900 species of animal to be saved. There are more than 4,600 mammals alone. Certainly, many, like mice and rats, would take up less space than cattle, while others, like elephants and giraffes, would require more. The average species would have to be about 20% of the size of a feed lot cow if they were to be squeezed into Noah's Ark. But then there are another 9,700 species of birds, 7,870 species of reptiles, and 4,780 species of amphibians to be housed. Where? The simple fact is, a few acres of deck could not possibly accommodate such an assemblage even if they remained immobile, stacked like cordwood, nose to butt, requiring no space for exercise or movement during more than a year of confinement aggravated by exposure to nearly 1000 hours of continuous torrential rainfall.

Another puzzling aspect of the incredible account of the great flood is the complete absence of any mention of the thousands of remarkable new animals that would have appeared at Noah's doorstep. It seems that anyone unfamiliar with a kangaroo, for instance, would make some note of a strange mammal that hopped out of the surf on oversized hind limbs with a transverse abdominal pouch aslosh with sea water after dogpaddling thousands of miles of open ocean with undersized forearms. And surely a pair of platypuses would have drawn notice, though they might have been brought onboard as living reminders of the consequence of depraved fraternization between unrelated species. Still, there was no mention of the tapirs or snakes with rattles at the end of their tails, or armadillos or anacondas, Komodo dragons or dodos. If this weren't an inerrant account of the Almighty, it would almost seem as though the omissions reflected a total ignorance of the vast bulk of the earth's fauna.

I have never seen a depiction of the Ark taking on anything except vertebrates, especially birds and mammals—yet they represent a small fraction of the earth's animals. More than 90% of all animal species are invertebrates—more than 850,000 types of insects alone, not to mention spiders, scorpions, centipedes, earthworms, snails and slugs, etc.—and God instructed Noah that these would have to be saved as well. So prominent are insects in the scheme of creation, in fact, that renowned British geneticist J.B.S. Haldane (1892-1964), when asked what he had learned about the nature of the Creator in his long study of nature, answered that "He must have an inordinate fondness for beetles." Hundreds of thousands of insects and other invertebrates have life cycles that are irreconcilable with such a flood. The adults live only a few weeks and conditions on the Ark would not be accommodating to their eggs and larvae. Take, as an example, the 17 year "locust," more accurately called the cicada, whose loud, undulating and sonorous droning is a herald of summer's end in much of North America. The vocalizing adults survive only a few weeks after emergence from their long slumber. They mate and lay eggs on certain species of trees and shrubs and then die. The eggs hatch within a few more weeks and the hatchlings drop to the ground where they will spend nearly 17 years sucking nourishment from plant roots. On the Ark, assuming the adult female cicada was broad minded enough to deposit her eggs in the vessel's gopher wood timbers, the hatchlings would drop into the drink or be trampled underfoot by rhinos and penguins while searching for soil and roots. Bummer!

And then the vessel would have to hold a 375+ day supply of food to satisfy the often uniquely specific needs of each of these millions of creatures—eucalyptus leaves for koalas, bamboo leaves and shoots for pandas, specific types of vegetation for countless ungulates, nectar for butterflies and hummingbirds, carrion for vultures, and many more than just two individuals of species that would have to serve as food for others: countless flies for spiders, toads for hog-nose snakes, ants for anteaters, and tons of specialty meats on the hoof for lions, polar bears, wolves and other carnivores. All of these provisions, of course, must somehow be kept fresh and dry.

Animal parasites—tapeworms and ticks—are also the beloved handiwork of the Creator and would have to be supplied with living hosts. Certainly mosquitoes, vampire bats and other blood eaters would feast well at the most comprehensive smorgasbord of life bloods ever assembled and neither Noah nor the members of his family would be allowed to swat any of the 6,168 mosquitoes, two each of all 3,084 known species, no matter how much discomfort or how many diseases they brought to the divine winnowing venture. Though there is no mention of the diet of Noah and his family during this trying period of boredom, motion sickness, slippery decks and athlete's foot, I can only hope it included plenty of fiber.

In turn, the consumption of so much food would cover the Ark's deck with enough manure and other wastes to make a garbage scow seem like a veritable Carnival Cruise. Unlike a feed lot building, the Ark had no slatted floors or provision for manure storage or management. Flies and dung beetles would be fat and happy, but most other life forms would find it difficult to abide, and all of their waking hours, Noah's family would have spent slogging along the decks feeding their menagerie or sweeping raw sewage into the ocean. Surely, they must have wondered on occasion how scraping platypus droppings from their sandals was part of a divine plan.

Enormous quantities of soil would have to be brought on board to satisfy the needs of the thousands of burrowing animals like earthworms, moles, spadefoot toads, mole rats, gophers and so forth and huge freshwater aquaria would be essential to maintaining all of the thousands of freshwater animal species that would die in the brackish broth created by 40 days of mixing fresh and salt water. I suppose you would have to accept as a given that saltwater creatures could withstand diluted ocean water since Noah couldn't begin to address that problem by keeping saltwater tanks; as all aquarium hobbiests know, they're just too difficult to maintain.

And what about plants? They, too, not just animals, would have to be spared drowning in a worldwide flood. And, since these immobile life forms could not report for duty like a pair of rhinoceroses, Noah would have to collect specimens of them all, from California redwoods and saguaro cacti to baobab trees and Australian tree ferns, as well as lesser types like mosses, liverworts, Venus' flytraps and bastard toad-flax—untold thousands of species—all potted in appropriate potting medium, of course. As a practitioner of the green arts, I would love to know how he kept all of these bathed in the sunlight they require, while simultaneously keeping their potted roots from drowning over a period of forty gloomy and rainy days.

Reducing the domain of all species to a population of two individuals that would thereafter reconstitute it? Such a loss of genetic diversity would so dramatically reduce the fitness of any resulting offspring that many, if not most, species would simply die out. The same applies to the predicament of Adam and Eve, which also fails the test of biological authenticity, but that's another story. And in either account, the small number of humans representing the species' sole procreative stock would necessarily be responsible for serving as carriers of diseases like deadly and highly communicable small pox for which there exist no non-human hosts. It seems surprising that there was no mention of the deadly epidemics that would have attended such a demographic bottleneck. And like someone who had painted himself into a corner, God would necessarily have to accept a good measure of incest as the price of employing such a short-sighted approach in restoring morality; the children of Noah's three sons would have to intermarry.

All of the foregoing assumes that 40 days of rain would flood the entire world. Perhaps the world known to the writer of Genesis, but not the world with which we've become acquainted by several millennia of investigation and discovery. There is, in fact, a finite volume of water on the planet, existing in solid, liquid or gaseous form. The only mechanism that would make so much water available for worldwide flooding would be thawing the earth's frozen water so it could be evaporated and then condensed into rainfall as has, in fact, happened in the past. If the total amount of water tied up in polar ice were thus transformed, all in 40 days, the world's oceans still would rise no more than about 275 feet, leaving plenty of dry land across the globe. Most of peninsular Florida would once again be consumed by the sea but anyone who dragged himself out of the surf onto the foothills of Georgia would find most of the remaining North American continent high and dry. And, after the great annihilation, exactly where sea level water would drain off to isn't exactly clear.

The fact is, any deity familiar with the workings of the natural world would find it far simpler to eradicate the relatively small population of humans unrelated to Noah than virtually all other life forms on the planet. A science fiction writer today might envision the introduction of a deadly and highly contagious plague to which Noah and his family were granted divine immunity. This would eliminate the need to involve billions of innocent life forms uninvolved in God's otherwise short sighted and heavy handed quest for retribution. Why throw out the baby with the bath water?

Why commit so much ink to demonstrating the impossibility of the Ark scenario? Two reasons, really. The first is to demonstrate what startlingly different conceptions of reality now coexist within the human family as a result of different belief systems arising from assumptions that have no verifiable basis. Many people of faith know with certainty that Noah built a boat that saved all animal species from a worldwide flood while many others know with equal certainty (and supported by the weight of logic and factual information) that it could never possibly have happened. But the first group has no interest in exploring the truths that led the second to its conclusion, so both certainties continue to coexist side by side century after century...two worlds sharing the same time and space. Where some see a patch of bread mold, others see a likeness of the face of Jesus; and others, the face of Rasputin.

The second reason to analyze the tale of Noah from a naturalist's perspective is to demonstrate something of far greater significance. Genuine miracles—parting the Red Sea, moving mountains, walking on water, etc.—are, by definition, events whose mode of action lies beyond the scope of established laws of nature so naturalists have no credentials to critique them. They are beyond the realm of human understanding and, therefore, not candidates for such a reasoned analysis; we either believe them or we don't. But the account of Noah does not invoke the miraculous, but rather describes a collaborative effort between God and man, with God providing the directions and Noah carrying them out. It employs natural phenomena— rainfall of specific duration, assembling one individual of each gender for all species (though there are some hermaphroditic species apparently unknown to the author of the account), felling trees of a specific type to construct a boat of specific dimensions, etc. These thing open the account to critical examination by those knowledgeable about such things, naturalists and biologists. It is this distinction that provides the opportunity for a reasoned assessment of the events described and, ultimately, a repudiation of the whole affair as a ridiculous fantasy reflecting the limitations of a human—not a divine—perspective. The entire account collapses under the weight of an illogical story line.

The significance of this repudiation is that the author of the account was Moses and that Genesis was only the first of four books to his credit. By the time he got around to penning Leviticus, he was a joyless wet blanket whose primary pleasure seems to have come from making sure everyone else was joyless as well, condemning everything that rubbed him the wrong way; wringing every drop of pleasure out of life; even denouncing the consumption of shellfish, among other things, as "an abomination." His ludicrous account of Noah, though, provides shrimp lovers, and, in fact, all of mankind's abomination perpetrators, a reprieve by providing demonstrable proof that Moses was putting words into God's mouth and not, as so many believe, the other way around. Among his numerous other edicts is one granting humanity the birthright of "dominion" over other organisms and the blindly faithful have cited it for centuries to justify unspeakable abuses to non human species and a shameful disregard for the natural world.

Moses was clearly winging it; and understanding this goes a long way toward explaining one of Christianity's great enigmas—how to reconcile the Bible's two startlingly contradictory depictions of a single God. If you ascribe literal truth to all Biblical texts, then the only possible reconciliation of Old and New Testament Dieties is medical; He is afflicted with bipolar disorder. As befits an infinite and immortal being, the alternating states likely require millennia for full manifestation so divine utterances during transitional states might well have been lost on mere mortals trying to get it all down. Treatment would presumably entail gulping a lithium capsule the size of the Milky Way Galaxy every two millennia or so.

Moses' ludicrous account of Noah, however, demonstrates that at least a good portion of the Old Testament cannot be taken literally and strongly suggests that the violent, intolerant, insecure and remarkably short-fused entity he speaks for is himself. I find this revelation comforting because I prefer not to revere a God who is so childish and mean spirited. This view is not universal, however; He is the vengeful God so often identified with conservative politics and is regularly invoked to maintain order in their ranks. The liberals' God of choice resides in the pages of the New Testament. He champions the welfare of the poor and disenfranchised and advocates love, tolerance, forgiveness and embryonic stem cell research. It has been more than 16 centuries since the First Council of Nicaea chose from the hundreds of gospels then circulating the ones that would become part of the Bible and be officially sanctioned as reflecting the mind of God. We have learned a lot about the world since then. Now that we better understand the nature of human existence, maybe it's time to take another look.

What moral the parable of Noah is intended to convey about the nature of God I will leave to those versed in theology and mythology. The fact is, many other ancient religious traditions have a myth about a worldwide flood—some with an ark of even greater proportions—and some of these, like the Sumerians' version, predate the Hebrew texts by thousands of years. But those who have acquired a familiarity with the earth and the circumstances of our existence would never think it more than a parable. A knowledge of the natural world can serve as a road map that naturalists can use in their search for truth wherever it might lead unencumbered by prejudice or predisposition or the untested truths of others to better know the true nature of God. The truth is out there and we've been endowed with a mind that can sort it out.

Of course, employing one's God-given mind to sort it out often leaves naturalists at odds with the substantial chunk of humanity that chooses the path of blind faith in preference to cerebral heavy lifting. Charles Darwin, like Galileo before him, incurred the slings and arrows of much of the religious establishment when he presented an overwhelming body of evidence demonstrating that natural selection is the force that has generated the enormous variety of organisms that inhabit the earth today. His theory of evolution has won universal support from those with a knowledge of paleontology, anthropology, geology, genetics and related disciplines and, in fact, has been further bolstered by a century and a half of additional research and discovery. Now that we can see the evolutionary process in action with the development of drug resistant super germs, it is time to dispense with the convention that categorizes evolution as a theory and accept it as an established fact.

The only basis for refuting the reality of evolution remains the same today as it was when Darwin's master work appeared in 1859; it is at variance with religious dogma, specifically, the Genesis account of creation that was penned by the undermedicated author of the tale of Noah and his Ark. Darwin himself was a devoted Christian who initially intended to enter the clergy after his monumental journey. But he was also a champion of reason, and it was his intellect and inquisitiveness that led him to the conclusion that there were simply too many pieces that did not fit the picture ordained by blind faith. Since the uncompromising orthodoxy of the day necessitated a choice, he chose reason over blind faith, embracing a concept that led to his widespread denunciation and a measure of domestic discord as well, since even his wife found the notion to be heretical. As a naturalist, Darwin never denied that natural selection might be the mechanism through which God achieved his handiwork; for that sort of personal conjecture is beyond the realm of science, and should lie beyond the reach of politics as well.

Belief in the process of evolution and belief in God are two separate matters and by no means mutually exclusive. But it makes more sense, at least to me, to determine His/Her nature by studying His/Her handiwork, even if that is often akin to examining a crime scene. Then we can at least engage in theological discussions with confidence that the evidence for our God, whether cosmological, biological or physical, is demonstrable universal truth and not simply a matter of faith or, as in many cases, actually at variance with established truth.

None of the foregoing is to deny the value of faith. The search for spiritual truth is life's most sacred quest and faith is sometimes all we have to bridge the deep chasms on that path. But when faith, however fervent, is blind or ignorant, it is not truly a bridge but a diversion, and a costly one since it can take lifetimes to retrace our steps and renew the journey. We have been endowed with senses that can assess the world and the capacity for logical analysis; surely it seems an affront to whatever God we acknowledge to abuse these faculties by ignoring what they tell us and believing something completely different because of groundless faith. It is important to invest faith wisely and judiciously in values and beliefs that are consistent with reason and the truths imparted by our senses as we experience life. A belief in angels does the soul no harm and may be a source of comfort; but to envision them as being of classic Victorian form is an affront to reason, since these are unnatural beings—unflightworthy six-limbed mammals with feathers. Why have faith in a belief system that has no reality in the world we know? If, in the end, we can offer no greater basis for faith than heritage or tradition, then there exists no basis at all.

My experience with phantom limb pain has led me to the believe that God finds humor in irony. So He must regard the sermons and exhortations of many spiritual leaders as stand-up comedy and many of the solemn quests undertaken in His name as truly peculiar vaudevillian farces. Whereas I can always rely on the brilliant '60s classic "Dr. Strangelove" to satisfy a craving for dark comedy, God, with His more refined and exacting standards, likely reminisces about the best of the Crusades, a lengthy campaign of terror and death undertaken solely for his gratification. And while my favorite line from "Dr. Strangelove" is President Peter Sellers breaking up a scuffle between one of his generals and the Russian ambassador with the line, "You can't fight in here! This is the War Room!," I would suspect that the acme of God's list of Crusades era dialogue would be a side-splitting quote attributed to Arnaud-Armaury. He was the Abbot of Citeaux and spiritual advisor to the Albigensian Crusade sanctioned by the virtuous Pope Innocent III to purge southern France of its Cathari heretics. When the Catholic faithful of the town of Beziers refused to rat out their 200 Cathari neighbors, Arnaud-Armaury told the crusaders "kill them all. God will know his own." It is regrettable that nearly everyone in town, over 20,000 people, had to be burned or clubbed to death, but then there is often a stiff price to be paid in maintaining the high moral standards God would expect.

Certainly our life experiences vary so widely that there must be countless different conceptions of God's nature. One of the most original known to me I must credit to one of the students in a biology class I taught at InterAmerican University in Hato Rey, Puerto Rico following a spirited discussion that compared the theories of evolution and divine creation.*

This young man seemed particularly captivated by the exchange and was asked whether, in his view, there was sufficient evidence to suggest that the world and all its cargo were created by a superior intelligence. His somewhat rambling response could be summarily paraphrased:

> When one sees the beautiful and wonderful array of different organisms and the earth's great natural beauty, he can unquestionably see the hand of a superior being at work. However, while it is readily apparent that He is a superior being, there is nothing to suggest He is of superior intelligence.

As I pondered his answer, I realized it had considerable merit. God as an omnipotent dullard; truly, that would explain a lot.

*When divine creation failed to be taken seriously as a complete explanation for the creation of species, its supporters put lipstick on the pig and began calling it scientific creationism, even though no science was introduced. These days, the concept of divine creation is masquerading in the guise of intelligent design, though still starkly identifiable by the stunning dearth of evidence.

20

Where Have All The Green Snakes Gone?

Where have all the green snakes gone? Back in the early Pleistocene, when I was young, these dainty and lovely little creatures, known to me as "grass snakes," were doubtless the serpents I encountered most frequently. They were certainly more common than black rat snakes and infinitely more abundant than the elusive and prized "salt and pepper" king snake. Their relative abundance seems a logical consequence of the fact that their principal food, insects, can be found everywhere and their slender green vine-like bodies are easily concealed in virtually any vegetation, whether creek side willow or boxwood hedge. And green snakes hold a very special place in my memory, not just because they were my first snake pets, but because of the nearly magical incident that made it so.

Near my boyhood home is a small sand bottom stream that proved irresistibly alluring to a boy of eight. My most direct access to this little Eden was afforded by a set of railroad tracks a few blocks north of my home. These twin rails led to a trestle overpass that provided an outstanding vantage point from which to survey the little stream and its environs. On most summer days, the brief trek was enlivened by a frantic, and generally fruitless, pursuit of the spirited whiptail lizards that raced along the tracks just out of the reach of even a boy as fleet footed as me. The little stream served as a backdrop for many of my fondest childhood memories, most involving fishing or catching snakes and turtles. It was here that a barely discernible circular form on the stream bottom was magically transformed into the pancake carapace of a perfectly camouflaged baby soft shell turtle when I scooped it up between thumb and forefinger, my first turtle.

On another day, something even more extraordinary happened when I walked down the embankment and under the trestle. The site had been flooded only a few days earlier and the receding waters had exposed two small objects, white and oval. I judged them to be eggs of some sort and cupped them loosely in my left hand to provide protection during my hike home. Having only one free hand available, I decided to forego lizard chasing and concentrated on maintaining my equilibrium on my one-rail balance beam as I hurried home.

Only a few minutes after setting out, I felt something wet and viscous in the palm of my left hand, the one carrying my twin treasures. I opened the hand to behold the tiniest vertebrate I had ever seen staring back; the minute head of a hatchling green snake protruding from a slit it had sliced in the leathery shell of one of the eggs. I was ecstatic, thrilled beyond measure, and immediately abandoned my iron balance beam to quicken my pace home to show off my prize. Then, just as miraculously, the other egg hatched. My days of snake husbandry had abruptly dawned. That autumn at our county fair, I felt a special kinship with the proprietor of a snake exhibit despite the disparity of our reptilian trophies, his 16 foot python and my two tiny green worms, since, after all, we were both snake collectors. The brush off he gave me was gentle enough to convey his respect for my passion but brusque enough to impart the important lesson that people keep snakes and other wildlife pets for many reasons unrelated to passion.

Throughout my boyhood, I encountered these elegant and slender green snakes with regularity. I learned that it was possible to wade along the center of the little stream at night and find them by aiming the beam of a headlight up into the vegetation where it was reflected by their coiled white bellies to betray their location. A friend employed another method for locating them. He would align his line of vision along the face of a boxwood hedge where the protruding heads of green snakes, weaving back and forth to simulate the movement of a vine in the breeze, could be distinguished from the motionless vegetative mass.

Today, green snakes are not so common. I spend a lot of time outdoors in suitable green snake habitat and seldom see more than one or two a year. As is the case with many animals, this population decline is anecdotal. Definitive demographic studies are lacking, but they are unnecessary to convince me, and others like me, that something is wrong. In this case, a probable cause, perhaps *the* cause, is the pervasive use of agricultural insecticides that are inadvertently infused into the tissues of the little snakes as they devour insects. But it's not just green snakes. Indigo snakes, truly magical reptiles, have nearly disappeared altogether despite being afforded protection as a federally threatened species. Sadly, this designation does little to protect them from the habitat destruction that attends Florida's breakneck development, robbing them of the large upland tracts they require.

There are countless variations on these tragedies and they tell the story of an ongoing collapse of the elaborate web of ecologic relationships that underlie the natural world. Across the earth, the pervasive reach of humanity is impoverishing natural areas while simultaneously diminishing their expanse. Because the process has occurred incrementally, we have adjusted incrementally; and have accepted our diminished circumstances incrementally as well. At every turn, there have been voices of caution and warning, always reminding us of what we are losing, that we are part of a larger system, that we cannot keep fouling the planet as if it were not our home, that a day of reckoning was coming. But the response to these warnings has been little more than lip service, even when something as fundamental as our own drinking water is at stake. Cleaning up our water supply would simply be too costly, so we began drinking bottled water. Bottled water! On a water planet!

And so the incremental losses continued to mount; as a result, we routinely see figures that would have seemed unimaginable only a few years ago. Since the advent of industrial scale fishing operations, ninety percent of the earth's fish stocks have been depleted. At the current rate of exploitation, they will be gone altogether before the middle of this century. A third of all amphibian species are threatened with extinction; a fifth of mammal species; an eighth of all birds. There has been a twenty percent decline in corals. Species are disappearing at a rate that is between 100 and 1000 times the extinction rate chronicled in the fossil record. These numbers would have been inconceivable to a 1960s era ecologist. It would not have seemed possible that so much could be lost so quickly or that humanity would stand idly by and allow it to happen. Who could have imagined we would surrender so much with so little serious protest? Had we not fought so valiantly to save the bald eagle and the whooping crane?

The only explanation for humanity's failure to take action to halt and reverse this terrifying trend is a pervasive arrogance and selfishness. Arrogance, because we clearly do not acknowledge the inherent right of other species to exist. And selfishness because we seem willing to sacrifice virtually any species or ecosystem to sustain a short term economic prosperity that will secure happiness, if only for today. Here again, we are witness to the damage that is attributable, at least in part, to values built upon widespread acceptance of humanity's birthright of dominion over all others species. How angry God must be at Moses for putting those words into his mouth. Our willingness to exploit the planet's natural resources today, leaving a bare cupboard for our children and theirs, is shameful and immoral, and no amount of semantic whitewash can mask that blot or absolve us of what is clearly unprincipled behavior. Do we not truly love our children? Hoping for salvation by technological innovation is a naïve pipedream, not a plan. And simply hoping the ultimate collapse doesn't occur until after we expire is selfish and reprehensible.

How is it possible for an intelligent and reasoning species to be so shortsighted? To behave with such recklessness, disregarding hard evidence of a looming collapse of the ecological systems that support our societies and all we hold dear? In effect, to saw off the limb we're sitting on? We know with certainty that we will run out of oil and that we pay dearly for every imported drop. We also know of no replacement for this critical energy source and yet we behave as though our rescue by technological innovation is a certainty; the better to justify the innate selfishness imparted by natural selection. What if we are wrong? Is it wise to buy and drive hummers, SUVs and other gas guzzlers when energy efficient vehicles are available? To leave the engines of huge buses idling for hours just to keep conditioned air flowing continuously while its passengers tour Kanapaha Botanical Gardens or snap pictures of Graceland? When oil is increasingly purchased with the blood of our youth?

The regrettable truth is that evolution is a limited process. It improves the prospects of any species, including humans, to face the challenges of the moment. But there is no mechanism for allocating resources for long term survival. And so, the advantage accrues to the individuals who are the most selfish for they acquire the most resources. Within the human family are prophets who have harnessed the power of the human mind to surmount these selfish impulses and give us a glimpse of the terrifying future that awaits us unless we control the earth's human population and fundamentally change our relationship with the natural world. But, buried beneath our glorious and convoluted cerebrum lies an ancient reptilian brain stem that still does much of our thinking for us and, as in reptiles, is selfishly preoccupied with matters of personal security and well being. Planning to sustain these comforts seldom extends beyond our immediate family and circle of acquaintances and seldom beyond the limits of our own life. We should be looking into the faces of our children to summon the courage to make the sacrifices necessary to secure their future. Instead, we are watching professional sports and eating Nachos.

True altruism, noble and commendable though it may be, is a behavior that carries negative survival value for the altruist. It is not surprising that those who dedicate their lives to aiding the poor and disenfranchised, protecting the environment, eliminating hunger and other noble and selfless endeavors find themselves at variance with social norms, where support for such concerns seldom extends beyond admiration and lip service when it entails the prospect of personal sacrifice. To humanity's true heroes, we give, not Porches and riches, but rather plaques, ribbons, trophies, certificates of appreciation and other commendations and trinkets. There is little doubt where our priorities lie.

Back in the 60s, when Jordan and I were doing graduate work in Hogtown's academic mill, the environmental movement hit us like a blast of cold water. Suddenly, we seemed to be bubbling in a broth of contaminated water and breathing polluted air, obsessed with the need for recycling, with fears about greenhouse gases, eutrophication of lakes and rivers, pesticide build up, species extinction and the destruction of natural areas. Those of us engaged in a study of the natural world had abruptly become invested with a new responsibility—to educate society about the need to rethink its relationship with the earth from which it draws sustenance.

Jordan and I and many colleagues leapt onto the bandwagon with both feet. Soon we were slogging through Lake Alice hauling out rafts of water hyacinth, a lovely but invasive exotic plant that was smothering Florida's waterways. We enlisted in the Florida Defenders of the Environment, a corps of volunteers being recruited by the indefatigable Marjorie Carr—Archie's wife—to stop the construction of the ill conceived Cross Florida Barge canal and consequent destruction of the wild Oklawaha River. We wrote letters, circulated petitions, raised hell and, in the process, learned a lot about the politics of special interests. But the seeming suddenness with which the environmental movement sprang upon us was puzzling. Why had so much gone wrong? What was the common thread that linked our crises with greenhouse gases, pesticide build up, ozone depletion and the rest of it?

There was, in fact, an answer, an alarm originally sounded by Thomas Malthus in 1798, and rehabilitated in the sixties by Dr. Paul Ehrlich in his book, "The Population Bomb." The common thread to all of these looming disasters was and is overpopulation; there are too many people in the world. Feeding, clothing and otherwise sustaining them is the primary cause of it all; the specific concerns are all secondary. With fewer people, we would burn less fossil fuel, cut fewer trees, clear less land, use fewer pesticides and fertilizers and resources generally. The simple logic of maintaining a balance between the size of the human population and the earth's sustainable resources was so compelling an argument that it seemed clearly destined to carry the day. We had, as a species, to simply rear smaller families; to have an average of 2.11 children to stabilize population size, less to bring it down to a truly sustainable level. I was one of four siblings and Jordan was one of three; these brood sizes were simply too large and our generation would have to do better. We lived in an age in which safe and convenient birth control agents were readily accessible so we needed only to muster the will to put it all into practice.

That was forty years ago. Back when Jordan and I were making these decisions, we naively assumed such an attitude was becoming the norm. We limited our family to two children, the responsible thing to do as part of mankind's larger family, only to learn that this number was, and remains, below the norm. It appears that the great explosion of enlightenment that shook our graduate school world caused little more than a ripple in the larger society. The real explosion has resulted from the population bomb. How naive we were.

Today, we routinely hear educated and relatively affluent young couples speaking of their plans to rear large families. Confronted with the concerns of others about society's need to control population size, they often tout their fiscal wherewithal to provide for the physical well being of their large broods, as if that somehow negates the increased demand their existence will wreak on the earth's finite resources. The greater one's affluence, in fact, the greater his negative impact on all of these environmental maladies. But Erlich said that forty years ago; Malthus, two centuries ago. Must we always learn the hard way?

It has been painful to witness environmental destruction around the globe that has resulted from incremental rises in the human population, all the while, fully cognizant that it cannot continue indefinitely. Most of the environmental changes that now cloud our future have occurred during my lifetime and we can't afford another lifetime of such shameful disregard for the earth. In the past six decades, I have watched the planet's human population bypass the four billion mark, then five billion, then six. And all the while, concern seems to center, not on the principal problem, that human population growth must be stopped and reversed, but on the challenge of feeding, clothing and housing these additional billions, as though they bring some new richness to the mix that offsets the tragic permanent losses that must be borne to bring them on board.

This is simply more arrogance; an arrogance that daily transforms thousands of acres of Amazon forests and other Edens into charcoal pits and cassava plots to provide subsistence livelihoods for the planet's next destitute and prolific billion. And yet again, we find that it was Moses, that imaginative author of Biblical fiction, at the bottom of it, or at least a part of the problem with his edict to be fruitful and multiply. In any case, that was advice for a mythical extended family at a mythical demographic bottleneck thousands of years ago and it has been fulfilled with such admirable enthusiasm that half of all humans who have ever walked the earth are alive today. Now it's time to cork it!

These rants may not seem qualitatively different from those of cranks who have been complaining for centuries that the world is going to Hell in a hand basket And it is easy to understand why we tend to remember our past with fondness; things change so quickly and we all find comfort in things that are familiar, even if they exist only in memory. It sometimes seems that we stay the same, in essence, while everything around us transmutes into things that are less familiar. Or perhaps we simply wish to experience the uncomplicated certainty and magic that pervaded our thoughts and beliefs in simpler times. Whatever the case, I do remember my youth with great fondness. The world was exciting and all of its creatures were new and unknown; and the boundaries between reality and fantasy were wonderfully indistinct. So there has always been talk of the good old days and how the changes wrought by time's passage have diminished life's richness. But we're talking now, for the first time ever, about the prospect of transforming the entire planet into habitat for one species and dispensing with tens of thousands of other species whose needs cannot be satisfied in that world. This is a terrifying vision, but one that acquires more substance with every passing day. We are standing in a mineshaft waist deep in dead canaries and are still digging.

The genius of the human mind is sometimes overpowering. It has created tools and technologies that have transformed the nature of existence on the third planet, some for better and some worse. When I see images of sacred whooping cranes pursuing piloted ultralight supercranes to learn anew their long forgotten ancestral migration routes, I take vicarious pride in being possessed of the genome that has made it all possible. What thoughtful, compassionate and inspired creatures we are to take account of shameful past transgressions and to do all of this to make amends!

But then, everywhere around me, I see a headlong rush for personal wealth that is destroying the planet. While whooping cranes, pandas, manatees, Siberian tigers and other high profile creatures are the beneficiaries of our attention and concern, thousands of less prominent species continue to be trampled underfoot. I have witnessed the destruction of millions of acres of natural Florida and have mourned the tragic deaths of countless frantic and terrified animals on Florida's roadways as they attempt to flee these newly ravaged lands, their erstwhile homes, to find somewhere—anywhere—else to live. Of course, there is no place else and the ones that die quickly under the wheel are most probably the lucky ones. It is a sign of spiritual evolution that we summarily evict and murder only nonhuman animals, and no longer aboriginal humans, for these purposes, but that is small comfort.

Diatribes like this one conventionally conclude with a message of hope; hope that we can change course while it is still possible to stop the toppling dominoes, expanding ozone hole and melting glaciers. Hope that love for our children will outweigh our selfish impulses, runaway depletion of the earth's riches and the shameful destruction of so much that we hold dear. But I am not hopeful. Humanity has seldom taken that sort of a proactive approach since it would cause pain and end the careers of political leaders who are at least as selfish as the rest of us. It is more our style, as a species, to try to disregard and minimize looming crises until they cannot be ignored and then apply a band aid that will result in the least short term pain. But we are running out of band aids; out of oil; out of forests to log; out of red wolf and elephant habitat; out of coral reefs and ozone; out of green snakes. The earth is finite and we've turned every stone.

Humanity has experienced dark moments before, but nothing like this. It is true, of course, that all dark moments are unique and that in many cases, men and women equal to the challenges of those times appeared from nowhere and turned the tide. I most fervently hope that this will be one of those moments. It's too late already for Carolina parakeets, dodos, Tasmanian wolves, passenger pigeons, Timuqua Indians and many others; but there is much more at stake. The future of wild creatures and wild places cannot be secured without sacrifice and we should bear it willingly with thoughts of love and concern for our children held first and foremost in our hearts and minds. The environmental costs associated with our actions have not disappeared just because we have neglected to pay them over the centuries. With the entire planet now subjugated, our "exploit and abandon" approach to development is no longer feasible and past debts are coming due.

We must drive fuel efficient vehicles and drive them less; turn off lights when we leave the room; install solar hot water heaters, eat less meat. Recycling should be a major religion. We must learn to get by with less and the expansion of lumbering, drilling, and mining operations brought to a halt. The use of off road vehicles, snowmobiles and wildlife terrifying air boats should be prohibited on virtually all wild lands except for emergency operations. The peril of our time necessitates limits to personal freedom. Protection should be extended to all endangered species and the sacrifices required to restore their populations willingly borne. These measures and a host of others must become our second nature if we are to avoid a collapse of the social order we now enjoy. A catalogue of the planet's decline and the necessary remedial actions we must take are touted daily in our newspapers and on broadcast news. The pity is that we're not watching The News Hour on PBS but "American Idol" on Fox Television.

Above all, we must remember that it is human overpopulation that is driving these many crises. It is essential that we do all we can to support organizations that promote worldwide human population control and insist on government policies that do likewise. Stabilizing, and then reducing, the earth's human population is our paramount challenge; everything else is secondary. The full range of family planning tools must be made universally available if we are to have control over the stabilization and subsequent reduction of the human population. We can no longer afford to allow religious biases to influence policies that are designed to help third world countries control their populations. The specter of hunger, starvation, child slavery and the loss of the planet's last remaining wild areas is too terrible to ponder. Demography is a realm of science and the few factors that determine population size have long been known. If we don't use our knowledge and will to limit the size of the human family by limiting natality, the dispassionate hand of nature—augmented by warfare—will do it by increasing mortality. There's no more "West" to go to, young man; it has all been used up. The key to reducing pollution, environmental destruction, human misery and species extinctions is to reduce our demand for the earth's limited resources by limiting the size of the human population, one smaller family at a time. What additional richness will another billion people bring to our lives?

For the sake of our children, there should always be magic in the natural world; bubble eyed salamanders under boards, fireflies giving pulse to warm summer nights, giant otherworldly Victoria water lilies to take away your breath and spadefoot toads slumbering underfoot while visions of drenching storms dance in their heads. It is essential that these natural treasures, and a million others, persist to stir passion in the hearts of those lucky enough to see and appreciate their magnificence—naturalists—so they can remind the rest of humanity what is truly at stake and how profoundly blessed we are. And for naturalists, there should always be green snakes to make the world complete.